D0184731

Quality through People

A Blueprint for
Proactive Total Quality Management

Quality through People

A Blueprint for Proactive Total Quality Management

Jon Choppin

IFS Publications, UK
1991

British Library Cataloguing in Publication Data

Choppin, Jon
Quality through People.
1. Management
I. Title
658

ISBN 1-85423-094-8 IFS Publications

Photo-typeset by A J Latham Ltd., Dunstable, UK
Printed by Short Run Press Ltd., Exeter, UK

to Jan

Contents

Introduction

Welcome to a new era of industrial life!

These modern times require a higher degree of understanding and participation by everyone. A concept of *industrial citizenship* will be developed, such that everyone can make a responsible contribution to their company, and hence to the whole community. Quality is the key and people are the means.

Throughout the book, Quality is written with an upper-case Q, to emphasise the role that this concept must play in our work.

This book stems from the conjunction of several beliefs. The first concerns the necessity to assist industry to prosper. The destinies of everyone are linked. The politicians struggle and fight within the realms of wealth distribution, often missing the point that if no wealth is created, there will be nothing to distribute. Many people have considerable worries about the future ability of the nation to create sufficient wealth to keep us, our offspring and the rest of the population in the manner to which we have all become accustomed.

Process thinking

This is not a political tome, but I believe it impossible to write anything about the organisation of men and women without political overtones. I see *process thinking* as being a much needed middle course between the hard-nosed capitalist approach of many senior executives and the Marxist perspective of an exploited labour force operating obsolescent machinery. For those seeking political inspiration, this book contains new thoughts. Those not looking for politics will not find any.

Success through people

My second strand of belief is that it is only through effective management of people that long-term success can be achieved within industry. Our salvation as a nation needs this long-term perspective in our planning and industrial operations. We have to reverse the recent tendency to view industrial enterprise as a short-term phenomenon and to settle for short-term gains at the expense of long-term losses. Unfortunately, in the past, such short-term *gains* have been manifested in the pockets of very few, whilst the community at large has often had to suffer the long-term losses, often through unemployment, lack of investment and soul-destroying jobs. Good personnel management is always an investment in the future. Education is essential.

Related to this is my belief that the greatest untapped energy reserve in the UK is the human resource within our workforce. It has been estimated that the average worker gives, or has extracted from him, less than 20% of his potential. This is not only very much to the individuals detriment, but also very much a loss to the nation as a whole.

My own stand-point here derives from Christmas 1987 when, after several days of eating, drinking and relaxing too much, I looked in the mirror and was shocked by the elderly, unshaven spectre who stared back. I reached a conclusion that has altered my life: that I was middle-aged. The outcome of this momentous occasion has been the resolve to enjoy every working day, for the rest of my working life. This announcement usually promotes grins of understanding from a fair proportion of most audiences, and it would seem to be part of our common make-up, that we not only *want* to enjoy work, but that we *need* to enjoy work. It is only a short step from this realisation, to a perception of the unlocked human potential available from a happy, motivated workforce.

Such a workforce needs careful managing, by managers who understand the inputs to the processes they manage. Often I feel that the least understood input to a process is the human involvement. I often make a plea for equality. If we could only give to the humans who work for us the same amount of care and attention that we impart to machinery, industrial life would be so much better. If this has any truth in it, it is pretty damning.

Please enjoy reading this book.

Jon Choppin,
March 1991.

Preface

The tool-kit approach

There are no universal solutions, and ready-made management packages are not the answer. So often, successful people are seen, not so much as rule-breakers, but more as rule-makers. They write their own agenda, set their own standards, and devise their own methods. Above all, they understand their own business.

The way forward has to be to absorb ideas, thoughts, theories, whatever you can find that has bearing on your business, and then use them to adapt your present situation and push towards your ultimate goals of success.

This calls for mental activity, not of academic learning, but of imagination. This book is not for the mentally lazy, but for those who wish to take the simple ideas, propounded herein, and develop them within their own businesses. You can be helped to ask the questions, but it is for you to find the answers.

Directions

This book is not a package of measures. There is no success to be obtained by buying management methods 'off-the-shelf'. The only successful way forward, for any company, is for the senior management first to appreciate exactly where they are, secondly to decide the direction in which they wish to proceed, and thirdly to move in that direction.

This may sound simplistic, indeed it is simplistic: all good ideas can be easily expressed. The one bonus to be gained from presenting simple ideas is that people can very quickly decide whether or not to accept or reject them.

The basic tenets of this book are:

1. Nothing in life is static. Business is constantly changing, not only in methodology and direction, but in values and relationships.

2. Industry is directional. This means that there are few beginnings and even fewer ends in business. Everyday life is developmental, moving in one or more directions.
3. The only adequate way to decide on a particular direction is to know where you are, and where you want to be, that is, your ultimate goal.
4. The only ultimate goal worth pursuing is unobtainable: it will be an aspect of perfection.
5. Management is about managing people. If we can optimise the actions of all the people involved with our company, we will find success.

The five tenets

These five tenets may not appear to have much relevance to your daily life at the moment, but their meaning will become clear as you proceed. If you find that you disagree fundamentally with these principles, you will reject much of what the book is suggesting, since the ideas expressed are based on them. Don't give up though. There is probably as much value in reading things that you disagree with, and identifying the faults in the expressed arguments, as there is in just accepting ideas as obvious truths.

This book is not a ready-made Total Quality Management (TQM) package. Rather, this book seeks to provide a framework of ideas and theory. Within this framework, any company, and that includes yours, can identify a more successful route. This will be achieved, first by learning more about your own company, secondly by developing a *management strategy* to identify and resource the company's intended direction, and finally by identifying the tools to achieve movement in this direction.

'Management' is stressed. Obviously, it is not only through management that we can achieve success; up-to-date technology is needed, the right products for the right markets need to be identified, and the one-hundred-and-one other things necessary for a successful company need to be done. Without sound management, though, these things will not be done successfully. You can do it by yourself but, as soon as others are involved, man management becomes necessary to co-ordinate the effort of all the people involved.

steel. This is typified as the 'Rolls Royce' definition of Quality. It has many adherents, particularly among the older members of our industrial workforce.

None of this is terribly helpful, but it does suggest that what is required is a statement or description of 'Quality' that is *useful.*

Quality as a useful concept

Collections of words, or even ideas, will be of little use unless they relate to everyday tasks, and present scope for decision-making and action. All concepts, within industrial management, need to consider usefulness. Such concepts are indeed man-made, and not natural phenomena.

There is a tendency merely to accept the framework and definitions for any situation that we find in life. When we are children, this is quite natural. We question, but are often easily convinced by 'this is just like this', or 'its the way of the world'. It isn't though!

There is no 'way of the world'. All social groupings, conventions, written and unwritten rules, relationships, ways of behaving, methods of doing things, etc., are human constructs; they are man-made. No human activity is static. Most are subject to continual evolution. This is vital, as it gives a choice as to how to conduct business affairs. It also presents the opportunity to control change, and constantly improve.

The present consideration is just such an opportunity. For a number of years there has been a very 'woolly' concept of Quality which has often meant all things to all people. An adoption of TQM presents the opportunity to grasp this concept in such a way as to maximise the benefit from it. Quality must be a *useful* concept.

Idea

Look carefully through your company paper-work and proforma,
to establish where and in what context the word Quality is used.
Ensure that it always has the same meaning.
Quality does not mean grade or type!

anything considered academic to an 'ivory tower'. This ensured that little original thought entered our industrial activities. In other words, we didn't ask the right questions, and would not have had the academic framework available to answer them even if we had.

Ignorance inhibits change

These prejudices, first for the oriental methods, and secondly against any academic approach, inhibit a clear understanding of what 'Quality' is. They also prevent its achievement. Industry lacks a definition or appreciation of a number of critical concepts including Quality, competition, productivity and even management. They are all in constant use, throughout all sectors of industry. Their lack of definition, leading to their ambiguous use, gives rise to considerable variation in priorities, decisions, actions and attitudes, within any company management structure. Few in industry, or elsewhere, deliberately produce poor 'Quality' by their own definition. It is the working of 'the system' and *'other peoples' results'* that produce poor Quality. The traditional saying, that a poor workman blames his tools, is probably relevant here.

Few jobs have a clear set of values, even if they have detailed job descriptions. The role of a teacher extends from that of the students' friend and counsellor, to that of an instructor or pedagogic tyrant. Likewise, the role of a policeman could be a warrior against all those who transgress society's norms, or a concerned individual seeking to assist the public.

Back in the 1950s, a bus conductor (sadly an almost extinct breed outside the metropolis) sang loudly and in tune, nearly all the time. Many really appreciated this cheerful man, who took such a delight in his task of transporting them daily. Where are such people now? Would they be permitted to transgress the norm?

Quality

The Oxford dictionary definition is: 'degree of excellence, relative nature or kind or character, general excellence'.

There are many who still refer to 'the Quality end of the market'. These perceive the gold plated as innately superior to the functional stainless

Tom Peters[1] identified the optimum company size as five. Effective management becomes very difficult in any company with a greater number of people. In other words, it is not just a question of managing all the people involved with the company, but also managing them in such a way that their talents, energies and results are all assisting the company in the same direction.

There are, in fact, two different, and possibly conflicting, considerations. Firstly, we have to maximise each person's contribution to the shared aim of the company. The concern here will be with motivation, and the encouragement of all individuals to give of their best. This individualistic approach may conflict with the results stemming from the activities of others. Thus, we have to ensure that the totality of this energy is directed solely towards the common good. Any conflict of agenda, value systems, judgement, or simple ignorance of others' activities, will merely soak up some of this hard-won effort. These thoughts will be pursued throughout the book.

The TQM Blueprint

A number of opportunities are presented in the book. They may appear as problems that need sorting out in any company – for example, ensuring that there is a common language in use. Often there isn't a single set of meanings and a particular word or concept can have as many meanings as people using it. The main thrust will be the framework of ideas that is called a 'TQM Blueprint'. These are based on four overlapping facets of management:

- Management of Quality
- Management of Processes
- Management of People
- Management of Resources

Chapter 17 brings these together with a host of suggested activities. The book has been written to be useful. Use it, if only as a door stop!

1. Peters, Thomas, *In Search of Excellence*, Collins, 1982.

Part
I

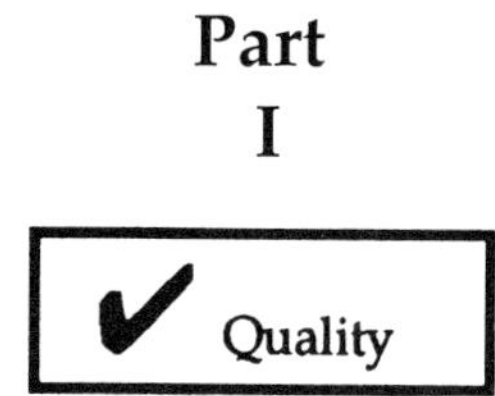

The Management of Quality

Chapter 1

Quality

Come give us a taste of your quality,

– Shakespeare, Hamlet II.ii.

Route-map

This chapter starts by considering the concept of Quality as a feature of everyday life, and then establishes that, with the right definition, Quality can be a useful management tool. An explanation and definition of the concepts of *Quality* and *Customer* follow. A link is made between the concept of the internal customer and industrial citizenship. Finally, brief explanations of the Quality Policy, Quality Management Strategy and the Quality Environment are given.

Questions

The two key concepts are that of **Quality** and **Customer**, and the key questions are: 'What is Quality?' and 'Who is the Customer?'. Indeed, the close examination and understanding of these questions can provide the basis of a commercial culture suitable for any company or organisation. The development of **Customer relationships**, based on the duty to supply **Quality** products and services to each other, is the driving force of the Total Quality culture.

Quality

The question, 'What is Quality?' invariably produces a range of diverse thoughts. A few are very useful, but most refer to meeting standards, being within 'spec' or being near perfect. Perhaps the most original came from a seminar at Leyland, where a delegate wrote 'Quality is a perception'. When asked what he meant, he replied that Quality could be all things to all men. *Quality* like *beauty*, was in the eye of the beholder. This is a useful start to the exploration of Quality, for this, like any other true concept, begins in the mind.

Quality as part of everyday life

Apparently, Quality is to be found in great abundance. The use of the word begins to rival *nice* as a universal description of every object or product of human activity. We live in a quality age. We have the opportunity to live in a quality home, full of quality furniture on quality carpets, eating high quality food from the quality supermarket, whilst our quality car waits patiently in the quality garage. Hovering, just out of sight, are a host of people waiting to give whatever quality service is needed, from a bank-loan, to a window-clean. These days, the one may be needed to afford the other!

In industry, the word is just as widely used. There is hardly a managing director who does not claim that the company is 'committed to Quality'. When questioned, virtually all will use phrases such as 'Quality is at the top of our agenda', and even 'we are proud of our Quality'. There are many factory gates emblazoned with slogans such as 'Quality begins here'. The early 1980s seemed to spawn these ideas. There are door-mats, encouraging the foot wiper with the thought, 'Quality is our business', and even the toilet paper, in some factories, vaunts its 'Quality' slogan. The 1980s saw many factories decorated with 'Do it right first time', 'The customer is king', 'Quality is everyone's responsibility' and even the blunt 'Quality is vital'.

The right and the wrong

These slogans give promises which are not only rarely kept, but which are seldom understood.

The right

They were right to highlight Quality as the central issue for consideration. Indeed, that is why Quality is spelt throughout this book with an upper case Q. Quality should be in people's minds, part of every consideration and involved with every aspect of the business. It is important to 'Do it right first time', 'Quality *is* everyone's responsibility', 'Quality *is* vital'.

The wrong

They were wrong to give bald statements with no education to explain the concepts used, or methodology to allow the ideas to come to fruition. At best the slogans were ignored. At worst they led to a great deal of frustration. Some people appreciated that not all was well, and that the posters held some sort of solution. Nothing actually changed, though, and no-one seemed to care. Those who saw the need for a Quality transformation, felt helpless. Traditional priorities, methods and attitudes reigned supreme, and presented an impenetrable morass of complacency.

Why Quality posters?

Why then, have slogans and posters proliferated? There are two motivations for choosing this route to employee participation in the 'Quality game'.

The first has been the tendency to turn to slogans and posters when there is a need to demonstrate that something is being taken seriously. Those remembering 'Mum's the word', not to mention 'Your country needs you', have probably been the target of thousands of such slogans during their lifetime. Most are now thoroughly hardened to the messages, if not actually cynical about them. For those responsible, though, the use of posters and slogans is a visible means of demonstrating to their peers that they are taking the whole business seriously, that they are doing their job and, that above all, money has been spent. What bigger commitment could a company make than spending money?

The Japanese provided the other major influence during the 1980s. Indeed, many managers became obsessed, in the mid-1980s, with the success of Japanese industry. They thought that their route to success must be emulation – 'If the Japanese do it, then we must do it'. Many in the West were envious of the oriental success, their worker participation, their Quality Circles, and even their early morning factory physical education sessions.

Unfortunately, neither the use of posters, nor the copying of Japanese methods, has produced the result so optimistically expected. Moreover, few middle managers really expected any dramatic improvement, some even doubting that improvement was really possible, or even necessary.

Beyond our control

British industry's problems were thought to emanate far more from outside influences than from any aspects within their daily control. The UK's ability, given the chance, to produce 'Quality goods' was not questioned. Great Britain had always been famous for its Quality. For years, 'Made in Great Britain' had been stamped on every item, as living proof that the world held such an accolade in awe.

Depending upon the person's position within a company's hierarchy, a selection from the following list could easily supply all the reasons necessary to explain a company's poor performance.

- Lack of government support.
- Lack of investment.
- Lack of proper leadership.
- World recession.
- High interest rates.
- The price of oil.
- The greenhouse effect.
- Poorly trained management.
- Poor industrial relations.
- Lazy workers.
- The unions.
- Poor foreign raw materials.
- Unfair competition from abroad.
- Dumping of unwanted foreign goods.
- Our winning the war.
- Even the British weather.

Everyone knew that British industry was held back by these problems.

The innate British arrogance ensured that the one question never asked was, 'are we doing it right?'. Another British trait was the relegation of

Quality as a management tool

The concept of Quality has considerable potential, when used by the management group of a company. Quality, therefore needs to be presented as a tool; as an idea that can be positively used by those managing. As such, it needs to have certain features.

It needs to be **robust,** in that it must be applicable to a wide range of situations. It must be able to give sound answers in all areas of business. It must allow managers to manage with confidence, by providing a sound answer to any question that may arise.

It needs to have **precision;** allowing exact and detailed results to flow from its use. Different managers, considering the same set of circumstances, should arrive at the same decision, provided they share the same basic philosophy, solid theory and conceptual understanding.

It needs to be **universal;** so that the same definition, or set of thoughts, can be applied by very different people, in many different circumstances, and yet adhere to an integrated management theory. The test of this will always be the common understanding between two or more managers, possibly from different companies, discussing a 'Quality' related point.

It needs to have **simplicity.** Any concept that is to be widely used must be simple enough for all to perceive it for what it is. Many would denigrate a concept for its simplicity, but this is to misunderstand the nature of human interaction with ideas and concepts. Einstein made a clear distinction between the need for clean, clear statements of a concept, that can be appreciated by the intelligent non-expert and the complicated justification of such a concept. The latter often requires expert knowledge and experience to be properly understood. Concepts, however, can be simply stated. In industry, concepts *must* be simply stated.

Quality as a central management issue

It is hard to perceive Quality as a peripheral concern, and yet this has been its position, in many companies, for many years. They have seen productivity, monthly targets and the current market share as being the critical management issues, whilst Quality has been considered only as related to the finished product. Inevitably, this relegated Quality to issues of customer complaints, public liability, indeed to a culture of 'what can we get away with?' Quality became only skin deep. Quality could be left to the Quality department. The Quality inspectors would check to ensure that we were not exposing ourselves to outside criticism.

This clearly hasn't worked. To many customers, outside industry, it seems fantastic that such a 'Quality credibility gap' could exist. How could a company continue to worry about its stocks and shares, its monthly production figures and its profits, with no regard for the object of all the activity, the actual goods and/or services being provided.

Generating wealth is the main purpose of any company. It is self-evident that this wealth flows from the products and activity of the company. Thus, the source of wealth is to be found, both in these products, and in the activity creating them. Value is directly related to the Quality involved, whether of product or process. Quality is thus, of central concern to management.

The adoption of TQM takes this further and makes Quality *the* central management issue. It subsumes all other concerns. It encompasses all other management activities. It must, therefore, be constructed on a sufficient body of theory, to give the confidence that it can produce the results, and can be relied on to lead a company to success.

Ubiquitous Quality (Quality as a multi-purpose concept)

The nature of business is such, that questions of Quality will be constantly under consideration, in all areas of a company, and in all groups of personnel. The theory and concept of Quality must take this into account. It must have both something of value for all within the company, and also a universality, such that 'Quality interpretations' from one area will be readily understood in another.

A similar consideration will apply between companies, and between a supplier and a consumer. Quality is of the greatest importance within all such inter-company relationships. Clearly, it is vital that all are explicit about their exact meaning of the term Quality, and how the concept is to be used.

Further, there is a web formed by raw material or component suppliers, selling to several different manufacturers, sometimes in more than one industrial sector. These, in turn, sell to customers, who also purchase from others. This web will involve a multitude of inter-company relationships. It will be inefficient, if not extremely expensive, for many different definitions of Quality to exist within these relationships. In reality, this web probably covers the trading activities of the UK, if not the rest of the world, in its entirety. The concept of industrial Quality will become ubiquitous.

If there is a multitude of inter-company relationships, there are an even greater number of interpersonal relations within each of these companies, which will be using Quality as an everyday concept. It is vital that the Quality definition sits as easily with these *internal customer relationships* as with the external, inter-company interactions.

Whatever Quality is, it must be applicable to all circumstances and situations.

The Quality definition

A definition of Quality is required that is:

- A useful concept.
- A management tool, that is robust, precise, universal and yet simple.
- The central management issue.
- Ubiquitous, fitting every situation and purpose.

The Quality definition must be inextricably tied to the main object of any company, that is the generation of wealth. Indeed, the definition must be **customer orientated**, since the only source of such wealth are customers, who exchange money for goods and/or services, that they value.

Customer orientated

Business is, in fact, meeting the requirements of the customer(s). A clear statement of what these requirements are will be part of the judgement of

Quality applied to any transaction. This transactional consideration is of particular importance. Whereas Quality will be seen as an integral part of every process leading to an eventual transaction (either between internal or external suppliers and customers), the judgement of Quality usually occurs at the transactional point.

This has led to the myth that Quality can be controlled, within this transactional situation. One of the most important messages from all those who have given serious thought to Quality Control, from Deming[1] to Ishikawa,[2] is that only the *inputs* to activities can be controlled. The Quality Control department's inspection activities merely demonstrate *where* control has been lost, rather than imposing any real control at all.

Thus, the stated requirements must be considered as part of the *transactional* activity. The term 'transactional' is used to ensure that it involves the many points during design, preparation, manufacture and distribution. When something is physically passed from one person to another, a transaction has taken place. At each stage of this chain, the judgement of Quality relates to the stated requirements of the next stage. In reality, such considerations move backwards, from the point of sale to the consumer, to the instigation of the product. Quality both starts and finishes with the designer, inventor or entrepreneur. These thoughts will resurface later, when the subjects of internal customer relationships and process capability are considered.

Customer requirements

These requirements will cover all aspects of the goods and/or services being provided. They will include the total number of an item, the presentation or packaging, the time of delivery and, of course, the price to be paid. All these aspects will be a judgement of Quality.

Such requirements are more clearly stated in some industries than others. Within the manufacturing sector, every dimension is not only precisely

Idea

The real inspector is the customer.

specified, but any leeway or tolerance is also written down. Other areas of commerce do not describe the customer's requirements so tightly.

In many instances, a subjective 'superlative' interpretation is applied; the best, the cleanest, the shiniest, the quickest, etc. Such a statement, either implicit or explicit, will always leave room for different interpretations, controversy about the Quality standard achieved, and potential dissonance between customer and supplier. It does not make clear *who* is the arbiter of 'the best'. Regrettably, suppliers, often with greater depth of understanding and knowledge of the actual product than the customer, apply their own interpretation to this subjective assessment. This assessment will be unlikely to coincide with that of the customer, without prior discussion and a clearly agreed statement of requirements. A 'Quality culture' demands such a clear statement of what standards are acceptable, in all respects, and at each transactional stage.

There is another danger, though. Specified tolerances, often referred to as 'spec', contain their own downfall in Quality terms. Spec is seen from very different perspectives by different people. The relationship between spec and Quality is considered later in the chapter.

Customer expectations

A statement of the requirements of the customer(s) is not a sufficient background to secure Quality, even though this may include the widest possible interpretation of requirements. Such definitive requirements will always be presented as statements, that is specified as part of a contract.

Such specifications will always represent a static, time-based statement of what the customer actually wants. Industry and commerce, like all other aspects of the world, move on. They are not static. Each day is a new day. Each situation is new. The customers' perception of the goods/services they are receiving will be tempered, enhanced, and even informed, by the host of experiences and messages that they are constantly amassing. Business must be understood through this changing and evolving perspective. What a customer expects of a product is also constantly changing. To give the customer Quality, we need to meet these changing expectations, as well as the originally specified requirements.

A bonus is available. The act of meeting customers' expectations on one occasion will almost certainly ensure their business next time. Indeed, by meeting the expectations this time, you are probably altering the specified requirements for future business. Your company is then placed in front of the competition.

The addition of *expectations* to the Quality definition creates a time base for the manufacturing philosophy. The UK industrial landscape is littered with the remnants, and empty factories of companies that knew that they did something well, and believed that all that was necessary, for the future, was to continue doing the same. They were wrong. They have gone, along with the wealth and employment they created. Tomorrow is always a new day. Tomorrow's desired Quality will differ from that of today.

How often expectations are shattered. The author's son recently returned from a holiday in America. He presented his mother with a small memento of his trip, a tastefully packaged small pottery dish. The words on the packaging described it as traditional pottery, of a type dating back to the early settlers. This was surprising, since the dish was clearly factory made, with the detailing coming from a printed transfer. Obviously, it was the result of mass-production techniques, unlike those of the early settlers. A small sticker on the base of the dish proclaimed 'Made in Hong Kong'.

Negotiated?

How are the requirements and expectations of the customer identified? There is a need to carry on a continuing dialogue with the customer(s). Without such discussions, the company can never be sure of the nature of these actual expectations. This constant dialogue is a negotiation.

This aspect of the Quality definition leads to intense debate among some managers. Negotiation would seem an obnoxious concept to many Quality managers. Many feel that Quality is not negotiable. Negotiation suggests a compromise and, in the wrong context, this would not be desirable. This attitude stems from a tradition of re-negotiation with customers, *after* a supplier has failed to meet the requirements laid down. This is a very different interpretation to that now being discussed. Definitions of Quality can never be satisfactorily arrived at after the event, and the negotiations suggested are to take place *prior* to any contract being agreed.

A satisfactory understanding of Quality can only be reached following the meeting of minds of the supplier and the customer. There will be two ingredients to such a meeting of minds. It must be recognised that the supplier is almost certainly the expert on the technical, indeed intricate, detail of the product to be supplied. Equally, the customer will be the expert on the *use* to which the product is to be put. The negotiation must involve a degree of mutual education, to resolve any differences of opinion arising from these two perspectives. However, should such differences be unresolvable, the final arbiter will have to be the customer. He must be provided with what he requires and expects.

At first glance this appears obvious, but there are numerous examples across British Industry where the suppliers assumed they knew best, and gave the customer what they thought he ought to have.

The Quality definition must:

- Be customer orientated.
- Take account of the customer requirements.
- Be aware of the customer's expectations.
- Be subject to constant dialogue (negotiation).

Hence:

Quality – meeting the negotiated requirements and expectations of the customer.

Who is the customer?

Some consider this an easy and obvious question. By ignoring all the customer relationships, other than those with the person who buys their products, they considerably reduce their ability to conduct their business properly and successfully.

For many others, this is *not* an easy question. A theoretical explanation is required, to enable them to pin-point all the actual customer relationships. A company may have a clearly defined customer or set of customers, but this does not identify the customer relationships for each individual employee. Most people within industry and commerce never have any real contact with a consumer. It is one of the inherited problems of industry that this contact is hived off to a specific group of people, the sales-force, who often have little contact with those who manufacture and handle the product.

To understand the *useful* concept of customer, it is necessary to appreciate what is taking place during any particular process. This is addressed in greater depth in Chapter 13. The aspect being stressed here, is that any process involves *change*. Something is changed by the process. The customer relations will stem from this change. The two questions applicable to everyone within a company, are 'From whom have I received that which I am to change?' and 'To whom will I pass that which I have changed?' Hence, I am the customer of the people who pass the results of their labour to me; the people I pass the results of my labour to are my customers.

At the shopfloor level, this may be easy to handle, but it is equally true higher up in any organisation. Managerial positions are typified by being involved with many processes, and, thus, having many customer relationships. It is part of the management role to handle these relationships effectively. In many companies, this aspect of management is often ignored. Quality is dependent on these internal customer relationships though, and it is part of the senior management's responsibility to construct the framework and systems within all areas of the company, and to allow the many negotiations necessary for healthy customer relationships to take place. Without them, Quality cannot be produced.

Internally then, the customer is the person who depends upon an individual's Quality outputs to do a satisfactory job.

Externally, the customer is the outlet for the company's outputs. This may be a wholesaler, supermarket or major manufacturer. Whoever he is, he will need to understand these Quality relationships, so that he can transmit the expectations and requirements of the eventual consumer back down the line to your company. Your future is in his hands. You do not have to sit idly by, in perpetual hope, whilst the 'big boys' manipulate your affairs, with your future in the balance. We all have a responsibility for the education of others. This mutual education cannot be separated from the negotiations involved with Quality relationships.

The person who pays the bill may well not be the actual *customer* in Quality terms. An example would be the spare part for your car. Most spares are purchased by the garage, and used by the mechanic during routine service. He will be far more concerned with the clear identification of the part, to ensure that time isn't wasted attempting to fit the wrong part, than with the attractiveness of the packaging. The manufacturer of the part will perceive his customer as the garage mechanic, rather than the car owner, who automatically pays for the spare part as part of the routine service.

Customer's duty

Logic dictates that the direct recipient, of any product or service, is in the best position to determine its Quality. The acceptance of poor Quality, particularly by an internal customer, limits the ability to purvey good Quality to the next stage.

It is at this level that the Quality battle is won or lost. In any company, there are a myriad of horizontal transactions taking place daily. Clearly, the acceptance of poor Quality, at any stage, lowers the ability of the company to deliver high Quality standards. It is easy to say that if only each recipient stood up and demanded good Quality, most Quality

Ideas

The customer is the person to whom you pass the fruits of your labour.

Customers are dependent on their suppliers for the Quality inputs necessary, to allow their tasks to be completed successfully.

We all are customers. We all have customers.

problems would be lost. It is the understanding of why this does not happen, together with an appreciation of the organisation necessary to achieve this level of involvement within in every employee, that underscores this movement towards Quality through People. The concept of citizenship is considered by many to be old fashioned, and yet what is needed, is the development of a type of **industrial citizenship**, in which everyone plays a vital and responsible role.

Industrial citizenship

It is your duty to demand good Quality!

A movement towards Total Quality is a movement towards the development of responsible internal customer relationships, thus ensuring satisfied external customers.

Quality and spec

The designer, draughtsman, architect (or whoever) constructs an idea on paper, and decides exactly what dimensions must be applied to each facet or attribute. Upon subsequent consideration of how this idea will be turned into fact, he reaches the conclusion that no-one can produce perfection. It is impossible to manufacture a number of items precisely to the same dimensions. A little leeway is needed, within which the manufacturer can operate. It is *not* that he does not care what results there are, as long as they are within *spec*, it is rather that he would like the nominal value to be achieved on each and every occasion. He expects each result to be as near to the nominal value as is possible. To him, the *spec* limit is the absolute bottom line. Near the limit is undesirable. On the limit is unwanted. Outside the limit is unacceptable.

Manufacturers, however, do not perceive *spec* in these terms. They see the specified tolerances as *licence* to produce anything they can, within these limits. They are no longer aiming at the nominal value, but aiming to get within *spec*. Indeed, anything within *spec*, or even on the line, is acceptable.

In many cases, the result is a mass of items that are within *spec*, but only just. The results are grouped at one end of the *spec* limits. Sometimes, of course, an item is produced out of *spec*. Usually it is found and safely re-worked, rectified or scrapped, leaving the batch of results all satisfactory. This is ill-conceived. It gives no tolerance to the inspection process and assumes it to be perfect. Of course in reality, it is no more perfect than any other process. When it fails, unacceptable results, that is out of *spec* items, slip through. The usually quoted figure for the accuracy of 100% inspection is 85%. However, this is of little value, since it fails to take into account the human factors at play.

In virtually all 100% inspection scenarios, boredom and personal involvement play a major role in efficiency. The operator who has little to gain, in the way of satisfaction or job enhancement, from detecting failure can only operate with diminishing efficiency. The expectations of the inspector will also play a role. Research has shown that where a particular proportion of failures is *expected*, sub-consciously, the individual involved tends to perform to that standard. Some good items from a process exhibiting improved performance may well be rejected, along with unsatisfactory results. Conversely, in a declining process performance situation, unsatisfactory items may be passed as acceptable. This is not 'human failure' or perverseness, or even laziness. It is the nature of 100% inspection. People perform to expectations, particularly their own expectations. The same behaviour has been demonstrated within trained animals; expectations are usually realised.

Automatic or computerised inspection, of course, considerably reduces this error. Machines are not prone to the same subjective behaviour as humans. They are more prone, though, to other types of failure and may not recognise obvious faults, because they have not been programmed to recognise them. Also complete reliance on computerised results has the danger of not recognising when the actual measuring instruments become inaccurate. It is, of course, possible to have computers checking

Idea

Any deviation from the nominal value is costly. Precision and accuracy are the least expensive modes of operating.

computers, but this becomes expensive and produces so much data that it may become impossible to recognise the signs of potential failure amidst the mass of satisfactory results.

The Quality policy

The centrality of Quality within the concern of any company is best expressed by means of a Quality Policy. It is not easy to present a policy that can be used. To be effective, it needs to be a proactive document, defining the value structure within which it is to work. As a statement, it must be self-explanatory. It should include explanations, demonstrating the concepts involved. It should exemplify the business environment in which the company seeks to operate, and have relevance to everyone involved with the company; the suppliers, the employees and the customers.

A useful Quality Policy can be compared to the American Constitution. It presents a value system that can be appealed to by anyone within the chain of relationships, from supplier to end-user. It establishes the customer's right to good Quality.

The Quality Policy will become an expensive millstone around the neck of a company which is not prepared to live this Quality Policy. The mere presence of the policy is sufficient to raise the customer's expectations, if not demands. It will expose the flimsy rhetoric of a company that

A test

Look at the folllowing paragraph for about ten secconds.

QUESTON

> Give yourself about ten secconds to do the
> the task of deciding "How many errorrs of
> of printing, spelliing ect. can you see in
> in this setence.

If you don't belief me, try it on a fiend!

continues in the bad old ways, whilst claiming to be fully committed to Quality. A sample Quality Policy is illustrated in Fig. 3.5.

The Quality Strategy

It will never be sufficient simply to state the Quality framework within which you wish the company to operate. It is always necessary to find the ways and means to achieve your goal.

The Quality strategy does just this. The development, and subsequent maintenance of the Quality Strategy is one of the key tasks of the company. It is strictly the preserve of the senior management group, indeed, the development of policy and strategy is their key task.

The considerations of the Quality Management Strategy are reviewed in Chapter 3.

The Quality Environment

It now becomes the task of every manager to ensure that the company 'lives' the Quality Policy. Quality considerations become part of every decision. This will, of course, have considerable implications for education

Test answer

The answer to the Test, was 15.

Look at the folllowing paragraph for about ten secconds.

QUESTION

> Give yourself about ten secconds to do the
> **the** task of deciding "How many errorrs of
> **of** printing, spelliing ect. can you see in
> **in** this sentence?"

If you don't believe me, try it on a friend!

and training within the company. There will be a need for everyone to have a common understanding of these concepts, for them to live Quality, and use the concepts and methods involved with Quality. Above all, a Quality environment demands intelligent, thinking people, with a common set of *values* and *attitudes.*

Establishing this may not be easy! Many may doubt the ability and sincerity of those with whom they work. Even more will question their attitudes. A 'unitary thinking' company is typified by the deep suspicion each of these groups has about the attitudes of the others.

The whole question of attitudinal change is explored in Part Two, Management of People.

Idea

Where there are attitude strata in a company, you will find values and knowledge also in layers, with little communication from one stratum to another.

Summary

The definition of Quality must be:

- A useful concept.
- A management tool.
- The central management issue.
- Ubiquitous.

And that is

- Customer orientated.
- Able to take account of the customer's requirements.
- Aware of the customer's expectations.
- Subject to constant dialogue (negotiation).

Hence:

Quality – meeting the negotiated requirements
and expectations of the customer.

The route to Quality is via:

A Quality Policy	stating the company's intentions
A Quality Management Strategy	identifying the means and the methods for achieving the policy.
A Quality Environment	in which the policy is 'lived' by everyone involved with the company.

Last thoughts ....

I believe Quality to be so important that we need the participation of everyone. Every consumer who accepts any product or service that is less than he expected, that is poor Quality, is assisting the decline of our industry. We all have a **duty** to demand Quality!

1. Edwards Deming, Dr W, *Out of the Crisis: Quality, Productivity and Competitive Position*, Massachusetts Institute of Technology, 1982.
2. Ishikawa, Kaoru, *What is Total Quality Control? The Japanese Way*, translated by David J Lu, Prentice Hall Inc., New Jersey, 1985.

Chapter 2

A Total approach to Quality

If Total Quality is implemented company-wide,
it can contribute to the improvement
of corporate health and character.

– Kaoru Ishikawa[1]

Route-map

This chapter examines why change is necessary, and considers the total reappraisal that is needed. It then examines four expressions of the Quality gap, and concludes with an explanation of the need for a total commitment to Quality.

Why is a change necessary?

We in Britain have always had a strange ambivalence towards the exchange of our efforts and work for money. This almost moral dichotomy, seems to be the basis of many of our problems. We prefer to be high-minded amateurs, rather than professionals.

For many, the essence of the amateur is that he works for pure motives. They believe that a task is best accomplished by someone who has a love for it, combined with an instinctive natural ability. This high moral ground should not be tainted by an excess, either of physical reward or of expertise. Until recently, breeding and character were of greater value than knowledge and experience.

Professional?

Why must industrial managers be professional? Indeed, what is meant by professional? The need for professionalism stems from the need for a management style directly aimed at fulfilling the company purpose, and based upon knowledge and understanding of what to achieve and how to achieve it. This has to include a full knowledge of the existing commercial environment and competitive position, both now and in the future. Management needs to be educated. The role of a manager should not be perceived as a birth right, or as a natural or instinctive gift, but as an activity stemming from an in-depth knowledge of the industry, the people who work in that industry and, above all, of the needs, requirements and expectations of the potential customer base of that industry.

There was a strange joke going around industry during the last Olympic Games. It had different forms, but in essence it suggested that if industrial management were one of the events, Great Britain would win, since, in the UK, management was our greatest amateur sport.

This traditional amateur approach to management within industry, has always sat uncomfortably with the ambition to succeed in a market-place economy. We have always been, and still are, ambivalent towards industrial success. We applaud the Victorian Industrial Masters, who appeared to rule the world with their manufacturing prowess, but we are unsure of the place of such success in society. We consider manufacturing industry, especially the older and dirtier industries, as having a lesser status than the 'professions'. It is easier to acquire recognised success, and often wealth and power as well, in the professions, such as law, accountancy, insurance, etc. Many within the 'heavy' industries have an in-built feeling of failure. Life has passed them by. They do not inhabit the real world of the city, but are the necessary, rather embarrassing face of an industrialised society, the trades-people. Through not having pursued a more academic route, via one of the professions, they have missed the real fruits of post-war Britain.

Historical attitudes must be overcome

They are wrong. In most countries of the world, particularly the UK's successful competitors, it is the industrialist who has the perceived high status. Such societies have an in-built understanding of their ability to generate wealth and live off its fruits.

Here in Britain there are two historical attitudes to overcome. Firstly, the class system has always seen a distinct separation between the functions of generating wealth and of enjoying its fruits. Secondly, the ability to manage was perceived as a gift. This gift was endowed from birth, something to be born with, possibly acquired over generations. Leadership was somehow transmitted through the genes.

This notion, which originated with the landed families, was introduced into industry during the Victorian era. It was founded on the paternal, family-based, autocratic managerial style that is at the root of many industries. It was compounded by the success of such companies. Such success was probably more to do with political exploitation of the Empire than with management skills, but the questions were never asked. No-one doubted the innate ability of the British to manage the Empire, or the new industries. The UK has always been blessed with an officer class whose education and breeding has created them natural leaders. Who needs knowledge?

The Empire had strong political controls, limiting any competition, industrial or military. Thus, whilst our industry served the Empire, this management style gave satisfactory results. Even as late as the 1950s, the UK industry's target was the expanding home market, still with little foreign competition. These management methods went unchallenged. It was not until our markets were opened, first to America and Europe and then to the Far East, that the UK's ability to manage its industry was shown to be wanting. The UK was not alone. Several leading Americans have indicated the lack of a coherent management style within the USA. Even as late as 1982, Deming commented,

> 'Western style of management must change to halt the decline of Western industry'.[2]

Whereas our Western colleagues have now largely revised their ideas of industrial management, many within the UK cling to the past. Perhaps our past glories were so glorious that it has taken more effort to move forward from them.

The much needed, but misdirected push!

The impetus for a movement away from past methods came with the onset of recession, in the late 1970s. This effort to change was too late for some companies, and they failed to survive. Those that survived changed by adopting and adapting ideas from abroad, sometimes in direct response to customers' demands. Whilst the ideas were sound, they were, for the most part, not fully understood. They became *attached* to the management style, rather than *integrated* into it.

The thought that the vast redundancies and closures of the 1970s and early 1980s were inevitable, is not only a myth, but a dangerous one. This era of British industry represents a vast lesson in industrial management. It is one so rich in examples of both good and bad managerial practice, and won and lost opportunities, that it should be studied in depth. Many messages will scream from this era, lessons which came too late for many involved, but which are still of great relevance today. There is a dangerous and misguided conclusion to be drawn, ie. that industry is beyond the control of those who administer it. A company is somehow mere flotsam on the waves of world commerce.

This dangerous mixture of national pride and fatalism leads to a passive acceptance of the inevitable. We may be poor and unemployed, but we are safe! It was fate, beyond our control. We do not have total responsibility for our future, nor for the future of those whom we employ. There is no need to question our ability to manage.

A task ....

Write down three or four of the most important aspects of your industry that have changed during the last 15 years.

For each one, ask yourself.

What caused the change?
Why was change necessary?
Could the change have happened earlier?
Was the change part of an overall strategy?
Does everyone in your company understand this change?

This is, of course, nonsense. Every nation trades under the same rules. Every company has the ability to foresee future markets, and meet them. Either there is an acceptance that bad management has led to the crisis, or another scapegoat has to be found. Unfortunately, it is easier to select from the reasons why the company has failed, listed below, rather than to question the ability of management to manage.

16 good reasons for the British industrial decline

- Lack of government support
- Lack of investment
- Lack of proper leadership
- World recession
- High interest rates
- The price of oil
- The greenhouse effect
- Poorly trained management
- Poor industrial relations
- Lazy workers
- The unions
- Poor foreign raw materials
- Unfair competition from abroad
- Dumping of unwanted foreign goods
- Our winning the war
- The British weather

This list may look familiar. It also appeared in Chapter 1.

Senior management have the responsibility to ensure success.

Excuses are not needed. What led to the demise of companies during the recession was not the recession itself, but poor management prior to the recession. Properly managed, each company would have foreseen the changing market-place. It would have planned and changed its operations to take advantage of the recession, rather than go under. This may seem hard, particularly in the older heavy industries - how could ship building and textiles be expected to compete with the cheap labour of the East?

The price of labour is but one of the many variables that need managing. It can be planned with investment in technology and the development of the full human potential. Where cheap labour exists, the use of ignorant masses replaces the skill and expertise of educated technicians with strong technology at their fingertips, who use knowledge rather than numbers. Where there is a large workforce, make more money by capturing a larger share of the world markets. Make people a resource rather than a millstone.

Senior management has the responsibility to put both people and plant to work to generate wealth. This means change. It will require the adaptation of other people's practice, and the development of new ideas and methods. If any market is possible, for any country or company, it should be possible for us. Japan has survived in the heavy industries, despite wage levels that are now equivalent to our own.

A total reappraisal

A total reappraisal of our business methods and management styles is needed. Reappraisal is an essential on-going activity to ensure that a company remains on course.

Active and passive knowledge

The reappraisal must be based on knowledge and experience. Experience is active knowledge gained from doing, from actual participation. This knowledge is often expensive, as the resultant mistakes have to be paid for. It is also extremely valuable, and a company asset.

Passive knowledge comes from the text book, and from academic study.

To learn from the active knowledge, that is from practical experience, it should be matched and tested against the relevant passive knowledge. This constant reappraisal of theory, by reference to the practical applications and vice-versa, will modify and improve the theory. There has been a gap between theory and practice in the past. Academics pursue theories in abstract, and are often unaware of the value, or otherwise, of their findings in industry, whilst the practical doers in industry base all their methods on their past practice and experience. Never the twain shall meet. Change is difficult.

Statistical Process Control (SPC) is an example of this gap. SPC was first introduced into the Bell Laboratories, during the 1920s, by Dr W A Shewhart. It was subsequently adopted into the academic side of industry, introduced into British Standards (600 and 1008) during the 1930s, and became a topic within university engineering degree courses. The number of students who learnt the theory of SPC at this early and formative stage of their life must run into many thousands. Yet the general integration of these ideas into manufacturing industry did not happen. The complete acceptance of this gap, both by the academics who taught these ideas and the students who became industry's managers, without finding any use for SPC, has to be surprising. We had to wait until SPC was made easy before we had a tool that was of use to industry.[3]

Improvements are on the way. University departments, such as the Industry Unit at the University of Wales, are developing and marketing the university's knowledge, in practical form, for industry. Also, Mal Owen's work at Bristol Polytechnic, with the Training for Quality Unit, has been a path-finder for many educational institutions aiming to bridge the gap between passive and active knowledge.

A coherent set of standards, theories and ideals.

Changing senior management attitudes can fill this gap between passive and active knowledge. A total commitment to learn, use the latest ideas and develop the company's theoretical expertise, will ensure that all decisions, priorities and actions reflect and incorporate the company policy to be the best. A Total Quality strategy can embody these ideals, and give substance and direction to the entire company. It will form all the company's actions.

Every question that arises can then be resolved against this backcloth of the management strategy. The knowledge, experience and theory, that combine to create the strategy, are available to everyone, at any time and at any place within the company. All decisions can be based on sound theory. The management of the company begins to have a total coherence. It begins to be the physical representation of a coherent set of standards, theories and ideals. Each employee, from the managing director to the newest recruit, has this tangible structure of theory and knowledge to draw upon.

The Quality gaps

The gap between academic theory and industrial practice is but one example of the 'Quality gap'. Most failure, in industry, can be seen as a manifestation of the Quality gap.

The gap between technology and industrial practice, as discussed above, can be demonstrated, in this way (see Fig 2.1).

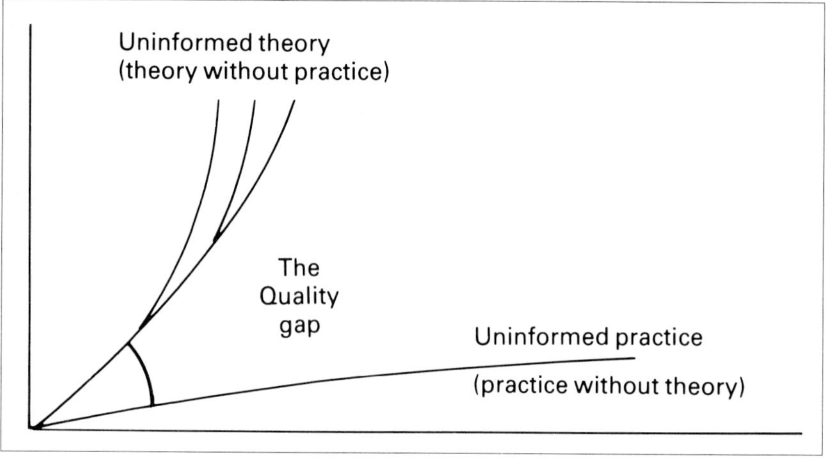

Fig 2.1 Quality gap - technology and industrial practice (open).

With a total approach to Quality, all practice becomes based on sound theory. The company becomes the research bed, at the forefront of the business, doing the job better than the competitors; the gap is closed, and Quality rises (see Fig 2.2).

Another expression of the Quality gap can be seen by considering how customer expectations are met. Obviously, all customers want the highest standards available to them, and usually expect the best. Indeed, their expectations are driven by the performance of the best suppliers. It was noted in Chapter 1 that the company with the highest Quality, sets the standard that others will have to follow. The Quality gap will, therefore, be the difference between the expectations of the customer and the performance of the supplier (see Fig 2.3).

Where this gap can be reversed, that is the supplier can create new ground and exceed the customer's expectations, a competitive edge will be created, ensuring continued business (see Fig 2.4).

Since good Quality is always less expensive to produce than poor Quality, the gap will have yet a further expression if price and Quality are compared (see Fig 2.5).

Improvement, from a poor base, will never produce the same results that would have been possible if total commitment to Quality had been present from the beginning. However, if Total Quality is adopted by a company, the achievements will be remarkable and may significantly narrow the Quality gap (see Fig 2.6).

Again, the activity of the competition, will be of the greatest importance. It should always be assumed that all the major competitors are undertaking process improvement activities, and that their performance is improving. The company, likewise, is constantly improving *its* Quality performance. The Quality gap, here, will be shown to be the gap between the rate of improvement by the best competitor, and the rate of improvement by the company (see Fig 2.7).

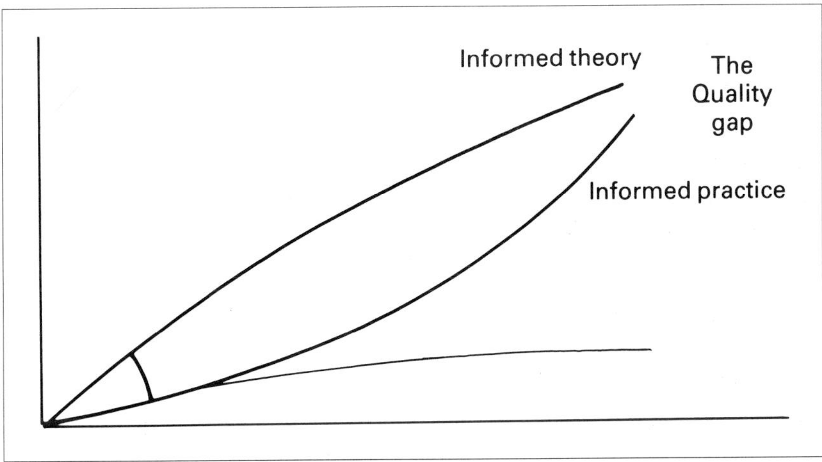

Fig 2.2 Quality gap - technology and industrial practice (closed).

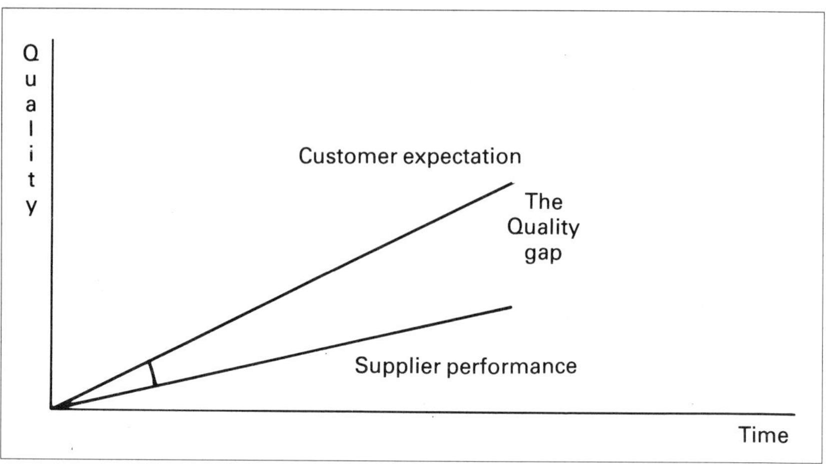

Fig 2.3 Quality gap - customer expectations and supplier performance (open).

Where the company can outstrip the competition, in terms of the rate of improvement in Quality standards, the Quality gap, again, becomes the competitive edge (see Fig 2.8).

Total Quality

Total Quality is the necessary component to survive. Total Quality is also the means to guarantee success. The commitment to Quality must, therefore, be total. This total commitment will have several expressions.

In-depth understanding

The total commitment to Quality demands a bridging of the gap between theory and practice, that is between passive and active knowledge. The company must become devoted to reason. All decisions must be based on the fullest knowledge possible. The company will need an on-going and in-depth knowledge of:

- Manpower - how to manage, motivate and obtain the full potential of the company's human resources.

- Machinery - understanding the latest in technology, how to maintain it, and how to achieve the greatest value from all the company's plant and equipment.

- Materials - being the expert in the use of the materials needed by all departments of the company.

- Methods - employing the latest methodology, in all areas of the company.

- Measurement - using the latest techniques to comprehend exactly what is happening with all the company's processes.

- Milieu - appreciating the effects of the environmental conditions in which the company operates.

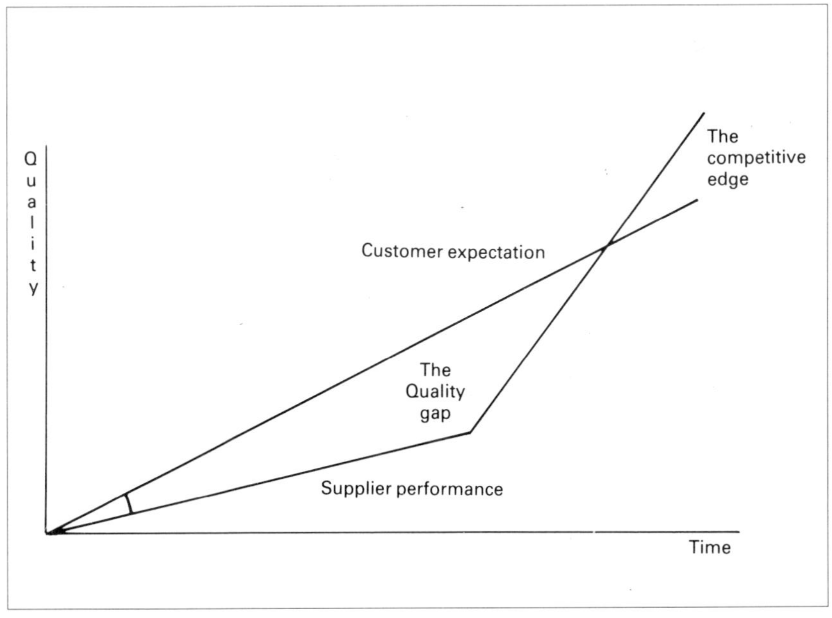

Fig 2.4 Quality gap - customer expectations and supplier performance (closed).

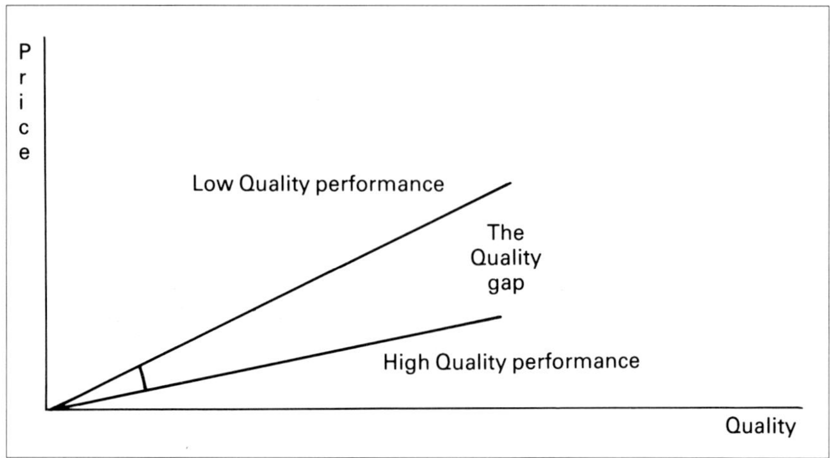

Fig 2.5 Quality gap - Quality and price (open).

Everyone

Total Quality needs the total commitment of everyone. Every member of the company needs to be informed of what is necessary, why it is necessary, and what their part in the company effort will be. No dissonance within the company can be helpful. Everyone must be orientated to work for the common goal. Everyone must be committed to Quality.

Fig 2.6 Quality gap - Quality and price (closed).

Every activity

This drive towards Total Quality must be integrated into every activity. The efficiency and cost of every activity must be understood and constantly improved.

Every decision

The concentration on a single goal, that of customer satisfaction, ie. Quality, will determine the priorities of the company, resolve differences, identify actions, and thus be the background to every decision made in the company.

Total commitment

Thus, Total Quality becomes the focus of the company's activity, energy and resources. Nothing is allowed to stand in its way. By orientating every member of the company, and indeed those beyond the company who effect its results, towards the same, easily understood and meaningful purpose, Total Quality is not only possible, it is greatly enjoyable. The force of a company of people with a total commitment to an ideal is unstoppable. That ideal is desirable, attainable and fun. It is Total Quality.

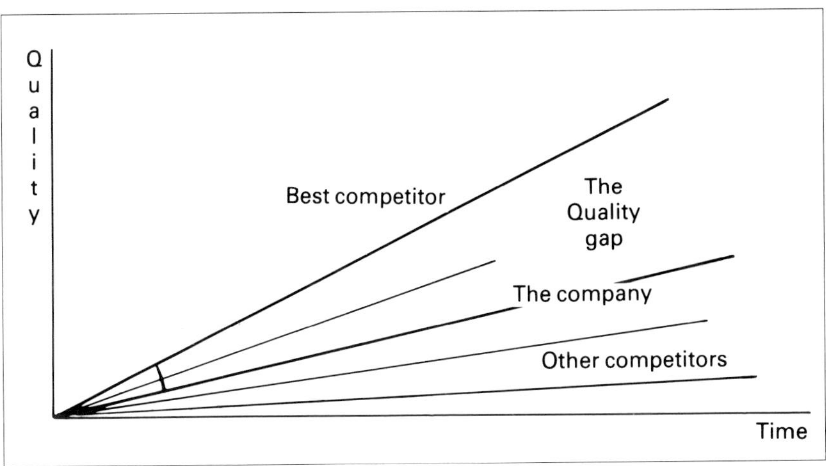

Fig 2.7 Quality gap - Comparative rates of Quality improvement (open).

Industrial citizenship

The role of each employee must be considered within this framework. No longer will there be a place for the unskilled, uninvolved mindless labour. A Total Quality company will require employees with a contribution to make, and an appreciation of the responsibilities and duties necessary to maximise the company's performance. Industrial citizens are needed.

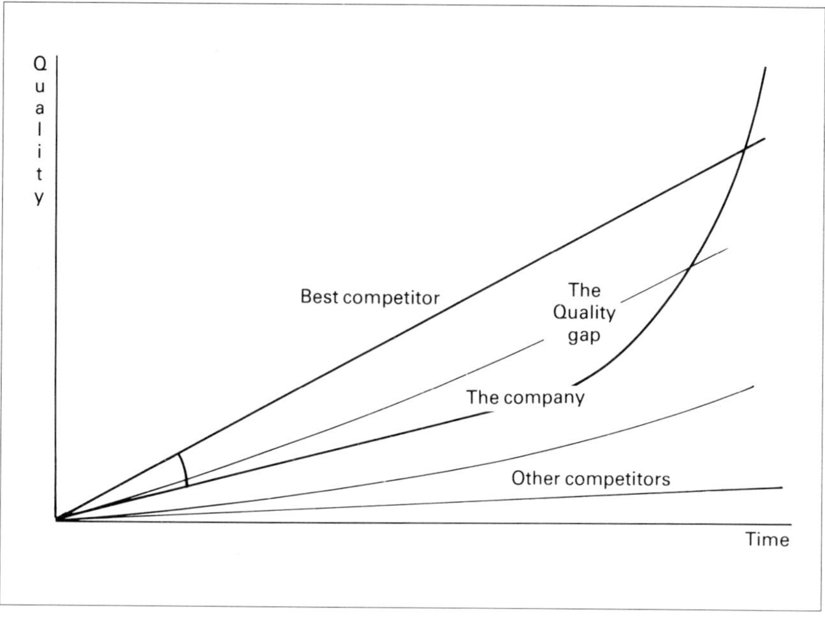

Fig 2.8 Quality gap - Comparative rates of Quality improvement (closed).

Summary

Change is needed via a professional approach to overcome historical attitudes. The Quality movement started in the 1970s and 1980s. Change is a senior management responsibility.

Total reappraisal considering active and passive knowledge, is also needed, providing a cohesive set of standards, theories and ideals.

Quality gaps concern

- technology and industrial practice
- customer expectations and supplier performance
- Quality and price
- Comparative rates of Quality improvement

Total Quality means an in-depth understanding, by everybody, in every activity, and every decision.

Total Quality simply means a total commitment to Quality

Last thoughts ....

What are the requirements of potential customers, seeing a sign outside a local stables?

Quality Manure

£2 per bag
Do it yourself £1

1. Ishikawa, *What is Total Quality Control?* The Japanese Way, p. 1, 1985.
2. Edwards, Deming, *Out of the Crisis*, p. 18, 1982.
3. Choppin, Jon, *SPC Made Easy*, 1987.

Chapter 3

A Management Strategy

Many things difficult to design
prove easy to performance,

– Samuel Johnson, Rasselas XIII

Route-map

The idea of a strategy is first explored and extended to a management strategy. There is then a more in-depth appreciation of what is meant by the concepts of management and strategy.

The main types of managers to be found in industry are typified as 'squareys' and 'roundys'.

The four 'A's of management are described as Access, Action, Attitude and Activity.

The chapter concludes with a consideration of the development of a Total Quality Strategy and a Total Quality Policy.

This book does not presume to be a comprehensive guide to business management, but rather, a useful tool for those seeking to develop a successful, Quality orientated business. To achieve this, the need for a management strategy is justified, and then the components are identified. Finally, this chapter will consider the methods involved, both in the development and the implementation of such a strategy.

The need for a strategy should not be taken for granted. Indeed, nor should the meaning of strategy be assumed. All companies have a strategy of some kind. It is often unwritten, unstated and in some cases, lacks real consideration. In its lowest form, a strategy could be, 'to continue past and present activities into the future'. This could be classified as a conscious decision, even if it is, in fact, a decision not to make any changes in direction, method or even understanding.

Why Strategy?

The word strategy is used to describe the conscious planning of the overall company aims, and the route to these aims. The whole act of doing business is always directional, in that, apart from the occasional dramatic event, such as liquidation, there is never any end point, finish or completion. Business is always on-going. This parallels the consideration of Quality. Perfection never exists: we can only move towards it. The research and exploration of the routes in this direction are the responsibility of the senior management group.

A definition of the senior management group is, therefore, important. Regardless of the company organisational chart, the small group who share the decision-making, are, de facto, the senior management group. In companies where the senior executive does not share this power, there is a senior management group of one. This has to be recognised and understood, both by the senior executive, and by everyone else.

A management strategy will have three stages.

The first will be an analysis and appraisal of all the information, theory and ideas, indeed the basic values of the company. During this stage, it is vital that an objective stance is taken to establish:

1. The exact status of the company, with regard to all the aspects held to be of importance. These will take account of the many internal features of the company and its plant and material, and resources, both human and financial, as well as the external concerns of the marketplace.

2. The direction in which it is desired that the company moves. Whilst this may be expressed in the convenient shorthand of goals and/or

objectives, it should be understood that such goals are the ideal. They can only be achieved step by step, rather than by any over-night transformation, and anyway, they will probably be re-assessed along the route. Thus, in reality, we think in terms of the direction in which we wish to change.

The second stage of the management strategy is arriving at the routes and methods to be taken. The third, but not final stage, is the implementation of the strategy, by relating the strategic direction, route and methods,to the everyday company activities and processes.

It is not final. The development of a management strategy is never a one-off, definite event, that is done for all time. The three stages are constantly re-assessed, as further evidence and information is taken into account. Once in operation, the direction should never need any significant alterations, rather just 'minor trimming', to suit changing circumstances. If this appears to be rather involved, it should become clearer as we progress (see Fig 3.1).

This rational approach has the benefit of coherence, whilst keeping the ideas simple and straightforward. The precise components of a strategy will be unique to particular companies, but each strategy will share certain basic ingredients.

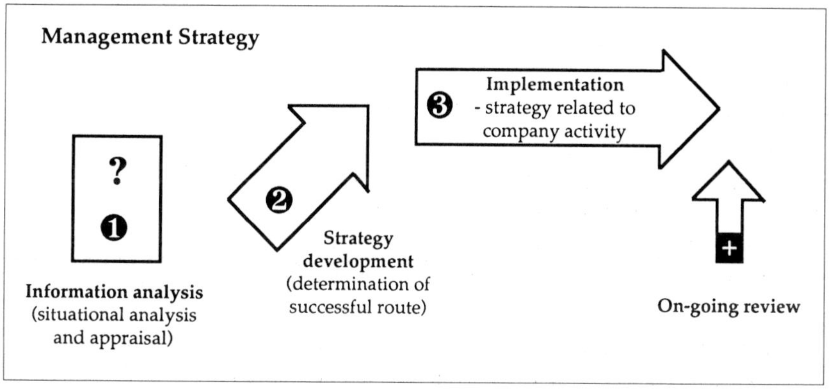

Fig 3.1 The three stages of a Management Strategy.

What is a strategy?

Strategy was originally a military term and was defined as 'the art of planning and directing larger military movements and the operations of war.' In business, this can be translated into 'the effective management of the company resources, to fulfil, and to continue to fulfil, the overall company purpose, to generate wealth'.

This is true of every company and corporation, not only in the UK, but throughout the industrialised world. The vast transformation occurring in the socialist countries, at the time of writing, is to some extent caused by the need for this main purpose within industry. They have yet to come to terms with the wealth generating aspects of their industry. The differences between capitalism and socialism can be expressed in terms of how this wealth is used and distributed, rather than its original generation. Sound wealth production methods are a necessity for either system. This may sound political, but wealth generation is the root of all industrial activities, and thus of any social system.

There are questions to be raised in relation to the service industries. They, with a few exceptions involving invisible exports, do not generate finance for the country as a whole. They represent part of the wealth conversion and distribution system. They are nonetheless valuable because of this but, within a manufacturing nation, should not be seen as a viable alternative to the manufacturing and export sectors of industry.

Service industries are not precluded from effective Total Quality Management (TQM). Indeed, TQM is as essential to them as it is to the manufacturing sector. The profit motive, the wealth generating purpose of an organisation, will in some cases be more difficult to perceive – it may be translated into wealth conservation, whilst fulfilling other purposes. It nevertheless must be there, in some shape or form, as the evaluative tool to be balanced against Quality. This is as true in a school or hospital as it is in a coal mine or car factory.

An alternative to wealth generation, as a definition of purpose, could be resource re-generation. In pure terms, these definitions are synonymous. A manufacturing company uses its wealth to purchase resources (people and equipment) to generate more resource, usually expressed in financial terms. Business is about skimming off the surplus to provide wealth for shareholders, employees, etc.

This framework still exists within the consideration of all parts of the service sector. The National Health Service, by using resources to satisfy its customers, promotes further political decisions to acquire taxes and revenue for further expenditure on health. There are more complicated customer relationships operating within any social service. For instance, is the customer of a school the pupil who receives the education, the parent whose child is educated, the community which pays the taxes that finance the school, or the local employer who uses much of the fruits of the education invested in the pupil cum employee, and who indeed generated the original wealth that enabled the community to indulge in education in the first place?

The main purpose of any business is the generation of wealth, and the Total Quality Strategy must be based on this purpose, but it must consider other available information. The strategy is produced from a synthesis of an understanding of the company purpose and all the available information about the past, present and future business environment within which the organisation is operating.

The company strategy should be firmly based on theory, not just on past practice. It will inevitably revolve around certain concepts, which

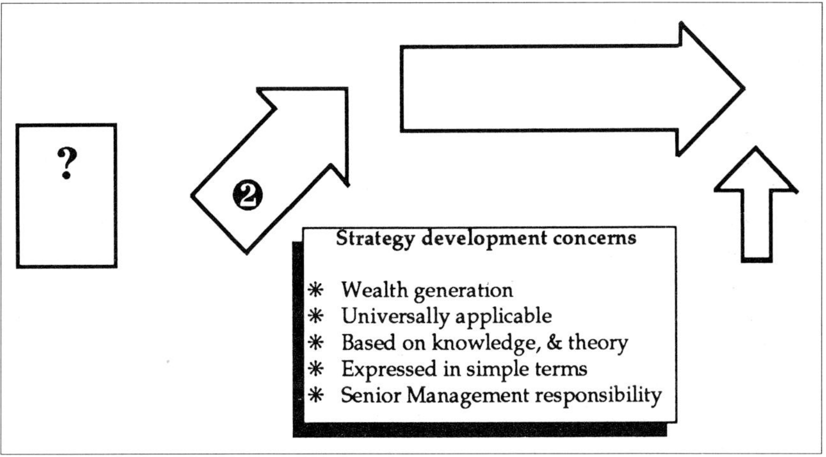

Fig 3.2 Development of a Management Strategy.

must be a common perception throughout the senior management group. This common perception should not stem from an automatic, non-questioning, received ethos of the company, nor from one person within the company, but should be derived from a constant interchange of ideas and debate in theoretical terms.

The orientation of the human resources of a company requires three inputs; stimulation, organisation and knowledge. TQM via the Total Quality Strategy orientates everyone towards the main purpose of the company. TQM provides the means of organising these brains; this is why it has to be managed. TQM must provide the knowledge base, in the form of sound information and ideas, founded upon commonly perceived concepts.

Why management?

Essentially, business must be managed. An appreciation of the theoretical inputs of this statement needs an understanding of the concepts of change and resources.

Change has often been said to be the only constant in life. The attitude to change describes two types of managers: the *squareys* and the *roundys*. In reality, neither style exists to the exclusion of the other. We are all a mixture of both; each invested in different degrees in all of us. Their description is helpful in understanding the world of industrial management. As you read, ask yourself the question, which am I?

The squareys

Traditionally, squareys have never been very good at controlling change, preferring to take the more comfortable route of endlessly coping with it. They are more able to shrug off the responsibility for the subsequent results as being beyond their control. The short-term benefits appear to be wholesome. They feel confident within a small world, expecting little to be different. Everyone, as well as everything, in its place, and a place for everyone and everything. This is an undemanding world.

This is because, squareys, both at a company and at an individual level, mostly just react; their actions are caused by the latest set of circumstances. Most decisions are pre-set, reactive, and are based on the short-term 'needs must' basis. There is often little choice. Time takes them step by step through life, with a sure inevitability that makes acceptance of the consequences easy.

There is even some pleasure in this way of living. Because so much is outside their control, it is exciting. The constant crisis is great for their adrenaline. Indeed, those who appear to cope best with this crisis management, and appear to devote the most energy to reacting to situations, are well thought of, become promoted and sometimes receive rich rewards. Squareys are loyal, straightforward and constantly reinforce the status-quo. They are the backbone of industry. However, the rich rewards are probably as much the result of co-incidence, as of calculation. There is a high casualty rate in middle age. For every single successful manager, there are many others who gradually become disillusioned and cynical.

The roundys

The roundys perceive the world as constantly changing. To them, the shape of their world can always be influenced and thus, to some extent, controlled. They are not subject to the inevitable. They perceive everything, and indeed everyone, as open to challenge. Ideally, they are concerned with the future, the present is rather boring and the past, except as a lesson, is totally uninteresting: everything is possible. This is not a comfortable existence. They tend to duck responsibility for the effects of their decisions, being more concerned with the future. Conversely though, they are involved with everything. The boundaries of each individual's thoughts, interests and activities are removed, responsibility becomes a shared commodity. Attitudes are developed to cope with these effects. Slogans, such as 'There is only one bad mistake – the one you don't learn from!', become commonplace. They shrug off concepts such as loyalty, and today's way of doing things. They live in the future.

Such people are difficult to live with. They make considerable demands on themselves, and on those near to them. They tend to be erratic, as new information and ideas reorientate their interests. However, they do positively attempt to control change, form the future, and actively manage the resources around them. They understand that management, to be successful, has eventually to become a long-term activity. A crisis is the result of poor management. There may be the immediate necessity to take a reactive, knee jerk decision, but this isn't good management. It is the result of poor management.

The fundamental dilemma

It is quite possible to perceive industrial organisations peopled with both types of managers. Clearly, since their whole ethos is different, they will be in conflict. They will fail to appreciate each other's point of view, and will be very sceptical about the other's ability to manage. The squareys are reactive. They provide only what is demanded of them. They are loyal. They are predictable. Above all, they are solid members of the community, since they perceive their company as fixed, rigid and unchanging, based upon well understood principles, methods and disciplines. They daily reinforce the status-quo. They, in fact, daily help to make the world, including their company, more in the mould of their perception – that is, squarey.

They are in conflict with, and often intensely dislike, the roundys, who perceive the company shape as more amoebic, constantly changing, expanding, contracting and not based on rigidly held values, true for all time, but meeting the ever changing challenge of tomorrow. Those of the younger variety of this breed, far from being content to accept the lowly position of an apprentice, learning the company's ways before reaching an opinion on anything, expound radical thoughts, ideas and theories, in a never ending jumble. They demand information, facts and opportunities to develop. Such demands are seldom met and their lack of experience, knowledge or real responsibility, often leads to some of these thoughts and actions to be lacking in justification, or even misguided. Indeed, often they may be in conflict with each other. Nevertheless, they are vibrant, concerned with the future, and looking for the opportunity to manage.

All too often, the conflict is resolved on a day to day basis, and at a relatively junior level of the company. The squareys don't rock the boat, ask uncomfortable questions or behave unpredictably. In short, they appear to be solid company people. They get promoted. The moment never seems right for roundys. Their talents are recognised, but they don't fit. As time goes by, the relative numbers of squareys and roundys swings towards the squarey perceptions.

They actually create the company constructed out of solid, static, rigid, rectangular blocks of thought, in the mould of their original perception. Being good status-quo people, who reinforce today's values and methods, they become more senior, with more power to do just that, and reinforce today's values and methods.

These are not really today's values and methods any more, but yesterday's. However, they don't notice. Before long the top of the company is peopled with squareys, who have few management strategies other than the desire to ensure that the roundys are kept safely in their place, away from any position of influence.

Breaking the mould

What is your managerial stance? Part of the value of implementing a TQM policy is that it breaks this mould. People of talent are allowed into the areas of real responsibility and planning. The conflict is resolved by a universally perceived notion of the company, its purpose and future. Properly constructed inter-personal relationships replace the hit and miss, 'sort it out at an individual level' regime that inhabits most of industry. The roundys' enthusiasms are captured, tempered with knowledge and experience, and then allowed to manage the future for the benefit of all. They are disciplined by the results of their actual responsibilities, and their own need to construct a present, as well as a future. In short, they become a little squarey.

The squareys are gradually educated, opened up and shown the inherent flexibility existing in all human relationships, and in time become a little roundy.

Essential management

As with most words and terms in industry, *management* is widely used, very loosely, with no real definition. If asked, people are often reluctant to accept the term, unless it is part of their title. The labelling of some and not others with the 'manager' tag, probably does more harm than good.

Most management is amateur in the extreme, as a brief conversation with any group of managers quickly reveals. Each acts out his own private theories and beliefs about the role of a manager, and is usually sure of his own managerial ability, whilst having grave doubts about his colleagues. There is no universally accepted definition, methodology or yardstick, with which to measure the effectiveness of management. Hence, it is described as 'amateur'.

Definitions

Senior managers – those who decide which processes are to be operated to produce results. The concept of process is expanded later in The Management of Process.

Managers – those who *facilitate* the processes for which they are accountable. That is ensure that all the process inputs (6Ms) of good quality are provided.

Process operators – those who have responsibility for the processes (they could be called the process experts).

Management is about decision-making, which is essentially the synthesis of known information, perceived priorities, immediate circumstances and desired outcomes. The result of the decision is action. It may be a decision to take no action, and such a deliberate negative action allows previous actions to be perpetuated.

The four 'A's of management

Behind every action, there is a decision. To control all the actions, there must be control of all the decisions. 'Ay!' as Shakespeare wrote, 'there's the rub'. It is only in circumstances that give rise to confidence, that the decision-making process can be delegated. It is hoped that, exposed to the same information, anyone would make the right decision; the right decision being the one we would take. Delegation thus moves the decision, but does not necessarily change it.

A for Access

The first step to management of people is to ensure that everyone has access to all the necessary information. Whilst this sounds obvious, it is the very opposite to many management styles. British society runs on ignorance. Knowledge is often equated with power, and thus it is restricted to a 'need to know' basis.

The company has nothing to fear from a spread of knowledge. Individuals may fear that their incompetences may be shown up if others have full access to information, methodology and people. Regrettably, ignorance often begets more ignorance. The terminology embeds the closed nature of the culture. People rarely refer to a closed management style, or closed government, but only as enlightenment spreads do we hear of open management, open government. The idea that knowledge is power is a myth.

Conversely though, ignorance is a stultifying force, and a very expensive presence in any organisation. Above all, it perverts or inhibits decision-making by people without free access to the required knowledge and experience.

Insecurity, stemming from ignorance, is the result of poor management. It is highly inefficient, and will ensure that a high proportion of decisions have below optimum results. It is neither by accident nor by chance, that people fear the competition of others in the organisation, nor is it inevitable. Such fear, by leading to wrong decisions, is extremely expensive. It is also self-perpetuating and destroys the essential trading fabric of the company by inhibiting any internal customer relationships. Individuals are not in competition within a company, any more than are the different departments, shifts, strata or activities. Every business has quite sufficient competition from outside, without constructing internal competition to consume its energies.

This trend towards ignorance, and coveted knowledge, is deep-seated throughout society. It may be challenged, at a national level, by the demands for a Bill of Rights, and a Freedom of Information Act. Locally, industry needs to move forward.

We cannot change the whole of society. We *can* change our company. We cannot create an open society overnight. We *can* give everyone free access to information, experience and to other people. We *can* set such a goal in our own area, and develop a management strategy that positively moves the company in that direction.

A for Attitudes

The culture of a company is really the result of the many attitudes held within that company. It was part of the common management philosophy for well over a century that a man's thoughts were his own, and that the company could only be concerned with his actions.

Such ideas have been reinforced by the two main political thrusts, through industry, since the industrial revolution. Capitalists were only concerned with outcomes, the results of actions. How they were achieved was of secondary importance. The man was indistinguishable from the machine. Marxists typified the industrial process as the purchase of a man's efforts for cash. Again, it was only labour that was considered valuable or part of the deal. The man's thoughts were his own. Both these descriptions are extremely simplistic, and will have caused offense in some readers, but they do have a degree of justification, though. In general, little effort is made to capture the hearts and minds of people in work. It is considered that attitudes are something to be lived with, rather than encouraged, informed and thus controlled. Such a large part of the decision-making process cannot be ignored, if the delegation of decision-making is to be as wide as possible.

Bad attitudes are a myth. Attitudes are the unconscious expression of the person's sense of reality. If there is a dissonance between two people's perceptions, they will hold different attitudes. Expose people to the maximum information and encourage debate, and these differences of perception will be reduced.

This not advocating brain-washing, indoctrination, or rigid selection procedures to ensure that people are all of like mind. Quite the opposite – opening up the access to knowledge and experience will allow the formation of attitudes. Lively debate will allow such attitudes to be tempered by the thoughts, attitudes and prejudices of others. Above all, there is a need for deliberate changes to be introduced into peoples' working lives. Changing the actions people take will change their perceptions of their job, their role, the company and their relationships. In other words, if people's actions are changed, so are their attitudes.

Rhetoric, slogans and posters are all designed to change attitudes, and usually fail. People do not have attitudes out of perversity, wickedness, or to spite someone else. Their attitude, just as much as our own, is an expression of their view of reality. Prejudices are only attitudes in others which we don't like. Some people describe prejudices as ill-founded fears, or opinion without evidence or reason. We never perceive a prejudice within ourselves. We have reason for our beliefs. People never change their view, or their beliefs, merely because they are told they are wrong. Slogans and posters may reinforce a changed attitude, giving a warm group feeling to those in the know, but they do not change the view of the disbeliever. They do not change attitudes. To change the attitudes of the workforce, change the actions they take.

A for Actions

Attitudes will only be permanently altered if they lead to changed actions. The two, attitudes and actions, are inextricably linked. Changed attitudes will not only determine which actions are changed, but how. Methods, effort, efficiency, and many other aspects of the actions will be involved.

Actions can be considered to be of two types. Those that are an integral part of the processes, involved in the business, and those that occur in an unplanned manner. Those that are part of a well managed process will be predictable, in that every possible action will have been foreseen. It is the unpredictable, often in a crisis situation, that leads to unforeseen circumstances.

However, actions of both types can be left safely in the hands of well trained, well motivated employees. The attitudes of such employees should be based upon knowledge and experience, and, therefore, their scope should be predictable.

A is for Activities

The activities of a company can be decreed. A set of values that will inform, and define these activities, can be promoted. The environment within which these activities take place can be influenced. In short, management's responsibility is to plan the activities of the company, thus making optimum use of the company's resources to fulfil the company's purpose.

Many companies rarely put their activities under any real scrutiny. Life moves from day to day, repeating yesterday's activities and methods. Quality management has to embody a long-term commitment, bringing each and every activity of the company into the overall strategy. To relate this theory to the Quality structure of the company, an activity is defined as a collection of processes. Each activity has its purpose, the generation of wealth, indeed, each process within an activity should be similarly directed.

In most companies, there exists an unofficial hierarchy of activities. Some see themselves as more important, or more actively involved with the product, whereas the activities of others are seen as peripheral. Often those involved even see themselves in the same light. In answer to 'What is your function within the company?', many people will start their reply with *I only* ... It might be *I only do this, I'm only in accounts, I just work in the admin. area, I just schedule the work,* or *I only sweep the floor.* The *I only...* implies their secondary perception of their activity.

The 4 A's of Management

ACCESS to information

ATTITUDES are altered

ACTIONS are changed

ACTIVITIES are improved

Fig 3.3 The four 'A's of management.

This *I only* syndrome is very damaging to the operation of a company. Whatever the activity, it is either an integral part of the strategy, to generate wealth, or it is not. If it is, it is vital. If it is not vital, it should be discontinued. The vital nature of a particular activity may well be time-based. It may form part of the strategy for a time, and then be discontinued in favour of another activity.

In practice, most activities evolve, rather than being specifically designed. Whatever the activity, though, and however the activity is carried out, the attitude towards it should be the same. There should be a neutrality, derived from each activity being considered as equally important as all others. This neutrality will convey similar messages to the people who work in these and other areas. They all have a right to feel *of value,* and to be in a position to gain satisfaction from a vital job well done. All activities are part of the company effort.

There is a tendency within the steel industry to have attitudes that mirror 'Irish' jokes. Instead of the Irishman, they feature the furnaceman. As you find that the Irish then tell the same jokes about the men from Kerry, so the bottom of the pile in the steel industry would seem to be the ladlemen. Naturally, the counter feeling has developed within steel-works, whereby the nearer to the 'hot stuff' you are, the higher your status as a real steelman.

The inevitable effect of diverse feelings of value will be that many personnel give considerably less than their optimum, both in effort and thought. Also, certain activities will develop the aura of being luxuries. They will be afforded in the good times, but will be cut back when money is short; very important when affordable, redundant when not. There are many such examples. Some companies treat their factory maintenance in this fashion, whilst to others the training department has a flexibility that would be thought criminal in a direct production area. Even the Quality department may be seen as expendable when times get hard.

There will always be short-term arguments for such cuts, based on expediencies and emergencies. Such situations are, however, all examples of the lack of a proper management strategy, if not, of downright bad management. Good management would have foreseen and negated the adverse effects before they occurred.

In truth, all activities play a part in generating wealth, and are thus part of production. If they don't contribute to generating wealth, they will be consuming it and, therefore, should be discontinued.

The Total Quality Strategy

The strategy will be all embracing, and will involve a fresh look at every part of the company, and, in particular, every activity. However, for it to achieve the desired results, it must be essentially practical. It must be based on sound theoretical statements. It must operate in defined areas. It must have methods available to achieve the intended activity improvements, and it must have the means of demonstrating that such improvements are real, rather than merely part of the company rhetoric.

The growth in company rhetoric has been a disturbing phenomenon of some perceived moves towards Quality. Pioneers of the new industrial philosophies, such as Deming,[1] Juran,[2] Crosby[3] and the like, have all produced a fair amount in print, with much that is quotable, and much that is quoted out of context. None of them desired or expected that their words would be taken, and preached as a gospel to the uninitiated. Regrettably, where this has happened, it rarely produces tangible improvements.

Without any *real* seed change in a company's perception, nothing else will radically change. More rhetoric, and yet more rhetoric, has to follow to cover the lack of visible success of the previous ideas.

Salvation is often found in 'back patting' sessions. Each group devotes energy to self and mutual congratulatory messages. Without hard evidence of either success or failure, they generate a warm feeling. Now we have the rhetoric, we *must* be on the right road. Rhetoric begets rhetoric, and fills the space better taken by reasoned argument. Developments must come from the starting point, the company.

You cannot buy Quality improvement off-the-shelf.

Idea

Everyone is a production worker.

The strategic team

Assemble a senior management team, with sufficient knowledge, experience and business understanding to be able to take the complete view of the company's long-term strategy.

The administration of this team will have important implications. The chairing of discussion groups is one aspect of inter-personal relationships that few companies have fully comprehended. The chairperson of a group, as important as the strategic team, should be chosen with several points in mind.

1. The chairperson should be perceived by the group, as being neutral, middle of the road and not whole-heartedly committed to any particular outcome. This is usually extremely difficult for any chief executive, whose daily life is one of being overtly, totally committed to every aspect of the business.

2. The person chairing the group can only take a minor part in the actual discussions. He has to devote at least half his attention to what is *not* being said by the more reserved members of the group, or to minority points of view. Clearly, to produce a flowing discussion, with a positive progression towards sound conclusions, and with the maximum of support, he will need to adopt a stance that gives little time for his own inputs.

3. It is never easy to keep discussions firmly rooted in objective theory and reasoned argument. This will be essential though. The chairperson will need to find an acceptable route between the rhetoric, the weight of the forceful and articulate members of the group, and quiet common sense. The objective is to end each meeting with a coherent plan to convert reasoned theory into practical reality, and this with a near consensus.

4. Some education in group dynamics will be essential, if the potential value of the group is to be realised. Those that consider the task of chairperson to be easy, and natural for anyone with a personal authority, have regrettably missed the point. There is a great deal of underplay in any group of intelligent people, and there are techniques for assessing where there is untapped value, and of ensuring the maximum participation on the broadest front.

Objectives, concepts, terms and definitions

The team will have a little ground work to accomplish before it can attack its main agenda. It must become aware of not only what it hopes and intends to achieve, but why. This *why* is often left unstated. Whilst it may be obvious to one or two 'in the know', to many others it may well be translated as the latest fad or gimmick. Indeed, it may be more to do with impressing potential customers, the board, the Department of Trade and Industry, or some other extraneous body, than with any real change of industrial methods. Without an appreciation of the full picture, possibly related to the type of steps your competitors are likely to be taking, there won't be the necessary 100% commitment.

It is at this point that the exposure of the group to theory and ideas from an outside source is very useful. An awareness seminar is a valuable input, to expand thinking beyond the narrow confines of the company's own past and present.

An exposure of some of the group to much of the literature on the subject would also be useful. Do not expect each of your senior personnel to spend many hours reading a long book list – you will be disappointed. It is much better to ask each member to read and research a particular book, author or even idea, and then to present it back to the group, in palatable note form, together with a quick overview. In this way, the group can quickly move from being immersed in the company's own vital daily affairs, to becoming excited by a range of possibilities not yet achieved by anyone. Just copying ideas rarely wins whole hearted support, at any level. Use ideas to develop your own, new way forward. There is a magic in treading new ground, particularly new ground that you have thoroughly researched, explored and prepared.

The basis of any successful management strategy is an understanding of the implicit and explicit concepts and terms. Avoid looseness, by establishing from the beginning, exact meanings of the concepts involved. Remember, you need to use concepts as useful tools, rather than as sterile, all embracing dictionary definitions.

Everyday language and terminology often militate against these developments. Even the very structure of the company contains misplaced words and names. The title 'production department' suggests that others have nothing to do with production. The provision of a 'Quality department' was perceived, by some, as relieving them of any responsibility for Quality. The group will probably inherit a company full of anachronistic ideas, terms and attitudes. The challenge is to keep their thoughts and ideas pure, and above all, use the right terminology in everyday speech. It is not unknown for a company to decide that Quality is meeting the needs of the customer, and yet continue to use the term 'Quality' to indicate the 'grade' of material.

The four fundamentals

The Management Strategy needs clearly defined lines along which it will be accomplished. Theory without clear lines for coherent action, will falter. The team will have to address the four fundamental sources of any management strategy.

1. Quality – the satisfaction of internal and external customer expectations. These ideals must be translated through the organisation, via internal relationships. Customer satisfaction, based on a sound understanding of Quality must become the driving force for all.

2. People – the workforce is the major source of energy within your enterprise. Effective management and motivation can realise the latent abilities and potentials within the workforce. The relationships between individuals and their work must be placed in a Quality context.

3. Process – only designs and processes can be controlled, not the results of the process. 'Process thinking', rather than 'unitary thinking', must become the norm. All processes are part of the company's activities, contributing to the overall fulfilment of the company purpose. Tight control of capable processes within all activities of the company is needed.

4. Resources – the generation and conservation of the company's resources can be a way of life, stemming from an understanding of the relationships between people's activity and the costs involved.

These four fundamentals are taken forward throughout this book and used as a basis for a 'TQM Blueprint' in Chapter 17. The methodology is to produce a strategy that demonstrates a route from theory to successful practice, within each area.

The four areas overlap. This is not a criticism, but an essential. There is one company, with one unique way forward. The four thrusts are part

Sample Quality Strategy

1/ A Quality policy will govern all decisions within relationships with suppliers and customers, including internal customer/ supplier relationships.

2/ Quality can only be achieved via company personnel. The attitudes and actions of personnel are the responsibility of management, thus Quality will result from management procedures, methods and style.

3/ Where possible, groups of processes will be operated by teams of multi-skilled operators, who control their own processes unless in need of additional assistance.

4/ An honest and open approach will be the management norm, such that an implicit trust will be developed between all managers and personnel within the company.

5/ Formal and informal communications will be developed to allow everyone to have the information necessary for them to do his/ her job and to feel ownership of the company activities.

6/ Tighter process control is the route to Quality within each and every process. The company expects improvement in every process to be constant and never-ending.

7/ It is the duty of everyone to demand Quality from every supplier, whether internal or external. It is also the duty of everyone to give Quality to every customer, whether internal or external.

8/ We intend to provide a working environment that will allow everyone to perform efficiently and effectively, to give of his/her best and to maximise his/her contribution to the company. It is understood that everyone has the right to job satisfaction.

9/ All staff must be competent to work in their department to be achieved by an on-going programme of education and training.

10/ The main purpose of the company is to create wealth for the mutual benefit of everyone within the company. It is a common responsibility to conserve wealth, materials and time.

Fig 3.4 Sample Total Quality Strategy.

of the same army into different areas and ideas. By ensuring smooth overlapping of these thrusts, there will be a united front. It will be perceived as 'The Company'.

The Quality Policy

As soon as possible, the company should declare to the world that it has a company Total Quality Policy. This will be a statement of the company's definition of Quality, and its relationship to it. As stated

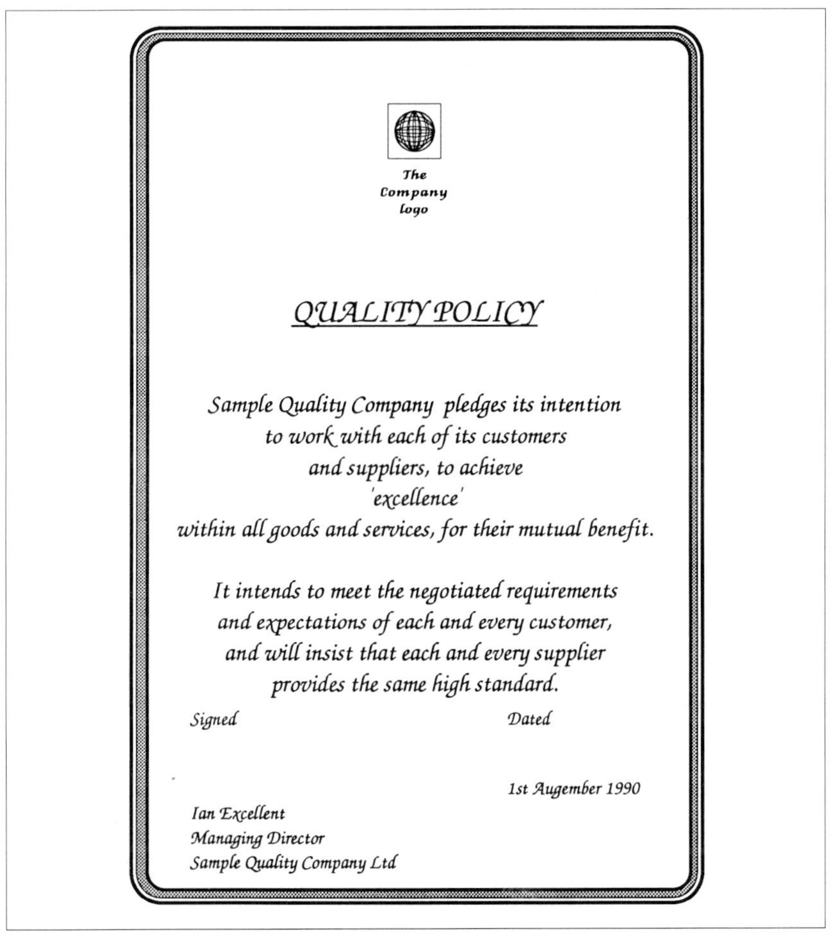

The
Company
Logo

QUALITY POLICY

Sample Quality Company pledges its intention
to work with each of its customers
and suppliers, to achieve
'excellence'
within all goods and services, for their mutual benefit.

It intends to meet the negotiated requirements
and expectations of each and every customer,
and will insist that each and every supplier
provides the same high standard.

Signed *Dated*

1st Augember 1990

Ian Excellent
Managing Director
Sample Quality Company Ltd

Fig 3.5 Sample Total Quality Policy.

earlier, it will be rather like the American Constitution. It will become the basis of appeal, by everyone involved with the company.

The publication of this Total Quality Policy will have profound implications, giving rise to expectations that will have to be met. Customers will expect this definition of Quality to be applied to all their dealings with the company, as a right.

Suppliers too will have their expectations formed by this statement, and, in many cases, the implications are as great in this sphere as that of the external customers.

The effect on the internal customer relationships will be most important. When the policy is fully understood, and this won't happen overnight, the essential rights of each employee to be able to work effectively for the company's good, and thus to have access to job satisfaction and

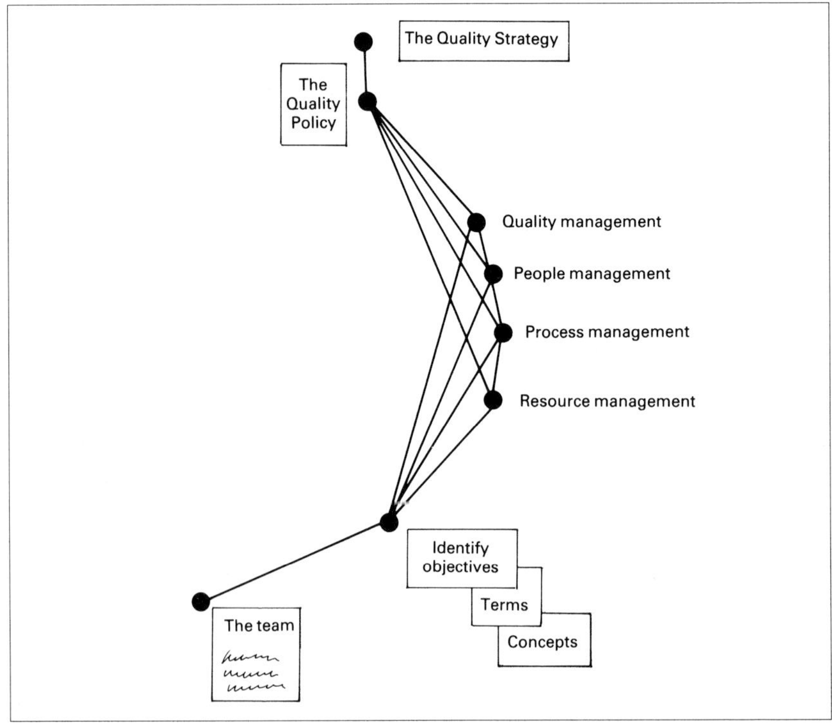

Fig 3.6 The Management Strategy action plan.

security, will have become enshrined. This will take some living with at first, but will eventually release human energy undreamed of by most.

The development of the Total Quality policy is further explored in Chapter 4.

Summary

Management Strategy

1. Information analysis.
2. Strategy development.
3. Implementation, plus on-going review.

The development of strategy:

- Aims to fulfil company purpose of wealth generation.
- Is applicable to all industries.
- Should be based on knowledge, sound theory and ideas.
- Should be expressed in simple terms.
- Is the responsibility of the senior management.

The fours 'A's of management

Access An intelligent management structure must be based on sound reason and argument. This can only flourish in an environment with open access to information and ideas, both from within and from outside the company.

Attitude Attitudes within the company must be controlled. They are based on individuals' reasoning and perceptions of reality.

Action The best way to change attitudes is to change what people actually do. Different actions produce a different view point.

Activities Every employee is engaged in processes that are organised into activities. These activities must be, and must be seen to be, essential to the fulfilment of the company's purpose.

Last thoughts ....

Slogans say what you mean, so that you don't
have to mean what you say!

A man of words, but not of deeds,
is like a garden full of weeds.

1. Edwards Deming, Dr W, *Out of the Crisis.*
2. Juran, Dr J M.
3. Crosby, Philip.

Quality through People

A Blueprint for
Proactive Total Quality Management

Part
II

People

The Management of People

Chapter 4

Quality through People

Banners bearing the legend,'We believe in Quality', adorn the walls; fine, some people believe in fairies.

– Frank Price[1]

Route-map

Quality can only be achieved via the effective management of people. To this end, this chapter examines the place of people within industry, in the past, present and future. This involves a consideration of the new way between traditions of Capitalism and Marxism.

The 'Quality Dream' is explored, and a 10-point plan to make the dream come true, is suggested.

The development of the people within a company is reviewed, with an example of a successful 'open learning centre'

The chapter concludes with a consideration of the concepts of leadership and followership, showing that they are intertwined with the customer/supplier relationship.

The place of people within industry (past)

There is little to be gained by spending too long divining wisdom from the past. We should be children of the future, putting even the present chaos behind us. Quite right, but we can quickly use the past to aid our understanding of the present. In this way, we can enter the future with confidence, comprehending both where we have come from, and whence we go.

Perhaps the first point to appreciate is that little real planning of the relationship of people in industry has ever taken place. Situations and relationships have evolved, often driven by forces and influences outside the factory gate. Indeed, it is part of the modern philosophy lurking in this book that we *can* and *must* understand and control the attitudes and understanding of the fellow humans that join us in our quest for wealth.

The industrial background of the UK

Historically, in Britain, such *thought control* was vested in the wider society. The schools played a major role in the formation of 'correct' and 'decent' attitudinal stances. Respect for authority, compliance with instructions, and taking a pride in repetitive work, were taught just as much as the three 'Rs'. This early education was reinforced by the church. Attributes, such as 'quiet obedience', 'respect for the law', 'acceptance of one's lot' and indeed, 'the acceptance of one's social position', were all considered essential for a good life. Throughout life, the worker was given to believe in the moral value of hard work. Salvation in the hereafter would result from unremitting toil on this earth.

Within the place of work, be it factory, farm or manor house, the employer tended to assume that all employees accepted these obvious facts of life, and for a very good reason. The vast majority did! The relationship between most employers and their employees was one of basic instructions, slavishly followed. Workers were seen as an extension of the machinery and equipment with which they worked. Indeed, they were often perceived as expendable items, in the same manner that we now view consumable items, such as fuel, paper, etc. Investment was placed in plant and machinery, not in people. There was an assumption that all knew their place and were content with it. It was the natural order.

Those interested in obtaining a deeper understanding of the position of industry during the early years of this century should read Robert Tressell's, *'The Ragged Trousered Philanthropists'*.[2]

The entrepreneurs

During this era of the subjection, deception and destitution of the working man, others in society with capital were investing, experimenting and advancing industry in a manner and speed hitherto unknown. Since much of the inherent wealth lay in land, it tended to be vested in families. The family business grew naturally from these roots, producing the patriarchal business model that still exists in many of our older firms. As companies grew in size, a larger management team than the extended family could provide was needed. It seemed natural to bring in trustworthy friends and acquaintances to fill this role. Thus, almost accidentally, the British class system was not only perpetuated, but strongly reinforced by the growth of industry. The old school tie became an almost necessary prerequisite for senior management status.

The two world wars, and other military adventures during this century, served to adapt this basic pattern. The middle manager, working up from the shopfloor by study and endeavour, echoed the non-commissioned officer and sergeant major of the army. These supervisors and managers were seen as the implementors and disciplinarians of industry. A middle class, but usually with little chance of breaking the real class barrier.

Until very recently, little basic theory, education or training took place within British management. The apprenticeship model was followed, whereby a manager was shadowed by his potential replacement, who thus learnt the job, well, badly or indifferently, from his predecessor. Thus, management was, and in many cases still is, an amateur activity.

Europe and the United States

Other European cultures have followed paths which, until recently, were like the British model. The divergence from this situation stems from the 1950s, with the post-war revival. Many countries re-equipped with updated industrial relationships, as well as new machinery. West Germany can probably be seen as a leader in this revival, but most Western European countries have developed, or are developing, professional management.

The United States has a very different industrial history. During the greater part of the nineteenth century, the USA stood for economic opportunity, rather than economic power. The 'New World' stood apart from the traditional distinctions of class and wealth. Individuals could be masters of their own fate. The American dream, of everyone being a potential millionaire, did have real meaning. This, perhaps, is no longer the case. The USA now stands for economic power. Opportunities are more limited. However, there is a classlessness that still offers chances to many, and whilst it guarantees that no-one has an easy ride, for most white Americans there are still chances. In the UK, we need to consider the relationships between people and their work, and the opportunities available to maximise people's talent.

The place of people within industry (present)

On the surface, the present relationships between employees and their employing company appear very different. However, the planning involved with these relationships is rarely any better than that of the past.

Most companies are still organised in vertical departments, with rigid layers of managers and workers. In the worst of these, the terminology still daily reinforces this stratification. How many companies refer to different groups of people by titles and terms, that are either supposed to boost their image and ego, or keep the individual in his/her place? The reader may be bridling, 'What's wrong with boosting people by giving them titles?' The answer is easy. Whenever you boost some, the same act relegates others, and we need *everybody.*

Everybody means including everybody

Most companies make large and damaging distinctions between those employees paid weekly and those paid monthly. The titles spell out clearly the esteem in which individuals are held.

Paid weekly	*Paid monthly*
Waged	Salaried staff
Workers	Supervisors
Operators	Officers
Operatives	Managers
Hands	Executives
Leading hands	
Process workers	
Production staff	

Shop floor
Hourly paid
Crew
Employees
Boys
Girls
or even just 'shop-girls'

The relationships between these strata are further aggravated by the conditions under which they are employed. The reader is asked to justify the existence of the following situations:

- Different toilets for different grades of staff.
- Different refreshment facilities for different grades of staff.
- Different holiday entitlements for different grades of staff.
- Overtime arrangements for some, but not others.
- Expenses for some, but not others.
- Individually negotiated salaries and nationally agreed wage rates.
- Incentive packages, company perks, etc. compared with overpriced cardboard cups from a drinks machine.

The consideration of job security is yet another divisive tool within industry. The weekly paid worker, in most industries, is still seen as an expendable item. In bad times, the wage bill must be cut. The first to lose their jobs are production operatives. Even in good times, companies see their way forward through cost reduction. Success can mean higher productivity, fewer jobs and inevitable redundancies.

This was brought home strongly to the author at the end of a training course for Welsh steelmen. The cost effectiveness of Quality methods had been expounded together with the common sense argument of tighter process control. 'We believe you boyo, but what will it mean for us?' He explained that every previous *improvement* at the plant had ended in more of his fellow work-mates being made redundant. 'I'm sure you're right. Yours is the way for the future, but I expect to see its results from the other side of the gate. You're asking us to work ourselves out of a job'.

Compare the traditional attitude to that exercised at the Honda factory in Swindon. Here, there is single status. Everyone is an associate of the company. Everyone wears the same style of overall, from the chief executive to the receptionist. Everyone is treated to the same respect, shares the same facilities and has the same holidays. It is possible.

Capitalism & Marxism

Many readers may shy away from the consideration of these 'ism's, and indeed any 'ism's. There is value, however, in appreciating that the industrial world to date has been true to both, and that the fundamental truths emanating from both have been born out. In other words, there is a need to understand, not only the parts of the industrial scene that they describe, but to see the gap in the middle that neither can cover. It is the covering of this gap that provides the major opportunity for the coming years.

This political exploration will be kept short and simple!

Capitalism is an economic system, based on free competition, with the means of production largely in private hands. The system is demand driven, in that, in the long run, the variety of goods and services offered will be determined by the effective demand of the potential customers. The system will be self-regulating, matching production to the wealth available to purchase it. Thus, it embodies not only wealth generation, but wealth circulation. It is in this context that the purchase of labour has been seen as a basic component of manufacturing. Money rules. The mechanism has been one of investment leading to a direct financial return. Plant, machinery and people have been entirely secondary to this working of the money market. Financially, this works.

Marxism understands this aspect of capitalism. However, it considers the place of the working and non-working people within a capitalist system. Inevitably, the few who own the capital will have to exploit the means of production to the full to be successful. Those without capital will be allowed only such wealth as is necessary for them to purchase the goods that are being created. Therefore, payment for labour will always be governed by these rules. It will work directly against the interests of workers, who, by definition, are without capital. Alienation from the work will result. Workers, inevitably, will be exploited. This scenario will be aggravated by the increasing obsolescence of both machinery and skills. The struggle to create new markets will push technology forward, rendering the worker increasingly unnecessary. Workers will become button-pushers of highly sophisticated machinery.

People become an extension of the machinery. People are just a commodity.

The results of communist experiments, often failed experiments, are usually assumed to be true communism. However, some have seen the intrinsic value in the philosophy, without necessarily understanding how best to use it. George Bernard Shaw defined a communist as an intensely proud person who proposes to enrich the common fund instead of sponging off it.[3]

The place of people within industry (future)

It will not be easy to establish new relationships. It is hard to convince people who have seen so many good, experienced and valuable people lose their jobs that they have a sound future in the industry. It may be difficult to convince them, but it is essential.

It is important that industry is seen as a partnership of all those involved with it. Each company should not only expect loyalty from its workforce, but deserve it. By centring on Quality, and aligning the interests of all the individual people concerned with the company, it should be possible to manage any business to continued success. Companies have failed, in the past, because they have had a self-image that they feel obliged to fulfil. Such an image is the responsibility of management.

If the approach is to use the expertise, skills, plant and machinery to generate wealth continuously and well into the future, intelligent management should foresee and overcome any difficulties. If the company's competitors can survive, survival should also be possible for the company. The one safeguard for everyone is 'being the best', which in effect means 'doing the best'. In an over production situation, it seems that the British response is to speak of rationalisation, decline and cut back. So often, this is to the direct benefit of the competition, which presses all the harder to gain more of whatever market there is. The aim is to make *money*, rather than to produce a particular product range. Wealth is created from the hard work and genius of the workforce. All employees, from the managing director to the newest apprentice, have a great deal to contribute. They should be viewed in this light, and referred to as contributors, company personnel, staff, or just people. The same term should be used for each. The sooner the idea that everyone is in the same boat is accepted, the sooner everyone will pull together.

The new way forward

Both the capitalist reality and the Marxist interpretation are right. They both partially describe the working of Western economies. Both are harsh and cruel, paying little attention to the individual, particularly those who have little to contribute. All Western societies mitigate this, to varying degrees, by introducing a mixed economy, in which the state plays a role, blurring the edges. This, inevitably, is seen as inefficient, since profit has to compete with compassion and caring, within the priorities.

There has to be a better way.

There is a better way. A new look at our activities is required. We need to be concerned more with the *process*, that is with the *doing*, rather than having an obsession with numbers, profit and results. From this perspective, it becomes obvious that the process of life *now* is an important consideration. There is little point in pursuing vast profits if we destroy the planet on which we depend, in the process. This is true globally, nationally and for every small community, including each company.

The new source of energy, and thus of wealth, is people. Rather than treat people as an expense (capitalism), as a sponge (communism – unto each according to his need), we must see people as a resource. Both the two '-ism's, concentrate on people's hands. The most valuable human part, (well, of most humans), is the head.

Idea

This is the basic message of this book, the future will see a better, fuller understanding of industrial relationships. Neither capitalism nor Marxism will be discredited. They are both partial views. They must be enhanced with a new perspective that seeks a path between these fundamentals. The concentration on process, on the centrality of Quality and on the orientation of people, will prove an unstoppable formula.

We can all benefit by considering the process of living, that is by using industry for the common good. Indeed, we can use capital for the common good, The Quality of life, now and in the future, is important. We can use the accumulated value of years of experience by enlisting everyone, as a team, in the quest for wealth. But first, there is a need to construct industrial relationships, whereby the company works for the good of all who are involved in that company; shareholders, directors, and employees. If everyone can be convinced that there is a common mutual interest in success, and logic is on the side of this argument, then, by aligning the efforts of everyone, success will be guaranteed. Any company can become the best, but only with the full cooperation and participation of each and every individual contributor. 'We need everyone, that is we need you!', should be the only poster on display in the factory. No, even that is unnecessary. In the well managed company, everyone will know this without the poster. Actions speak louder than words. Processes speak more intelligently than results.

Quality relationships within industry and commerce

Total Quality Management starts with the realisation that it is relationships that need to be managed – the relationships between departments, the relationships between individuals and the company, and the relationship between individuals and their work. It is for this reason that Quality management is chiefly about managing people.

It has taken the Western world some time to reach this conclusion. Some see industry as the area of society that tends to set the management patterns. It is, after all, the area that has to account for the investment and produce a profit. Very often, the management methods of one decade become integrated into the service industries, social services and other related parts of society during the next decade.

Management concerns since the war

By charting the major concerns of industrial managers in the USA and Europe since 1950, we can understand the lack of cohesive people management during these decades.

The 1950s

World trade was in total disarray following the second world war, but the rapid development of technology, not least in aircraft, presented enormous possibilities. The 1950s became the decade of booming markets. Those countries whose industries survived the war girded their industrial loins, and attempted to meet the ever-increasing market demands.

The main aim was to capture and hold on to part of this market. The situation can be likened to maintaining a sector of an expanding balloon. The constant pressure was to produce more. It was necessary to match the increased market with increased production to maintain a market-share.

Make it and ship it! Make it and ship it! Make it and ship it! There was little time to consider the finer things in life, such as accuracy, Quality or tomorrow. These times were exciting. Industry was being rebuilt, at the same time, each company was coping with unprecedented demand.

Meanwhile, Japan and West Germany were not involved with this boom. Their industries were in no position to continue work after the war. They had to be rebuilt. Fortunately, help was at hand. Via the Marshall Plan, the US supplied the necessary finance and expertise.

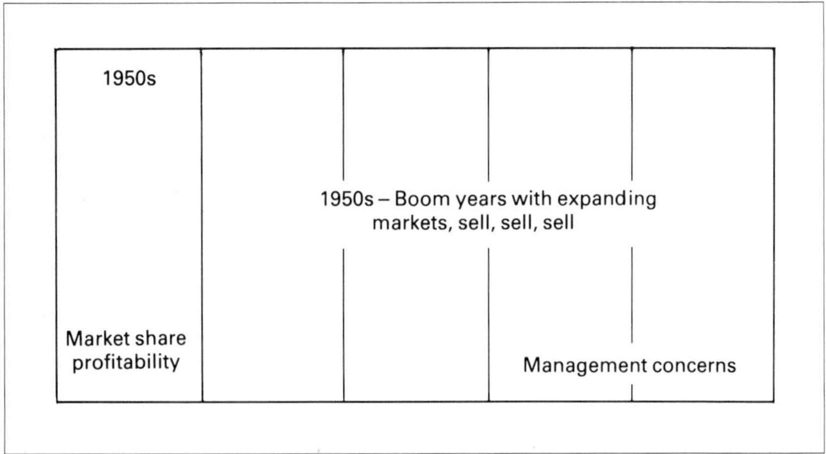

Fig 4.1 Management concerns, 1950s.

Neither Japan nor Western Germany were yet in the game, but both were in the process of an industrial rebirth that included different personnel relationships.

The 1960s

The balloon reached its full size, the growth declined, the markets stabilised. The 1960s became the time of re-assessment as additional markets were not so available. Profits were not made from expansion. There was little additional revenue to be made, money must be saved. The major concern of industrial management during the 1960s was to reduce costs.

Meanwhile, in the East, the Japanese began full-scale production and started to export, particularly in the automotive sector. The Datsun became a familiar sight on British roads. These cars were very like the equivalent European models; the Datsun Bluebird estate was similar to the Ford Cortina estate, and so on. But they were cheaper. Not only were they cheaper, but, in some respects, they were better. Tinted windows, radios and items considered extras in the home market, were standard fitments. There were the suggestions that the Japanese industrialists could not be trusted. Clearly, the Japanese were cheating. They were dumping their over-production on the British market, at less than their production and transportation costs.

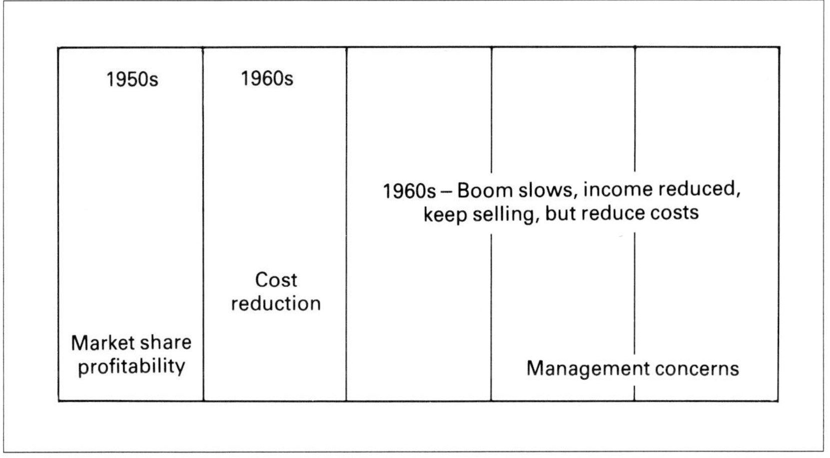

Fig 4.2 Management concerns, 1960s.

This competition began to hit the home market. Industry was already trying to cut costs by using cheaper materials, thus relying more on designed strength than material strength.

The British public were unaware of this pending industrial and economic downturn. They believed themselves still in the economic post-war miracle. Harold MacMillan brought the Conservatives back to power with the slogan 'You've never had it so good'. People expected more, and demanded it. Now was the time of the good life! We who were around at the time entered the 1960s with Guy Mitchell, wind-up gramophones, cold pantries, lino, long waits at the bus-stop and a week at a Butlins holiday camp. We came out of the 1960s with the Beatles, televisions, refrigerators, fitted carpets, a car, foreign holidays, and a consumer society that expected the material things in life.

The wage bill, in industry, grew to be a major factor during the 1960s.

The 1970s

The crisis began to loom in the 1970s. Economic downturn was now a reality. People began to speak of recession. People were spending more than industry was earning. Industrial management turned to productivity. The only way to justify the payment of higher wages was to demonstrate that more was being earned. More output from fewer

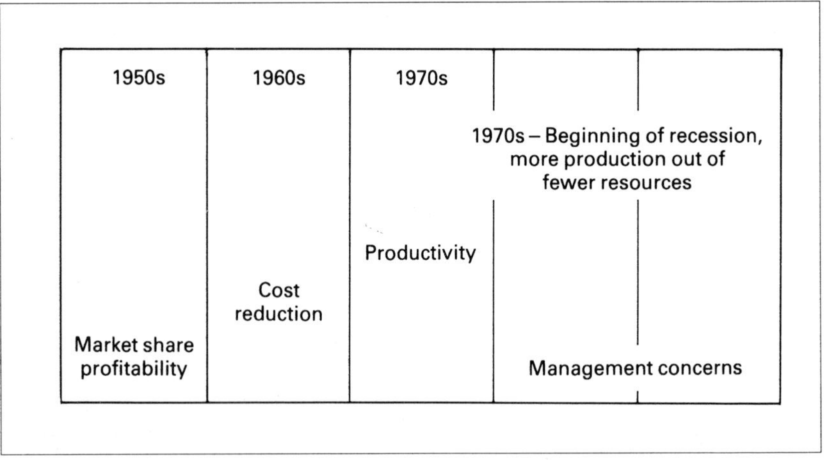

Fig 4.3 Management concerns, 1970s.

people. The shaking out of unwanted labour started, and the term *structural unemployment* began to be used to describe the movement of people from older industries to newer technologically-based industries, as opposed to the normal pool of labour created by *frictional unemployment*.

Higher productivity was sought from the machinery, as well as from the workforce. More was to be produced from less. Additional life was expected from worn-out and out-of-date machinery. Investment was not available to replace it.

The fundamental management errors continued. Decisions were still based on numbers, on results, and short-term results at that. Considerations of Quality were of a lower order. In companies with any Quality input at all, it was treated in the same way. Quality was *numbers-based*, a question of sorting the good from the bad to ensure the production targets were met.

Meanwhile, in the East, a different path was being followed. With the help of Western consultants, the Japanese car industry, followed by the electronic and other industrial sectors, grasped the importance of Quality. Dr W Edwards Deming, an industrial consultant who had suffered frustration within the United States during the 1940s and 1950s, instructed them on the important considerations. His 14 points for management represent the basis of the Japanese industrial revival. In Japan, Quality had become the central issue![4]

The 1980s

The recession came. Many companies went under. Those that didn't file for liquidation realised that something was wrong. Many turned to Quality. Quality began to be the subject of conversations, the slogan, the solution. Many reinforced their Quality Assurance departments and turned to stronger inspection methods. Some even considered modern Quality methods, such as Statistical Process Control (SPC) and Just-in-Time (JIT). A few companies reconsidered their stance, their decision-making procedures and their management styles. People such as Philip Crosby,[5] in the United States, emphasised that a Total Quality approach was necessary. A different form of management was necessary and a new way of doing business was essential.

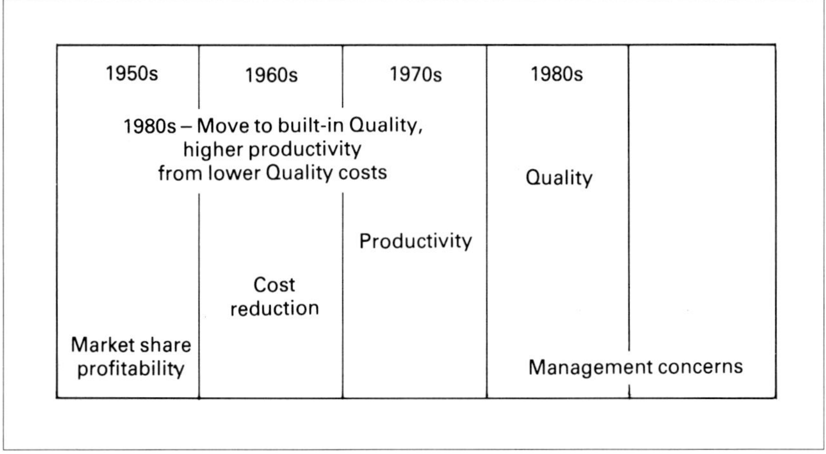

Fig 4.4 Management concerns, 1980s.

However, for most companies, this was too radical. Quality standards were largely considered in terms of 'approval' standards. British companies obtained BS5750, ISO9000, or whatever approval was necessary for their particular type of industry – Lloyds registration, Ministry of Defence AQAP, Civil Aviation Authority BCAR, or whatever. Each of these approvals carefully examines the systems in place that allows high standards of Quality to be achieved. Such systems are essential, but they do not guarantee Quality. They tell the customer that the company is capable of producing Quality, not that it will. More is needed. Neither the systems, nor the approvals and registrations are enough.

The 1990s

The necessary change of emphasis was charted by several major companies, typified by Ford. They were not only concerned with the systems, but demanded an input and assurance about the methodology and the processes that were being used. In 1984 it became part of the purchase requirement of the Ford Motor Company that their Q101 standards were being achieved. This made many process measurements and control methods mandatory. It became a contractual condition that capability studies and other Statistical Process Control techniques were used in all areas where Quality was deemed to be critical. More

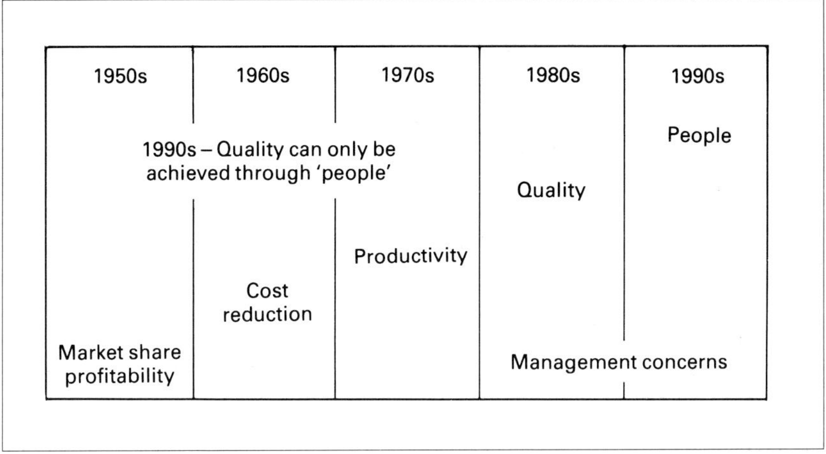

Fig 4.5 Management concerns, 1990s.

recently, this has included Failure Mode and Effects Analysis (FMEAs) on items with a safety implication. This customer pressure often produced more movement within the supplier base than within the company's own plants.

The 1990s will be typified by the enhancement of people's work. It will become increasingly obvious that continued success will only be possible by harnessing the full potential of each and every person within the company. In the 1980s, industrial management learnt that Quality was the central issue. In the 1990s, they will learn how to achieve it. They will find that Quality can only be achieved through the successful management of people.

People and the 'Quality Dream'

Some can describe a picture of keen and enthusiastic people, joining together without any thoughts of status or company politics, happy and confident in the knowledge that their future is assured by their tight personal control over their own activities, within a Quality orientated company. Most who hear such a description, describe it as a dream, some even revert to stock 'put-downs' such as 'cloud cuckoo land', or 'cloud nine'.

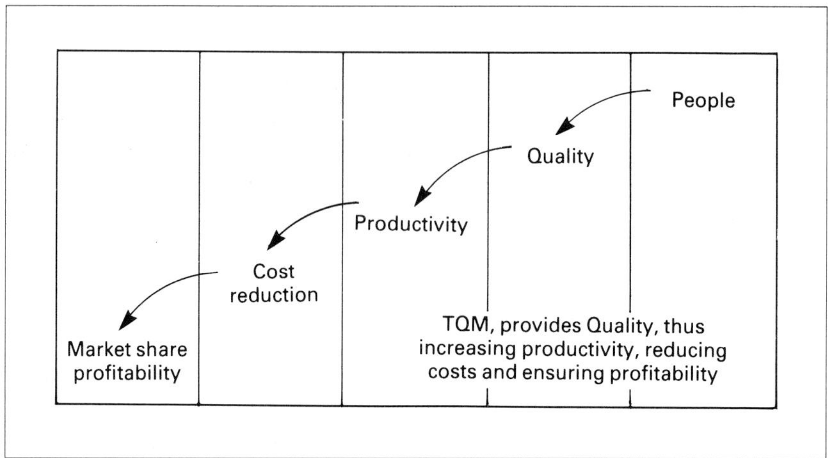

Fig 4.6 Management concerns, 1950s-1990s.

For most companies, it may be a dream at the moment, but it is a dream that can increasingly become a reality. Quality is a direction. The senior management task is to decide the direction, and the values on which the direction is based.

The ingredients of the dream are logical. They are also economically sound. The problems result from an inability, firstly, to create such an environment, and then to manage it.

By concentrating on the management of people, the gap between the desirable and the possible becomes narrowed. It becomes finite. A finite number of people are involved with the company. The larger the number, the greater the problem, but it nevertheless remains a containable problem. The bigger the company, the larger the scale of resources that are available to assist the cultural change.

A possible route

The following is not offered as a definitive route, but as a logical line to follow, to achieve the unified organisation, in which a Quality culture might grow.

1. Commitment of the Chief Executive

An essential starting point. Commitment should be tempered with understanding. It will be essential that the chief executive is fully able to carry the company into Total Quality Management. Most chief executives have a variety of commitments, but their commitment to Total Quality will have to supersede all other concerns.

2. Formation of Strategic Quality team

Such a team will probably comprise of half a dozen senior managers representing the breadth of company activities. Their function is to consider the broad direction of Total Quality Management, and to suggest ways of moving in this direction. They will have to be educated in the ways of Total Quality, and be conversant with the current company situation, as well as clearly perceiving its future direction.

3. Development of the Quality Policy

This will involve the close definition of all the terms involved, and the meaning and implication of all parts of the policy. This is a key document.

4. Ratification of the Quality Policy

It is important that the whole senior management team understands, has ownership of, and feels a strong commitment to, this document. It may make minor modifications to the proposed document. However, its major contribution is likely to be in the background values of the company, and in the meaning and implication of the policy.

5. Development of the Quality Strategy

The strategy is the means to achieve the policy. It is the way by which the company will continually move towards the ideals that are implicit and stated in the policy. This is dealt with in greater detail in the last part of this book.

6. Senior management education

It is essential that every senior manager fully understands, not just the direction in which the company is moving, but the value structure and implied priorities that this direction demands. Each member of this group will need assistance to translate this company objective and strategy, into his own area. This is not the time for the senior manager to duck, and delegate this 'Quality stuff' to some subordinate. There has to be a solid commitment, based on thorough understanding by each member of the senior management team.

7. Cascading education

Within each department, the policy and necessary actions, based upon sound theoretical argument and understanding, must be disseminated through middle management to every member of the shopfloor staff. New methods and responsibilities will be involved, as well as new meanings and priorities. Above all, new relationships between people and between an individual and his/her work, will be created.

8. Development of teamwork

This is the most sensible way in which to organise any significant number of people.

It allows:

- Process control at the point of operation.
- The operation of internal customer relationships.
- The maximisation of employee effort.
- Strong pro-active management.
- Realistic and constant process improvement.

9. The overt corporate image

As these components come into place, it becomes easier to function as a unit. The promulgation of this corporate wholeness will be vital, and communications will be developed to feed the growing appetite for company information.

10. Continual reappraisal, modification and improvement

    As the company improves, there will be increasing opportunities to gain tighter process control, and achieve yet higher degrees of customer satisfaction. Remember that the management of Total Quality involves:

    - The Management of Quality.
    - The Management of People.
    - The Management of Process.
    - The Management of Resource.

The Quality Policy

A common company objective will emerge as a policy statement. It may not be called that, but it will give an essential framework for all decisions and actions emanating from the company, or indeed from any individual within the company. If Quality is to become the dominant concern of the company, and a purpose of this book is to convince you that it should, then you need a Quality Policy.

Such a policy for the company will need a great deal of careful thought. It is not sufficient to arrive at a simplistic statement such as 'We are going to be the best', 'We are committed to Quality', or 'Excellence is the bench mark of this company', though these are all admirable sentiments. The policy has to embody some of the means of achieving the desired aim.

The Quality Policy must:

- Mean something to everyone concerned, that is, it must have a significant purpose within their daily working lives.

Idea

Quality must be the central issue, and this can only be achieved via effective management.

- Be relevant.
- Have an obvious intention.
- Be capable of exact and clear definition.

Above all, the Quality Policy should become a *bill of rights* for everyone having dealings with the company, or indeed in the company. It should be a clear statement of what the company holds dear, and is prepared to stand by. Any customer, supplier or even any employee, should be able to point to the Quality Policy and demand the attention, service, and Quality embodied in it.

The damage done to a company which makes such a statement, but clearly and repeatedly fails to live up to it, cannot be over-estimated. When sights are set high, failure to achieve success each and every time is understandable and, indeed, acceptable. What is unforgivable is the failure of *intention*, exhibited by a lack of commitment to the high ideals.

Examples of directional statements

We can all think of declared policies of large organisations. Many are thrown back at them when they have been perceived not to work. Two such examples spring to mind:

Several cartoonists grasped the British Rail slogan, 'We're getting there', to illustrate the first day of the recent 'rail strike', amending it to read:

not
'We're^getting there!'

This public statement, displayed on station platforms, where people waited for late or non-existent trains, probably did more harm than good. It would be interesting to know how many were subject to graffiti, with such comments as, 'Lucky you, I wish I was!'

Another example that appeared to back-fire, was the Commercial Union's claim for easy efficiency, when dealing with claims. An agent for this well known insurance company, told the author that she was accused of 'making a drama out of a crisis', on average, three times a day.

Intentions and endeavours

When companies take directional goals, such as 'perfection', 'excellence', 'zero defects' and 'complete customer satisfaction', they will fail.

What impresses customers is that the company is *trying*. Can it be seen to be always trying its hardest? Is it constantly striving to improve its performance? Many remember the Avis Car Hire slogan, 'We try harder'. It was not an insignificant part of that campaign that their staff members all wore that badge, thus giving them a sense of being an active part of the company activity.

Thus, it is the *intention* of the company that will impress the customer. This may be embodied in the Quality Policy, with phrases such as 'The company will endeavour to ....', 'The company intends to .....', or 'The company continually seeks to improve .....'.

It should be remembered that these statements are being made internally, as well as to the outside world. What is intended when considering the account of the major customer, will also form the dealings between two sections or departments of the company. In many ways, it is within this latter type of relationship that it is harder to achieve the real meaning of the Quality Policy. Without success internally, though, real satisfaction of external customers and end-users will be impossible.

People development

People are the main resource within any company. Thus, the opportunity for personal development of each individual is of the highest importance. Many understand that the progress of individuals

Idea

A Quality Policy declares to the world that you are serious about Quality.

within the company is also an opportunity for greater corporate achievement. It would seem sensible, and in most cases cost effective, for the company to assist with this personal development. Indeed, in its own interest, effort should be taken by the company to help an individual's programme of self-improvement.

There are now many companies offering such self-help schemes. Jaguar's policy of providing open learning centres at each of their plants is typical. A wide range of courses is available, using appropriate delivery vehicles. Interactive Video programmes (I/V), and Computer-Based Training (CBT), coexist with formal lectures and distant learning techniques. The subjects are nearly all those needed in some part of the company, but all are available to each employee. For example, a typist can learn welding, a salesman can learn first-aid, and the welder can learn French. The take-up at Jaguar was remarkable, with nearly one third of the workforce registering for a course in one year. The company meets the costs, but all the learning takes place in people's own time. The result is a much better workforce, more able to play a full part in the pursuit of Quality.

The 'One more' theories

There are two complementary 'One more' theories.

The first 'one more' theory suggests that the company should always have at least one more person with a particular skill or experience than it needs at present. This person can not only cover for absence, holidays and further education, but is available when the original person is promoted. Changes in staff can be fluid, occurring without any disturbance to the normal flow of business.

The other 'one more' theory suggests that each person should be attempting to acquire an *additional* skill, responsibility or area of

Idea

People are the main resource
within any company.

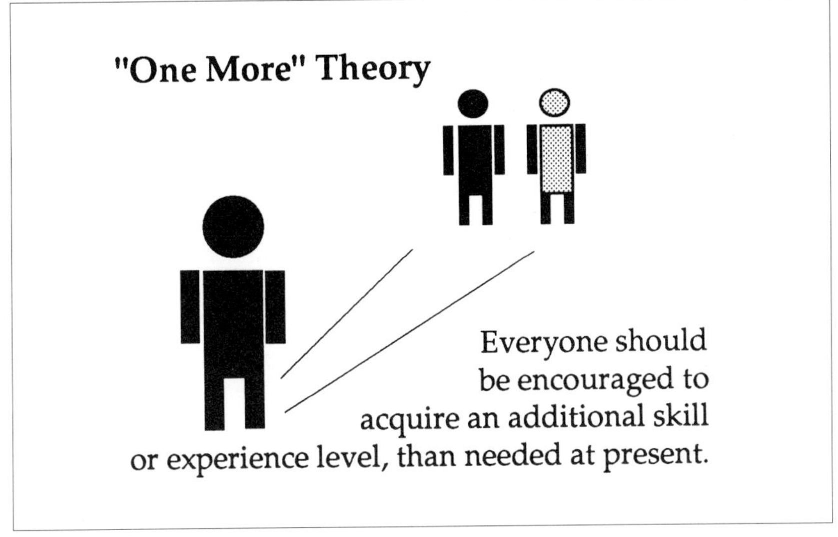

Fig 4.7 One more theories (a).

experience. This will inevitably be beyond that required for the present job. This theory sees the latent ability and value of each individual as being only partially tapped. In a well managed company, the dissonance between what is advantageous to the company and what is beneficial to the individual will be reduced to a minimum. Thus, the development of individual talent will be of mutual benefit.

In these ways, personal development will be an on-going part of the company's life, and personnel mobility will be achieved.

Flexibility within the management of the company is also an additional benefit. People have holidays, are occasionally ill, have days away from their normal work for education and training, and, indeed, resign or are promoted. Fluidity within the personnel of any company is not a luxury, it is a necessity.

These theories are in opposition to two oft-found practices, inherent in British society. The first is a desire to label everybody, and limit their potential to the scope of that label. When a person holds a particular post he is thus labelled, and expectations are limited to the requirements of that post. There is a need to perceive an individual's

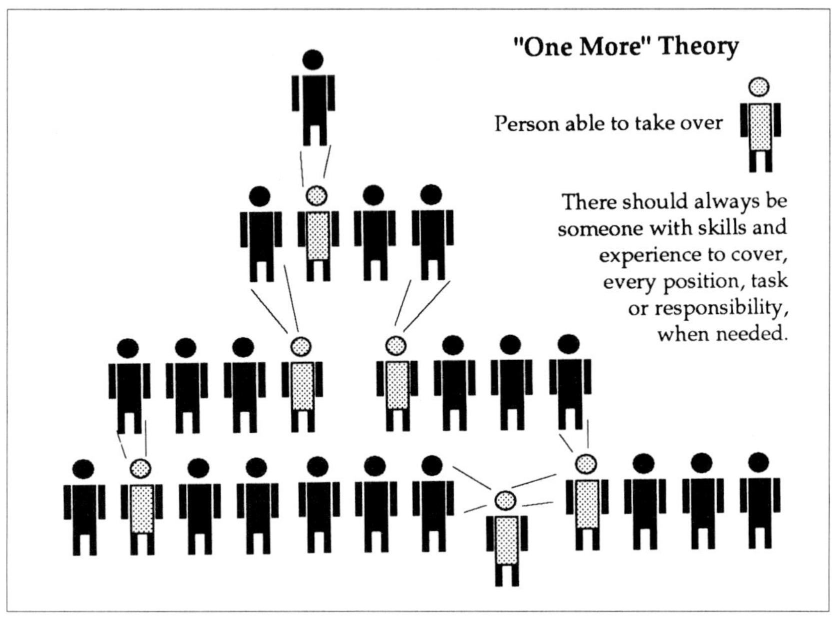

Fig 4.8 One more theories (b).

talents as separate from the demands of the particular job. A craftsman may have managerial abilities that have yet to have an outlet. Most have abilities that go far *wider* than are exhibited by their present tasks. Where this width of ability exists, the depth can be achieved by education and experience.

The other common failing is to believe that the grass is always greener on the other side of the hill. Many people in all walks of life can relate stories of how home-grown talent is ignored in favour of young hopefuls from elsewhere. The brief glimpse of an unknown character, backed by an optimistic curriculum vitae and positive references, is pitted against an internal candidate, whose name is firmly linked with the present lower grade job and with his past successes, failings and mistakes, sit side by side.

Leadership and followership

It is of the highest importance that relationships between people are fully understood. In the past, rank and status have defined most

An exercise

Consider the following statements about your present company, in the light of the comments above.

How strongly do you agree or disagree?

Statement	Strongly disagree	Disagree	Don't know	Agree	Strongly agree
1/ For every task, in the company, there is an additional person with the required skills and experience, to be called on, when necessary.					
2/ The company is concerned to ensure that there is another person with the skills and abilities, shadowing every important position.					
3/ The company never finds itself in crisis as a result of a person suddenly being promoted, resigning or becoming ill.					
4/ The company actively encourages personal development for all employees.					
5/ The company provides in-house facilities, or funds outside agencies, to educate any personnel that request additional skills opportunities.					
6/ Most people are actively developing their skills and experience.					
7/ Most people have changed their role, within the company, at least once in the last five years.					
8/ Most people have held more than one post within the company.					
9/ The company usually appoints internally, if possible, and rarely advertises for outside candidates.					
10/ The company provides opportunities for its staff to gain experience outside the company, whilst retaining a future inside the company.					

What improvements would you recommend in the area of personnel development, within your company?

Fig 4.9 An exercise.

relationships, prescribing the value to come from either the relationship, or from the individuals involved.

These inter-personal relationships are very much more complicated than is at first observed. Each is not only different, but each relationship changes with time. The relationships are, in fact, transactional. That is, they are created each time a transaction of some form takes place. This will have credibility, wherever and whenever the transaction occurs.

There are two types of involvement, occurring within each such transaction:

- Customer/supplier involvement
  In each transaction, something changes, something moves from one side to the other. It may be information, it may be instruction, or it may be something physical. There will be a customer and a supplier involved.
- Leader/follower involvement
  Rarely is a relationship entirely neutral, in this respect. One side of the transaction is perceived as possessing more authority, knowledge or drive. The other is prepared to follow the perceived lead.

Neither involvement is as straightforward as it may appear above. In each type, there will be a two-way mechanism at work. The customer will be in receipt of the goods, service, information or instruction, but

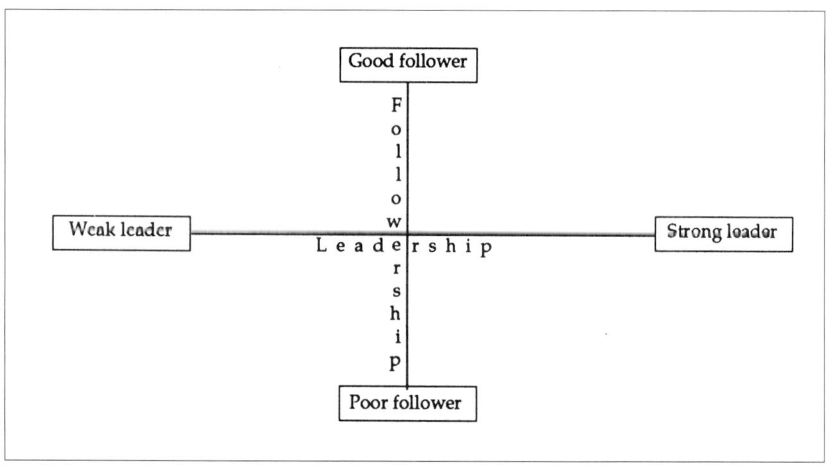

Fig 4.10 Relationship grid (a).

the customer also initiates the transaction with a request or instruction. The Quality of this request will be the customer's responsibility, and the supplier, now a customer himself, is entitled to demand a clear input. Following the transaction, there may well be some converse activity. The customer may need to return some information, packing materials, or, in the case of an outside relationship, some payment. The relationship is now reversed; the customer becomes the supplier. External customer relationships are always two-way. There is the transfer of goods and services in one direction, and money in the other.

A similar balance is found between the potential for leadership and followership. Rarely is anyone merely a leader or a follower. We all tend to follow a strong lead, whilst exerting a little influence to modify the direction. Equally, the good leader, understanding the value of group work, will probably be a good *follower* as well. This will occur, even whilst he is leading; that is, the good leader is prepared to accept advice and suggestions from those being led.

We can look at these involvements on a relationship grid.

These ideas are particularly valuable when considering internal customer/supplier relationships. Every relationship can be plotted on the grid. The balance of the customer role and the supplier role can be assessed for each participant. The degrees of leadership and followership involved can also be assessed.

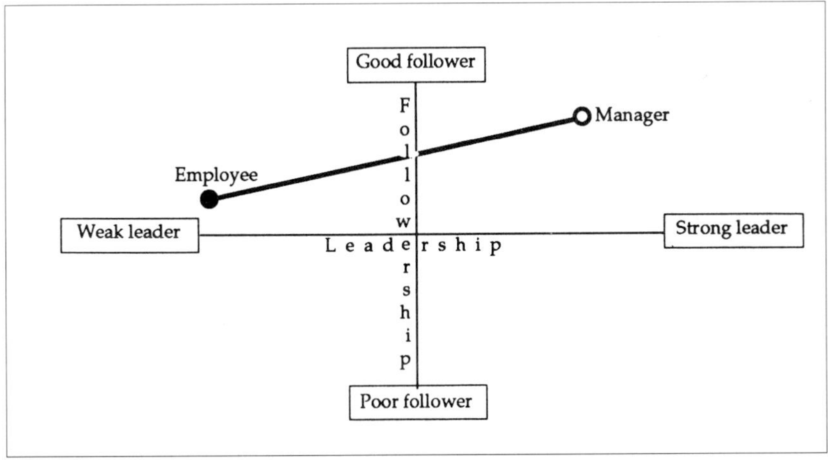

Fig 4.11 Relationship grid (b).

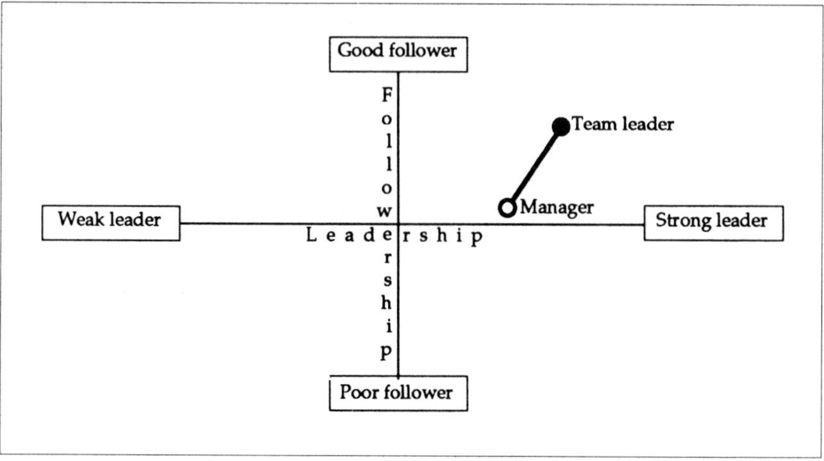

Fig 4.12 Relationship grid (c).

The position on the grid of a relationship between a manager and an employee can be assessed.

Fig 4.11 shows a dominant manager receiving little in the way of input from a subservient employee. Fig 4.12 shows the relationship between a manager and the teamleader of a workteam. Most of the leadership needed for the team is forthcoming from the teamleader. The manager has to supply very little. The team is clearly almost self-sufficient and needs little in the way of management from the manager, thus the teamleader is largely a supplier.

Summary

This chapter explored:

The past place of people within industry

The industrial background of the UK
The entrepreneurs
United States and European development

The present place of people within industry

Everybody within the company is needed
The capitalist and Marxist split
Industry looking for a new way

The future place of people within industry

The new way is via Quality and people management
Quality industrial relationships
Management concerns since the war

1950s	Market share profitability
1960s	Cost reduction
1970s	Productivity
1980s	Quality
1990s	Quality through people

People and the Quality Dream

A possible route

1. Commitment of chief executive
2. Formation of Strategic Quality Team
3. Development of the Quality Policy
4. Ratification of the Quality Policy
5. Development of the Quality Strategy
6. Senior management education
7. Cascading education
8. Development of teamwork
9. The overt corporate image
10. Never-ending, continual improvement

Quality Policy = bill of rights for:

- all customers
- all suppliers
- all employees

The relationship between individuals can be assessed by using the leadership/followership vs customer/supplier grid.

Last thoughts ....

A senior manager of a major company, a household name, proudly boasted to me that it had spent £25,000 on Quality Management training. Every manager had been bought a book, and had attended a series of seminars about Quality. The whole exercise had taken two and a half years.

Impressed, I asked, 'What improvement has it given you?'

A surprised face replied, 'Well, none yet, but its early days isn't it!'

1. Price, Frank, *Right First Time,* Gower,1984.
2. Tressell, Robert, *The Ragged Trousered Philanthropist,* Granada Paperback, 1965.
3. Shaw, G. B, *Man and Superman, 1903.*
4. Edwards Deming, Dr. W, *Quality and the Competitive Position,* Massachusetts Institute of Technology, 1981.
5. Crosby, Philip, *Quality is Free,* New York, 1979.

Chapter 5

Organise for Quality

I kept six serving-men
(They taught me all I knew)
Their names are What and Why and When
And How and Where and Who

– Kipling, The Serving-men

Route-map

This chapter opens by considering two types of company organisational structure; diffuse and integrated structures.

It then suggests methods of unifying the company.

The chapter concludes by considering the concept of internal energy, and by deciding that Quality is the key factor in its limitation.

Structures

The industrial company is a human structure of departments, hierarchical positions, authoritarian relationships, inter-related tasks, frameworks, responsibilities, accountabilities, dislikes and sometimes (hopefully) even friendships.

Traditionally, the structures of responsibility and authority have owed more to evolution than conscious decision. Indeed, the 'needs must' reasoning will be found behind most of the decisions that have been made. People have perceived the necessity of carving out their own sphere of influence, of developing their own activities and creating their own set of objectives. Departmental structures have often been dependent on one or two strong personalities developing their own ideas and careers. Many companies find themselves as a collection of mini-empires. Inevitably, this has left a legacy of irrational staffing levels, particularly at the managerial level, together with diverse budgetary arrangements and differing objectives.

Each company can undergo a little self examination by considering these three questions:

1. Are the managerial staffing and salary levels in each department proportional to the wealth generating capacity of that department?

2. Is there a common budgetary arrangement for all departments, and are these arrangements common knowledge across the business?

3. Does each department have a set of stated aims and objectives, and are they related to the work of the department, rather than to the work of the company as a whole?

It is not unusual for different activities within a company to be staffed by groups of people with little in common. They come from different backgrounds, have different concerns, and are judged by different standards – they even speak different languages. The accounts department is often an obvious example but, in larger organisations, there will be a long list of such different groups.

Diffuse organisations

'What's new? This is the way big business operates!'

To those who have grown, and prospered, in such organisations, it seems abundantly self-evident that this is the nature of big business. Obviously, each department will have its own concerns, indeed its own aspect of the business. Unfortunately, though, these differences are not minor and unimportant, but are detrimental to the overall business aims. They are costly, inefficient and mitigate against future success.

The dangers, resulting from a diffuse organisation are many and varied. Whilst they may not be present in all such organisations, they will tend to develop unless positive actions are taken to prevent them.

Inbreeding

The work of any individual within the organisation may be seen as a step within a career pattern. Such an understanding will inevitably be centred more on the activity than on the company. Our opinions tend to conform with those around us and reflect common cultural aspects. This may result in the individual feeling his loyalty divided between department and company.

A greater danger, however, is from the 'mental inbreeding' within a group of specialists, be they accountants, designers or Quality engineers. They will mix and confer with people of like background, training and thought. By talking the same language, with the same set of implicit values and meanings, they will constantly reinforce these group values and attitudes. Their personal development, indeed their social existence, both within and outside the company, will tend to be with similar people. A mental separation from other departments within the company would seem almost inevitable.

Diverse values

Opinions, judgements and assessments always relate directly to the values underpinning our belief structure. Where such opinions stem from a group of people, a section or department, rather than from the company as a whole, such values reflect the common culture of the group. All too often, such judgements become simplistic, especially when referred to other departments and people. They become expressed in easily transferred numerical values, such as monthly sales figures. The immediate pressure on an individual is to perform within these stated group values. The individual is measured by the standard expected by the department.

In such circumstances, conflicts may arise between the good of the individual and the benefit of the department. Such conflicts will tend to benefit career-minded individuals, who will perform to the expectations of those deemed to be advantageous to their careers. They will exploit differences, play company politics, and generally increase, rather than diminish, such conflicts. They will look after themselves, not the company.

Likewise, when there is a conflict between what is in the best interest of the department and the best interest of the company, the outcome is inclined to favour the smaller organisation. Rarely are these conflicts overt, or even understood by those involved, but the routine method of reaching a decision is likely to disadvantage the company in favour of those involved.

Conflicting priorities

What is considered important to one department may not be recognised by another. There will be no clear overall 'game-plan' for the company, and no over-riding value system on which it can fall back. Each area of activity continues, oblivious that others have very different perceptions of the world they inhabit.

Different language

In many instances, not only do the various groups use different words, but they speak with different accents and their speech patterns differ. Where they use the same words, they often use them in a different way, and with significantly different meanings.

Diverse expectations

The lack of knowledge of one department about the people, aspirations, or even daily work of other departments, leads to poor expectations. These are at first erroneous, but through constant reinforcement, they are eventually fulfilled. It is a sad fact that in industry suspicions are usually justified, and prophecies are usually self-fulfilling.

Divergent life styles

All these differences add up to people having vastly diverse appreciations of the company environment. They not only see the company as different, they live these differences daily. No one individual lives anything other than the expected life pattern, but many notice that the shopfloor, the senior management, or particular groups, wear different clothes, work different hours, eat at different times and places, and don't even share the same toilets. The differences are reinforced. The divisions become wider. Communication, which occurs naturally with people who see each other daily, becomes ever more contrived or scarce. The cost, to the well-being of the company, becomes daily a greater percentage of the wealth generated.

Status orientated

As observed before, one of the effects of poor Quality management is the confusion stemming from the concept of competition. The diffuse organisation breeds internal competition, rather than cooperation. The perceived position of the individual within the company is an overt characteristic of this competition, and thus diffuse organisations will be status orientated, and be overburdened with levels of management and authority, titles, job descriptions, privilege and status symbols, most of which add nothing to the overall ability of the company to perform its function successfully.

Rigid structures

The framework between the diffuse areas of the company have to be, of necessity, fairly rigid. Such a structure quickly becomes thought of as entirely natural and inevitable. The rules, values, positions and privileges of yesterday are assumed to be those of tomorrow. Internal competition abounds, consuming vast quantities of energy, time and resources, often referred to as the company's 'internal energy'. The successful in these competitions relax, having reached the limit of their ability (or as some would have it, the level of their incompetence). Those engaged in this career struggle, make it their personal priority. Thus, they expend any amount of energy to meet the competition, that is the people working along side them. It is all very wasteful, expensive and soul destroying!

Examples

Take five minutes to consider your own company organisation, with respect to each of the above points. Try to identify examples that illustrate each one. Discuss the nature of your company with others. Does everyone perceive it in the same way?

An example from the author's own experience demonstrates one of the many petty concerns that often typify a diffuse company structure.

'A chief concern of many within larger companies would seem to be the rules governing where employees park their cars. When I worked for a major car manufacturer, such debate usually produced venom, aimed at some of the non-managerial staff who dared to park inside the perimeter fence, reserved for managers, rather than use the workers car park just outside the fence. A suggestion that the fence could be moved to permit room for everyone inside was met by a stunned silence, followed by the sad shaking of wise heads, who better understood the value of status and privilege.'

Family businesses

It may be that the historical background of much of our industry has led to this diffusion. Paradoxically, the origins of many of our major companies, and thus our corporate psyche, are rooted in the completely integrated paternalistic model of the family business.

Many family businesses started in the Victorian era, when many assumptions of power and authority went almost completely unchallenged. The unique method of organising a business around a family, with virtually all standards, values and decisions, emanating from the family head, was both:

- Thoroughly integrated, and
- Responsible for the lack of any deliberate structure.

Money operations

The gradual demise of the family firm, to be replaced with larger structures, has probably contributed greatly to our diffuse organisations. The situation is further aggravated by today's entrepreneurs. We have seen or, more accurately, are seeing the growth of the 'money operation'. This leads to many companies being bought, sold, amalgamated or hived off, principally for the sake of short-term financial gains.

Integrated structures

How can an integrated company organisation be achieved? The overall answer to this question must always revolve around people. That is, integration will grow from a common purpose and set of values.

It is not difficult to list the essential ingredients.

Single objective

It may appear to be simplistic to suggest that the single, most important objective of any company is to generate wealth, but this, within industry, is true. In most companies, this objective needs strengthening. The consideration of the process of wealth generation must include a time element. Good business practice will always look to the long-term, once the short-term is secure. The generation of wealth is not enough. The wealth must be conserved. Real wealth is the sum total produced, after expenditure and losses have been taken into account.

Common culture

The culture of a company stems from the shared values of those managing the company. Few company executives take time out to examine the values involved with the daily company activity. Indeed, we need to examine the values implicit behind every act or decision. The culture of the company can be developed through discussion and open management. An open culture will always display honesty and a sense of freedom. It will be exercised by people who perceive *task* as separate from *person* – it is acceptable to criticise the task, but not the person.

Effective communications

Implicit in a common company-wide culture will be the interchange of ideas, knowledge and values. Much of this will appear to happen informally, and much can be done to promote such informal communication. The planning of time and space can either inhibit informal meetings or promote them. The social mix and the basic respect of one individual for another will affect the growth of a healthy and informal communications environment. Whilst only so much social engineering can be achieved, staffing decisions and organisational detail can help, or hinder, this growth. Such informal relationships should never be seen as replacing the need to organise formal communications.

Educated personnel

To some extent, only those educated in the business of the company will be able to share the unified objective and culture. I do not mean educated in the formal sense, but rather that they are knowledgeable about the company's activities and all aspects of their own particular role within them. From this standpoint, everyone from chief executive to shopfloor worker can be considered educated, provided the input has been made to enlighten them. Uneducated people, at any level, will considerably inhibit new ideas. Those not understanding the company's principles and values cannot fully contribute to its normal working. This is a particular danger, in areas served by professionals, such as accountancy, engineering, etc. Such people can easily confuse their high level of overt educational qualifications, with being well-educated within the overall aspects of the company.

Respect for the individual

A company is a collection of individuals, each of whom devote part of their lives, effort and brain power to the company objective. Whatever the perceived position of an individual within a company, he or she deserves respect and trust. We usually both respect and trust people we know, however much the cynical may smile and mutter, 'you don't know so-and-so'. Lack of respect, indeed lack of consideration bordering on contempt, usually stems from a lack of contact and real knowledge of the individual people within our company. Tom Peters[1] describes the problems of organising large numbers of people, and to him any number over five is large. Our systems and organisation must be constructed in such a way that everyone is well known and respected by someone within a chain from the chief executive to every other individual.

Trust

Allied to the respect for each and every individual, is trust. We must construct our human organisations on the assumption that people are honest, and will give of their best, unless this is shown not to be so. This is preferable to living under the cloud of mutual suspicion, except where an occasional ray of honesty breaks the pattern.

Company orientated

The focus of concern within an integrated organisation will be the 'company good'. Everybody can share the pride in the unified achievements of the company. The ability of everyone to contribute effectively to a common objective will create a sense of *ownership*. This does not happen by chance. Indeed, the competitive forces internally, for resources perceived as scarce, or the internal struggle to achieve promotion in front of another employee, can be present in any organisation. It will require a totality of approach to subvert such natural competitions, for the common good of the company. Company politics and Quality are uneasy bed-fellows.

Fluid management

The management of change, together with the concentration stemming from being process-orientated, will produce the fluidity to avoid the normal internal struggles and squabbles. Any company will use a certain amount of its energy and resource for its own organisation. This wasteful internal energy should be minimised, thus allowing the maximisation of concentration on the real competition, that outside the company.

Domestic arrangements

The domestic arrangements of a company can convey many messages. A good test of a commitment to informal communications is to consider where and when people *eat*. Meal-breaks are an ideal time to allow the interchange of ideas and information. Many companies, though, not only allow people to shuffle off to eat with their own small peer group, but actively encourage them to do this. Management dining rooms and toilets are still common. The artificial barriers between managers and the managed are still maintained.

A senior executive of a major UK company gave the author his habit of judging a company by its toilet arrangements: 'I have visited many toilets in factories and offices. I believe the provision of clean accommodation, to meet the personal needs of the staff, is indicative of the respect in which the individuals are held, and thus the potential of the company.'

Perhaps each reader should consider the arrangements for eating, etc., that provide a background to their everyday life. What judgements would the above quoted senior executive make if he were to visit your premises?

Unifying the company

The responsibility for unifying the company has to sit directly on the shoulders of the chief executive.

The concept of unifying the company is concerned with optimising the efforts of the many individual people who form the company. In a diffuse organisation, individuals and groups will adopt a variety of objectives and directions. Whilst they will rarely be directly in opposition, there will be minor differences in direction. This will lead to the adoption of different priorities and standards. In more extreme circumstances, decisions leading to different consequential actions will result.

Effects of internal dissonance

There are several reasons why such dissonance will be damaging to the company.

- Wasted effort

  Any divergence in direction will lead to human effort becoming less than one hundred percent efficient. Such effort is described as the company's internal energy. Some internal energy will be necessary for the maintenance of the company's systems, and this must be conserved. It is as vital as all other representations of the company's resources.

- Conflict

  Even minor conflicts of interest, ideas or loyalty, can have a profound effect on the efficient operation of the company. Conflict leads to competition. Conflict also inhibits relationships within the workforce.

- Stress

  Stress always produces less than the best from people. Stress aids and abets crisis management. It produces a flow of adrenaline that can upset the normal, careful analysis of information leading to a rational decision. In such circumstances, it can have catastrophic results.

- Loss of morale

  One clearly defined company objective provides each member of the workforce with a scale upon which to measure their own efforts. It is the source of job satisfaction and pride of workmanship. The lack of such an objective will operate as a demotivating agent, with a consequent loss of morale.

Value of a unified approach

The value of a unified approach might be thought of as self-evident, and in many ways stemming from the reverse of the above list. There will, however, be additional benefits.

- Better corporate image

  Greater confidence will be inspired within your customer base, and indeed within the public at large. Everyone from the company will talk the same language, and present a unified set of standards and commitments.

- Improved internal relationships

  The concepts of cooperation and compromise for the common good will become the daily norm. With a shared ownership of the decision-making process and its outcome, there will be a differentiation between person and task. People will no longer assume that criticism is a slight on their personality, but see it as an attempt to improve the company's effort.

- Easier communications

  The common objective provides a common agenda, or central concern, for everyone within the organisation. This will become the focus of most communications, both formal and informal.

- Higher productivity

  Again, the common objective will focus the company efforts, leading to better Quality levels being produced, with lower Quality costs. This will lead not only to a more productive company, but to an expanding scope of enterprise. More human resource will be released to be re-invested in the company.

Internal energy

The concept of internal energy compares the sum total of the energy, time and expense administered within the company to maintain itself, with the total energy that is available.

An exercise

Question the use of 'internal energy' within a company, known to you. Consider the company's diffuse nature, in each of the areas identified. Make an assessment on a scale of one to five, where 5 denotes a considerable expenditure, and 1 virtually none:

Area	1	2	3	4	5	Comment
Inbreeding						
Diverse values						
Conflicting priorities						
Different language						
Diverse expectations						
Divergent lifestyles						
Status orientated						
Rigid structures						

Fig 5.1 Use of internal energy.

It suggests that there is a finite amount of such energy available within the company. The more that is expended within the company, the less there is available for the real purpose of the company – the satisfaction of customer requirements and expectations.

Each of the areas highlighted in the description of the diffuse company will be rich in the use of this internal energy. One aim of the unified company is to minimise the internal energy, thus maximising the external energy available to defeat the opposition.

Daily examples of the misuse of internal energy can be found in most companies. It is often salutary to remind those engaged in internal conflict *who* is the customer.

Internal energy should be minimised, thus leaving the maximum effort available to satisfy the external customers, beat the competition and generate wealth.

Quality is the key

The message on virtually every page of this book is that Quality is the one tool that has a *significance* at all levels, in all activities, within all decisions and at all times. The constant and ever-present movement towards higher Quality levels in everything done, and in everything made, focuses the total energy of the company.

It is a simple and easily made mental jump, from the objective of the company to generate wealth, to the state of being the best and achieving the highest Quality levels. Everyone within the company, and indeed everyone connected with the company as a customer or supplier, must make this mental step and take on board seriously the *commitment to excellence*.

How the company is organised will make a significant contribution to this Quality focus. It is not sufficient to merely organise the workforce in a particular way. Such a re-organisation has to grow from the need to work in a way that is perceived as essential in the pursuit of Quality.

The route to Quality is both time consuming and exhilarating. It is essential that a firm hand controls and directs the activities, not to determine and prescribe the outcomes, but to maintain a momentum and ensure the climate necessary for a successful conclusion. It will be vital and stimulating.

Speak Quality

The first step can be to change the language of the company. Many find it irritating to have loose language pointed out to them. They complain that they did not mean exactly what they said, and that everyone knows that Quality is important. It must be continually emphasised that this is *not* so, and that the way to live Quality is first to speak the Quality language. Loose talk conveys wrong impressions.

Speak Quality, live Quality, produce Quality.

Summary

Company Structures

Diffuse organisations	Integrated organisations
	typified by .....
Inbreeding	Single objective
Diverse values	Common culture
Conflicting priorities	Effective communications
Different languages	Educated personnel
Diverse expectations	Respect for individuals
Divergent life styles	Trust
Status orientated	Company orientated
Rigid structures	Fluid management

Unifying the company

Effects of internal dissonance	*Value of a unified approach*
Wasted effort	Better corporate image
Conflict	Improved internal relationships
Stress	Easier communications
Loss of morale	Higher productivity

Internal energy - is the effort expended by people within the company on maintaining the structures and internal operation of the company.

- should be minimised, thus leaving the maximum effort to be available to satisfy the external customers, beat the competition and generate wealth.

Quality is the key

Speak Quality, live Quality, produce Quality.

Last thoughts ....

The technical director of a well-known company explained their attempt to be the best. 'Ah,' I said, 'You are the Rolls Royce of the plastics industry.' 'I'd rather be the BMW,' he replied.

1. Peters, Tom, *In Search of Excellence*, Harper & Row, New York, 1982.

Chapter 6

Team work

The complexity of most of the processes which are operated in industry, commerce and the services places them beyond the control of any one individual.

– John Oakland[1]

Route-map

This chapter examines the concept of team work. It demonstrates that it is a great deal more powerful than just people working in groups.

Teamwork is identified as the route to effective management, and the following are considered:

The team work concept
Why work in teams?
What is a team?
Sharing responsibility
Team responsibilities
Role of team leader

Team work

The basic unit of a well organised company is the team. The team consists of a small group of people, sharing a joint responsibility for their activity and contribution to the company. Such groups can be created at all levels and in all departments.

Some consider it easier to create teams within certain types of company, but the basic ideas are relevant to all. The team work theory perceives teams working *in relation to each other* – the very embodiment of the customer supplier links that are so necessary for Quality.

Why teams?

Better control

Processes are controlled better by teams than by individuals. The team members supply a joint effort, and support, at the time and place demanded by the process. The process receives control when it needs it. A team can service its own manpower needs, ensuring consistency and constant attention.

Easy management

Teams allow an easy management style, with one manager being responsible for several teams, rather than for a large number of individuals. Good managers develop an easy relationship with the team, overtly delegating as much responsibility to the team as it appears able to handle. The manager is able to vary the amount of overt management activity according to the needs of each team. The well orientated, motivated and able team, will require little attention, leaving the manager free to concentrate on the team that is not functioning so well. Team work leads to efficient management.

Work rotation

Team work allows a work rotation pattern, or other such formal devices, that best suit the people involved. Thus their efforts are maximised. The team organising its own work will integrate the needs of the company and the needs of each team member, giving the most efficient working environment for the team.

Social needs

People are social and have a psychological need to belong to a small group. This applies to working relationships as well as to social and domestic relationships. Each individual team member will grow to value the strength stemming from such relationships.

Group instinct

There is a natural desire to be part of a team or group. Indeed, I would suggest such groupings naturally occur within any working environment. Without organisation, they are unlikely to be work orientated, and could well be counter-productive. Whilst this team instinct may be natural, the means of working effectively together in an industrial or commercial organisation are not. The working of a team has to be taught, so that the purpose, the responsibilities and the implications are understood by all, both within and outside the team.

Recognition

People need recognition for their work, and it is more possible to recognise group efforts. The working of the group will always be greater than that of an individual, and the team can share praise and appreciation. Also, many opportunities for a reassuring word, or for reinforcement, are missed in the wider company organisation. Team members can give, and do give, immediate recognition to the work of other team members. The appreciation of people, mutually respected, is always a very valuable commodity.

Supportive

The team will play a supportive role, smoothing the ups and downs of working life. Nothing ever goes smoothly all the time, and each individual will have a 'bad' day. The group protects and supports the individual when it is necessary.

Discipline

Discipline is best achieved through peer pressure. The most effective discipline is self-discipline, and this regulates most of us, most of the time. Where this 'being responsible for one's own person and activities' is insufficient, the pressure exerted by those nearest is often the most effective, the most immediate and the most acceptable to the misguided individual. Often the occasional rebuff is taken from friends, when it would be fiercely rejected and fought, if coming from someone more distant, someone in authority.

On-going improvements

Teams build trust, confidence and responsibility. The team is an excellent natural formation, within which on-going improvements, via Quality improvement projects, problem-solving and process development, can occur. The team will become more knowledgeable about their own processes, those involved at previous stages of manufacture, and the design aspects effecting their work. They will also understand the requirements and expectations of the customers, both internal and external.

What is a team?

The concept of a team needs to be actively developed within the individual company. The answer to the question 'What is a team?', becomes, 'A team is what your company wants a team to be'. The

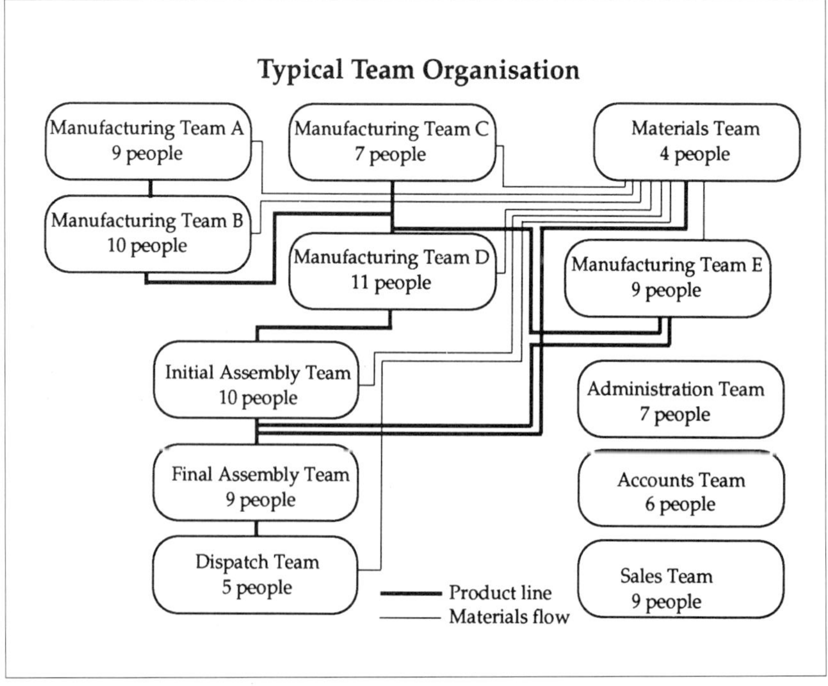

Fig 6.1 Typical team organisation.

definition important to you is not that which you may find written here or elsewhere, but the meaning and common understanding that you can create behind the concept. The team is an 'industrial tool', to be formed and used, not worshiped.

This is a generalised interpretation of the concept.

> *A team is usually comprised of between four and 10 people, who share a group of activities or processes. Each team member is multi-skilled to enable him to do any of the tasks of the team. The members of the team share responsibility for their work.*

Central to the concept of the team will be the idea of *sharing*. This will be typified by the shared responsibility that the team develops, or is given, for aspects of its daily working life. Such responsibilities, and the relationships that result, are even more difficult to describe. Indeed, it is not helpful for a company to define a list of responsibilities. The list would probably be small, being the least expected from the worst team. It could deny the full value of team work to those teams able to wield it.

Multi-skilling is important, as it not only allows the most flexible use of manpower, but enables all individuals to maximise their potential.

The company should not prescribe these responsibilities. They emanate better from the relationship between individual managers and the team concerned. They must reflect the abilities of the team members, individually and collectively.

It is more valuable to describe the areas in which the team could be *expected* to wield responsibility. Having arrived at such a list, the management group should highlight the *limits* of the team's responsibility in each area.

In general then, the team has a joint responsibility for:

- The production of the work from the team.

  Clearly the ability of the group to meet targets must be enshrined in the team methodology. This, after all, is the main purpose of the team. Living the company's Quality Policy by meeting the customer's requirements and expectations, will be the prime target of the team.

- The control of the processes.

  Only those directly operating a process can effectively control the process. The ability of the team to control a particular process will depend not only on the members, but on the measurement of process inputs.

- Organising the work within the team.

  The sharing of the work to maximise each individual's interest and satisfaction, whilst also achieving the required output, is best left within the aegis of the team.

- Quality.

  The team should take full responsibility for the Quality of its work, in all respects. No-one else can wield this responsibility with as much effectiveness.
  The team will have **customer relationships** with other teams and individuals. The concept of 'industrial citizenship' is as important for the team as a whole, as it is for individual members. Each member has responsibilities and duties to the team. Each team has responsibilities and duties to others.

- Problem-solving of all problems created within the group.

  The solutions to all problems lie in the heads of those most concerned with the processes from which the problems emanate. The team is the ideal basis for problem-solving activities.

- Constant and never-ending process improvement.

  For this to become a way of life for the company, it must involve everybody. This is much easier when operating with a team organisation. The team is the natural basis for a Quality Improvement Group, Quality Circles, or any other formal activity. Also, it can daily live the never-ending improvement philosophy on an informal basis. Either way, the team will need the requisite skills to enable this function to be successful.

In short, the team will probably have responsibility in these areas:

- Work production.
- Process control.
- Organisation of the team.

- Quality.
- Problem-solving.
- Never-ending process improvement.

Sharing responsibility

The key to team work is sharing. It does not matter in which part of the organisation the team operates, its success will depend directly on the ability of the team members to *share* the responsibilities of the team as a whole. It is this joint nature of the activity and responsibility that provides the cohesion of the team, raising it from being a group of individuals, to being a powerful team.

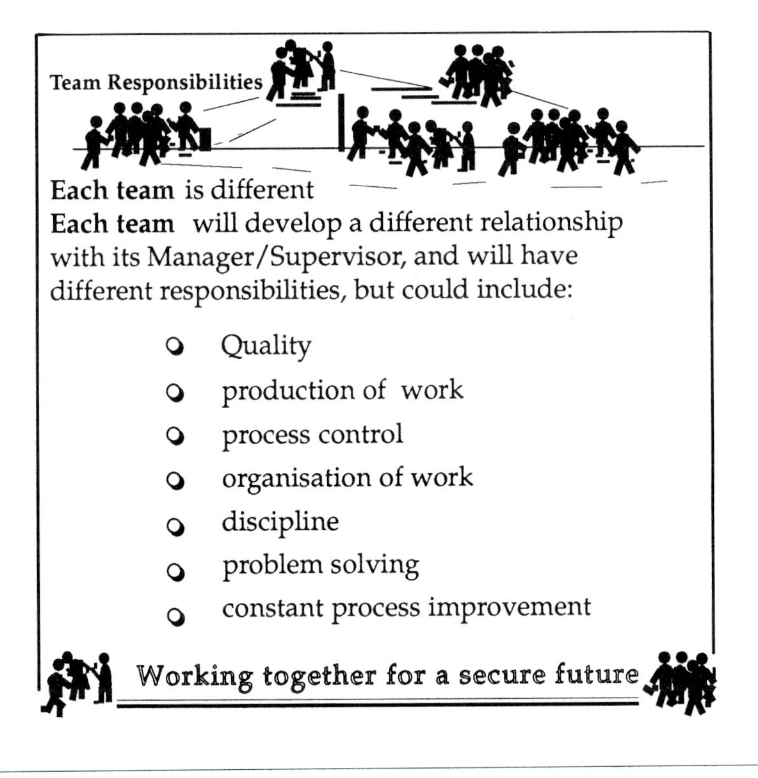

Fig 6.2 Team responsibilities.

A well organised team will share: responsibility
knowledge
skills
interest
friendship

Secondary teams

There may be secondary teams at work within the organisation. A secondary team is a group in which the members may not be working at the same location, or at the same activity, or within the plant. Its members will share an overall, plant-wide responsibility. This may be to provide a service or back-up to the main company activities. Electricians, maintenance, caterers, and so on, are all typical examples of secondary teams.

Some people may find themselves members of more than one team, or secondary team.

It is most important that each secondary team is well aware of the negotiated areas in which it has responsibility. Time and education will be needed to establish such teams. Indeed, the full effectiveness of the team will not be possible without this initial input. Once in operation, the secondary team will require time and space to be able to remain a cohesive force.

Many small companies do not possess the logistical arrangements for such group activities. It is difficult to find time for the team to come together, and sometimes even more difficult to find a suitable room or space. Such problems *must* be overcome. The lengths that the company is prepared to go to to ensure the effective operation of teams, will be indicative of its commitment to Quality.

Management teams

The senior management team is a secondary team, using the definition above. Each member will have a considerable daily work load, based upon his own area of activity within the company. Together, though, they will need to act, and be seen to act, as a team. As with all team work, it should not be assumed that this will occur automatically, and with no conscious input or organisation.

The effectiveness of the management team can be judged by the manner in which it shares the responsibility for the company activities. This will be the key to the company's ability to achieve Quality.

The use of teams blurs the basic definition of a manager. The introduction of team work delegates immediate responsibility for action and organisation to teams, often comprised of people with no wider responsibility. These people, in other circumstances, would be termed and viewed as operatives or shopfloor workers. The modern approach to the working situation, gives everyone some responsibility for themselves and some responsibility for the work of the other members of the team. Thus, team management is part of the shared responsibility. Everyone is a manager to some extent.

A distinction between levels of management function may be helpful. This can be seen in terms of process control.

Team operation

The team should *not only* be perceived as being part of a customer/supplier relationship chain with other teams, but should actively *live* such a relationship.

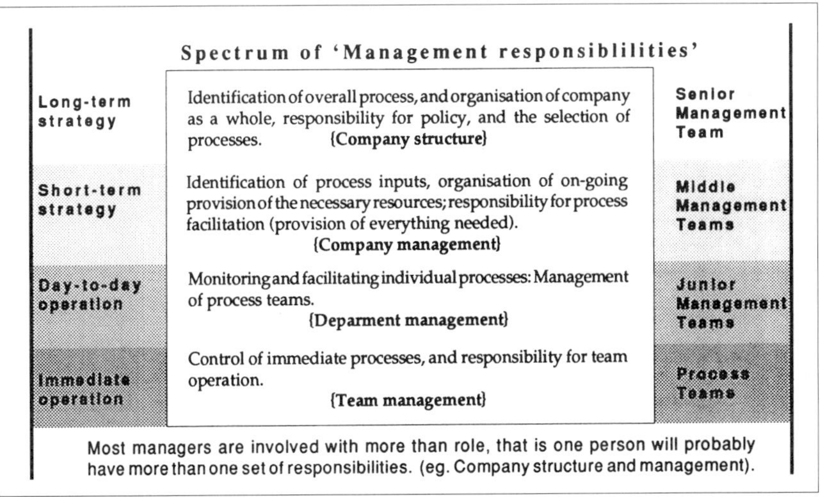

Fig 6.3 Spectrum of management responsibilities.

Horizontal communication

A communications framework between the team and its suppliers and customers will be vital. This may be formally organised, or may be left to the more straightforward, old fashioned method of people daily talking together, as and when necessary. Whether formal or informal, it is sensible to think through the channels of negotiating throughout the whole chain. The essential links will be horizontal, crossing department and activity boundaries, and will usually exist between people of equal status.

Team negotiations

The questions to consider will be in these areas.

- What does each team require and expect from other teams?
- How will such negotiations operate on a daily basis?
- What physical spaces or barriers will have to be overcome?
- What authority barriers and/or company-made inter-departmental barriers will have to be overcome?

All such questions can, and should, be considered well in advance of implementing a team organisation. The questions may stem from the Quality Strategy Team, but the answers will be more the responsibility of the management within each area.

Semi-autonomous teams within a secure framework

The team should function as a self-sufficient autonomous unit within a strongly structured framework. It will seek assistance only as and when it is required, whether this assistance is managerial, engineering or whatever.

No team will ever be totally self-sufficient. When in need, it should readily ask for assistance. Again, the provision of assistance is part of the customer/supplier chain.

The engineering department supplies a service to the process, when it is needed. The training department supplies skills to the team and/or team members to meet not only the team's needs, but the personal needs of each member.

The team may well require the assistance of the manager to accomplish something beyond its control. This could be external to the team, such as securing finance for a process improvement. Equally, it might be internal to the team, for example asking for the managers authority, to obtain the compliance of one or more team members to the declared team activities. The manager becomes the supplier of management, and the team is the customer. The company Quality definition, policy or statement, will be as important here as it is in all other areas. Each team has a right to Quality management.

It may be that the management, carefully observing a team, proffers advice and direction prior to the team actively seeking assistance. Such a decision cannot be made by anyone other than the appropriate manager. The task of managing the team involves maintaining a sufficiently close relationship to know when such assistance is required. There is no question of the manager abrogating accountability or personal responsibility for the team's activities and performance. The manager remains accountable for the activity, processes, and results of the team. The best way of meeting this accountability is to delegate much of the day to day responsibility to the team itself, whilst maintaining an intimate knowledge of its internal operation and performance.

The ideal team member is:

- ❑ **good tempered**
- ❑ **thoughtful**
- ❑ **consistent**
- ❑ **reliable**
- ❑ **able to get things done**
- ❑ **capable**
- ❑ **able to talk to people easily**

Fig 6.4 Who make good team members?

Clearly the manager will share with the team leader, and the team itself, the task of *motivating* the team. This aspect is examined in more detail in the next chapter.

The role of the team leader

The exact responsibility of any individual team leader must be the result of a negotiation between the manager and the team. In the end, it will be the embodiment of the relationship between the team leader and the supervisor or manager.

As a basic principle, the team leader's role should be negotiated so that:

- The team leader is confident in the role.

  Clearly, this may not be a static situation. The team leader can be expected to grow in confidence and experience. The role will, therefore, be subject to change and re-negotiation.

- The supervisor, or manager, is happy with the role.

  This has to be an essential if the accountability for a process is to be separated from the daily responsibility for its operation. Again, confidence will grow with experience. The relationship between team and manager will develop and, hopefully, strengthen with time.

- The team understands and accepts the team leader's role.

  There is a subtle difference between a manager's role and a team leader's role, and only time and practice will develop the leader's capacity to lead from within. It is, of course, an excellent training ground for future management.

There are other points to be born in mind during the negotiation of the team leader's role. The team leader:

- Has a coordinating role.
- Contributes to the organisation of the work.
- Ensures the social well-being of the team members.
- Calls for assistance when necessary.
- Coordinates all the Quality improvement activities
- Is firstly a team member, and secondly its leader.

Team Member Profile

Subject:

Assess characteristics:

Characteristic	**Not at all**	**Hardly at all**	**Average**	**Only a little**	**Very**
1/ Capable					
2/ Skilled at your job					
3/ Quick at your job					
4/ Reliable					
5/ A consistent worker					
6/ Good time-keeper					
7/ Responsible					
8/ Able to work when tired					
9/ Interested in new ideas					
10/ Ambitious					
11/ Good tempered					
12/ Get on with people					
13/ Able to talk to people					
14/ Show initiative					
15/ Thoughtful					
16/ Able to get things done					
17/ Able to solve problems					
18/ Happy					
19/ Able to share a joke					
20/ Work easily with others					

Fig 6.5 Team member profile.

Team size

An essential requirement of the team organisation is a degree of stability within the workforce. Team structures are quickly broken down if people are constantly being moved from one team to another.

Instability of the workforce

The team structure can militate against any inherent instability. A loyalty is easier to develop within the small team, than within the department or company. Absenteeism becomes more difficult when the main sufferers are your fellow team members. This internal disciplinary pressure can be cited as one of the major benefits of team work.

There are implications here for staffing levels. Each company needs to achieve a balance between an acceptable level of overtime, the personal disruption caused by working overtime, and an increased payroll. Most don't. Most make decisions based on the assumption that people are never promoted, leave suddenly, are ill, are trained or have holidays. In other words, when any of these events happen, a crisis situation ensues, and crisis measures are implemented. As a result, there is little long-term planning of overtime as a manufacturing expense. Overtime is usually the easy way out of a temporary production problem, again, and again, and again.

The two major effects are *staff movement* between jobs, teams and activities, and *paid overtime*. Both affect the life of the shopfloor worker more than anyone else in the company. Often the effects go beyond the factory gate to affect the employee's family and friends. These types of additional demand, probably contribute to staff instability, thus perpetuating the crisis situation.

Overtime bill

Any high overtime bill is a drain on the resources of the company, and should be perceived as a 'Quality cost'. The company pays for a worker and a half, and receives only one worker, usually tired, working considerably below par, and with extra worries because of his enforced separation from the home. The company rarely gets value for money at the usual rate, let alone at time and a half. Quality will suffer. The customer will not have his requirements and expectations met.

This is poor management. If a company perpetually has an overtime bill, it is not employing enough people.

There are many advantages to be gained from employing slightly more people than is at first apparent. The reduction in crisis management will be considerable. Smooth and efficient working, in the absence of crisis, will considerably improve efficiency, Quality standards and customer satisfaction. Employees do not, in general, benefit from overtime. Where they perceive it as essential to make ends meet, the wage structure needs attention.

The mathematics are relatively simple.

An example

A team of 10 employees, working 40 hours a week, for 50 weeks of the year, will need:

$$10 \times 40 \times 50 = 20{,}000 \text{ working hours}$$

Assume that:

- Each employee has 10 days holiday (from the 50 weeks).
- Each employee is ill for seven days per year (on average).
- Each employee receives 10 days education/training per year (on average).
- Three of the 10 employees will leave suddenly and not be replaced for two weeks.
- Two of the 10 employees will be promoted suddenly and not be replaced for four weeks

The team has lost :	800	working hours (holidays)
	560	working hours (illness)
	800	working hours (education/training)
	240	working hours (resignation)
	320	working hours (promotion)
	2720	working hours of normal working.
This would cost	4080	working hours (overtime @ 1.5 rate)

This is equivalent to more than two additional employees (4000 working hours).

An alternative calculation

The alternative plan would be to employ a team of 11, on the understanding that the team manages to be self-sufficient and covers at least two absentees at any one time. Indeed, the flexibility inherent in team work produces extra resources. The team, by sharing responsibility, can cover for absence, sometimes with no additional manpower. Holidays can be arranged such that there is never more than one member on holiday at a time, and education and training commitments can be largely organised around these holidays.

The mathematics would now be altered.

Theoretically, the team still need the work of 10 employees, working 40 hours a week, for 50 weeks of the year:

10 X 40 X 50 = 20,000 working hours

However, we now find that:

- Each employee has 10 days holiday (totally covered by the team).
- Each employee is ill for seven days per year (six of them covered by the team).
- Each employee receives 10 days education/training per year (eight of them covered by the team).
- Three of the 11 employees will leave suddenly and not be replaced for two weeks (assume half-covered by the team).
- Two of the 11 employees will be promoted suddenly and not be replaced for four weeks (assume half-covered by the team).

Calculated on a team basis, the figures are (ch = coverage hours):

0	working hours (holidays, 880 ch)
88	working hours (illness, 528 ch)
176	working hours (training, 704 ch)
120	working hours (resignation, 120 ch)
160	working hours (promotion, 160 ch)
544	working hours of normal working.

This would cost	816	working hours (overtime @ 1.5 rate)
+	2000	working hours (for additional employee)
	2816	working hours

{* the cover provided by the team amounts to 2392 wh, which is covered by the additional person plus the flexibility gained from team work.}

This is a saving of 1264 working hours on the wage bill, equivalent to more than half an additional employee, plus all the additional benefits of smooth normal working. With simple logic like this available, why do companies insist on crisis management?

A rule of thumb

For any team of eight employees, it is usually cost effective to employ nine and expect the team, exceptionally, to be able to cope with two absentees (for whatever reason).

For any team of 12 employees, it is usually cost effective to employ 14 and expect the team, exceptionally, to be able to cope with three absentees (for whatever reason).

The benefits of working slightly enlarged teams.

- The team can cope with absenteeism, holidays and training activities.
- Instead of crisis management of moving staff, the team will usually find a little more effort for the rare occasions that it is needed.
- Staff are not moved and remain in their teams, thus becoming more valuable employees.
- The wage bill is reduced.
- Staff only work normal hours. Loss of Quality through tiredness is eliminated.
- All the benefits of team work become possible.

An extra team

The team organisation is an excellent way to introduce new recruits to the company. An additional team, called the Training Team, is introduced, with a nominal membership determined by the size of the company and the staff turnover.

Recruits are placed in this team during an initial probationary, training period. They not only receive formal training, but can be used as a pool of labour to replenish any other team, temporarily requesting additional workers. This not only ensures that other team members are never removed from their teams, but that new recruits obtain a wide experience in many areas of the company's activities before settling down in a particular team. These team-members-in-waiting are thus instantly available the moment a vacancy appears in one of the regular teams.

Summary

Team work

Why teams?

- Teams control processes better.
- Teams aid an easy management style.
- Teams give better work rotation patterns.
- People have a psychological need to belong to a small group.
- People have a natural desire to be part of a team.
- People need recognition for their work.
- The team has a supportive role.
- Discipline is best achieved through peer pressure.
- Teams build trust, confidence and responsibility

What is a team?

A team is usually comprised of between four and 10 people who share a group of activities or processes. Each team member is multi-skilled to enable him to do any of the tasks of the team. The team shares responsibility for the work.

Team work is sharing responsibility

Team responsibilities:

- Work production.
- Process control.
- Organisation of the team.
- Quality.
- Problem-solving.
- Never-ending process improvement.

Team operation:

- Horizontal communication.
- Team negotiations.
  What does each team require and expect from other teams?
  How will such negotiations operate on a daily basis?
  What physical spaces or barriers will have to be overcome?
  What authority barriers will have to be overcome?
- Semi-autonomous teams.

Team size:

The case for additional employees, rather than a high overtime bill.

Last thoughts ....

There is a chinese proverb about heaven and hell. In hell there is plenty of food, but all the chop sticks are five feet long. People cannot feed themselves, and everyone is starving. In heaven, there is also food and five foot long chop sticks, but people have learnt to feed each other.

1. Oakland, John, *Total Quality Management*, Heineman,1989.

Chapter 7

Motivating for Quality

It is not that men are ill fed, but that
they have no pleasure
in the work by which they make their bread, and
therefore look to wealth as the only means of pleasure.

– John Ruskin ,'The stones of Venice' (1885)

Route-map

The first part of this chapter examines the theoretical basis for motivation, by considering:

The need for motivation
Motivation on several levels
The Protestant work ethic
Why people work
The myth of money as a motivational force
Needs-driven motivation

The practical applications of this theory then include:

Job satisfaction
Financial reward
Recognition of superiors and peer group
Three other parallel factors:
advancement, interest and responsibility

The chapter finishes by considering practical advice on how to motivate staff, and explodes the myth of 'boring jobs'.

The need for motivation

The subject of motivation has come to the fore in recent years. The 'Enterprise Culture' accepts the need for 'incentives'. Within capitalism, no-one does anything for nothing. The bonus system, and productivity related pay, are both heralded as means of achieving the best from the workforce.

The author whole-heartedly rejects these theories as a way of achieving Quality. In reality, many people do a great deal over and above that for which they are paid, that is, for nothing. What inspires people to give of themselves completely is vision. People following a dream accept no bounds to their possible achievements.

George Eliot, in Daniel Deronda, comments, 'What makes life dreary, is the lack of a motive.' The traditional working man giving honest toil for the sake of his pay packet, has always been a myth. The Victorians knew that people would not continually endure hardship for *only* money. They enlisted the support of the Protestant church, and many vicars gave Sunday sermons on the goodness of honest toil. The Calvinists had a deep anxiety about their *certitudo salutis*, or their certainty of achieving salvation.

Motivation at several levels

1. Society and the State

Effective motivation always requires a simultaneous input from several levels. There can be state factors that totally subordinate the company and individual efforts. High taxation, a state of war, a break down of law and order, will all demotivate anyone striving to achieve a safe and secure future. Clearly, the societal framework will always have a considerable effect.

Where there has been state involvement in a business sector, there may be more powerful forces present than the influences of an individual company. In such circumstances, motivation may be extremely difficult, as any action of the individual company may be outweighed by the influences resulting from external decisions. There are many clear examples here. A widely publicised statement by a government minister, describing ambulance drivers as mere taxi drivers for the disabled, was a demotivating force. This undid many months of painstaking managerial work in many individual ambulance stations.

State monetary policy can have effects on an industry that may last for decades. The lack of investment at Ravenscraig, British Steel's major Scottish plant, left the privatised company with the impossible task of motivating a workforce that has no belief in its own future.

The 1970s and 1980s have seen several examples of the depressing effect of the government's monetary policies. Investment in government-owned enterprises, such as gas, telephones and the railways, was included under the general heading of public expenditure. Such investment became an important item in the Public Sector Borrowing Requirement (PSBR), and, as such, conflicted with the government's declared aim to reduce the PSBR. However, once privatised, the same investment in gas and telephones was warmly applauded, thus removing the depressing effects of lack of liquidity and cash flow, and making motivation of the workforce a possibility, and in the event, a reality.

2. Company level

The framework of the company or organisation will be ever-present. It will dwell within the minds of individual managers and employees. There is, therefore, the need to create a climate in which it is possible to motive people.

Every company creates a climate within which people work. Consciously or unconsciously, it will encourage or discourage employees giving their full effort to the company's tasks.

These environmental, or company-wide, forces will be considerable, when compared to those exerted by individual managers. Power is perceived by individual workers to be at this level. Thus, the company motivational climate is of a higher order than the actions of individual managers.

Employees may respond to company motivational stimuli, or, in their absence, be unmoved by the actions of individual managers. In a company with poor morale, the employees may be convinced that they are not in a winning situation, and that no effort from them can influence the outcomes. The question, 'Do you expect good work from this out-of-date machinery, in this filthy place?', is difficult for individual managers to answer. In a poor company situation, motivation may be impossible.

However, it is often only at the departmental level that consideration of motivational factors takes place, since the higher levels may well be out of the manager's control. It is, therefore, imperative that the total working environment is considered.

3. Personal motivation

A further consideration must be 'self motivation'. The creation of some of the greatest works of art and most momentous human feats have occurred against all odds, without a helpful environment and with no motivational intervention. People such as Anne Frank,[1] Mozart[2] and Captain Oates,[3] typify the human spirit that supplies self motivation, when there is none coming from elsewhere. It is, however, not very helpful to expect our employees to exert such abnormal effort.

The Protestant work ethic

It is important to consider the background to people's expectations, and indeed their orientation to work. To appreciate this, it will be necessary to look back to examine the origin of our feelings.

The Protestant work ethic that grew from the Calvinists' concern with the hereafter, saw work as essentially a *good* activity, and laziness and idleness as *evil*. The proverb 'The devil finds work for idle hands' has its

Idea

The valuable effects of human endeavour are realised most when motivation at all three levels are considered simultaneously.

origin here. This work ethic also heavily reinforced the idea of authority. The power of others to give orders, and receive, not only obedience, but respect, was continually reinforced to ensure social order. The motivation offered during the dire years that followed the industrial revolution, was two-fold; *survival* in this world, and the possibility of *salvation* in the next.

It may be thought cynical to suggest that the major employers enlisted the support of the church to motivate the workforce, but then the suggestion that the employers were not aware of the churches' assistance in maintaining a docile workforce, just above the starvation level, could be thought to be naive.

The main reason for mentioning the Protestant work ethic, is that parts of it still abound within our society. The feelings of many of the unemployed could be attributed to this cultural heritage. This work ethic should be considered by anyone seriously attempting to understand the psychology of his workforce. A positive stance can then be taken to motivate it.

Very few of us ever stop to question our motives. Indeed, we seldom have a straightforward, single motive for any action. We are complex creatures, bound as much by habit as by logic. If we are to manage others successfully, we must attempt to see the world through their eyes, to share their perception of the company and its work, and to understand their motivation.

Why do we work?

This has to be the first question.

Logically, with many people excluded from enjoyment or pleasure in the work situation, and earning only just enough to survive, it might be sensible not to work. Perhaps the growth of 'hippy' communes during the 1960s was in response to this logic.

The consideration of why people work, may result in the first false steps for those interested in understanding the motivation of their workforce. It is unhelpful to expect all employees to share the management's desire to further the prosperity of the company. It is more helpful to understand that what motivates management may be very different from the motivational forces operating within the rest of the workforce, even though the fundamental personal motives may have a great deal in common.

Many see motivation as the satisfaction of a series of needs. We all have the same set of needs, and hence motivations, but we may be at different points in the series. Hence, we have different needs and motivations at any one time.

Some might suggest that men and women have different needs, and thus will be differently motivated. Indeed, such prejudices, if that is what they are, are reinforced by some psychologists. Michael Argyle noted that:

> 'Men and women tend to seek different things in their work. Men will want to have a job that is well paid, secure and gives prestige; they are quite happy working with things rather than people, and do not mind risk. Women are more concerned with self-expression and creativity, want to work with people rather than things, and to be helpful to others.'[4]

This example suggests that we all need to examine our own prejudices and beliefs when determining our attitude to the motivation of others. It is all too easy for deep-seated prejudice to become embodied in related attitudes, without any realisation that the outcome lacks logic.

The myth of money

The major concern of working people in the UK would appear to be *pay*. It has been the central issue in almost every trade dispute since the war, and is the on-going concern of government and unions, in looking for a balance between the current inflation figure and pay settlements.

This is a myth. Money is not people's greatest concern, and it is degrading, and damaging to morale and efficiency to pretend that it is.

The Taylor legacy

The damage was done at the start of the twentieth century, when F W Taylor developed his theory of 'scientific management'.[5] This identified an advent of job specialisation accompanying the technological innovation of that time. Taylor believed that this led to the requirement for men to work increasingly like part of the machinery. He saw a great deal of inefficiency, stemming from workers having too much opportunity to decide exactly how a job should be done. He believed that the managerial task of planning work included the exact method by which it was to be performed. This led to a decrease in the amount of individual control over work methods. His approach, the forerunner of time and motion studies, envisaged workers doing a repetitive job in an identical fashion, again, and again and again.

The individual's motivation for allowing himself to become an automaton was seen to be money. Money was perceived as the only reason for people to work. Taylor regarded men as individual machine-like units, as sources of energy. To combat low output, men should be carefully selected, totally controlled, and their desire for money exploited by making sure that their needs were never met. Hungry families made for compliant workmen.

Taylor's methods are described in this oft-told story of his study of a Pennsylvanian Dutchman called Schmidt.

> Schmidt was one of 75 labourers loading pig iron onto railway wagons. Production averaged twelve and a half tons a day, a figure that Taylor felt he could increase by using more efficient working methods. Taylor told Schmidt he could earn substantially more money by doing exactly as he was told. He was interested, and Taylor gave him exact directions to walk, to lift, to put the iron down, to rest and so on. At the end of the day Schmidt had loaded forty-seven and a half tons of pig iron, and continued to load this amount daily, for the three years he was under observation.[6]

Many since, have doubted the contribution of this Schmidt. Most time and effort studies produce a momentary improvement that then evaporates rapidly. It is hard to envisage this emigrant Dutchman happily slogging away in this fashion for three years.

Whilst Taylor has been long since discredited, there is still a prevalent belief that money is the highest motivating factor. Most readers will acknowledge that this is untrue for them. Most managers will claim that they enjoy their job, face the daily challenges with confidence, and obtain a real sense of achievement. We often assume that we are alone in having these needs for job satisfaction, and yet the author's experience is that we are not.

General perceptions

The author has asked what is the most important issue or concern of almost every group of people that he has met in seminars and courses over the past five years. He has yet to find a group that suggests that money is the highest concern. It is usually about number three, following job security and job satisfaction.

The reasons why unions place so much emphasis on money are complex, and have much to do with the need to find mass bargaining counters. Each individual is in a unique relationship with his work, and thus job satisfaction can never become a bargaining counter. Similarly, job security depends upon the company enjoying continued success into the long-term. No-one can offer this at the bargaining table. With most poorly run companies, it is out of the hands of the company executive anyway, with market forces seen to be the driving factor. Inevitably, it is money that is thrust forward. If a worker has no control over his work, and to quote Eliot, if 'life is dreary for want of a motive', then it seems obvious that emphasis is to be placed on the non-working life, ie. that financed by earnings.

Motiveless lifestyle?

Consider this conversation between a long distance lorry driver and an acquaintance whom he had not met for some time:

Lorry driver:	I thought it was you.
Friend:	It must be years now.
Lorry driver:	Yes, I'm not around much these days.
Friend:	What job are you doing now?
Lorry driver:	Driving heavy goods for about 70 hours a week.
Friend:	How much do you get?
Lorry driver:	Not much, and I have to pay most to my ex-wife.

Friend:	You separated then?
Lorry driver:	Yes, she didn't like my job. She made my life a misery. I miss the kids though.
Friend:	Do you like the job?
Lorry driver:	No, but its a means to an end.[7]

Most readers can supply similar stories of people, who apparently chased a particular goal, only to lose it in the chase.

Needs-driven motivation

A more scientific approach stems from the early 1940s, when the American A H Maslow developed a theory presenting human needs as a hierarchy, that has been accepted by most social scientists since.[8] He argues that most people's needs can be arranged in a hierarchy, starting with basic needs, such as shelter, food and clothing. Until these lowest-order needs have been satisfied, other needs remain relatively unimportant. Once satisfied, the lower needs lose their importance, and the next level of needs become the major concern.

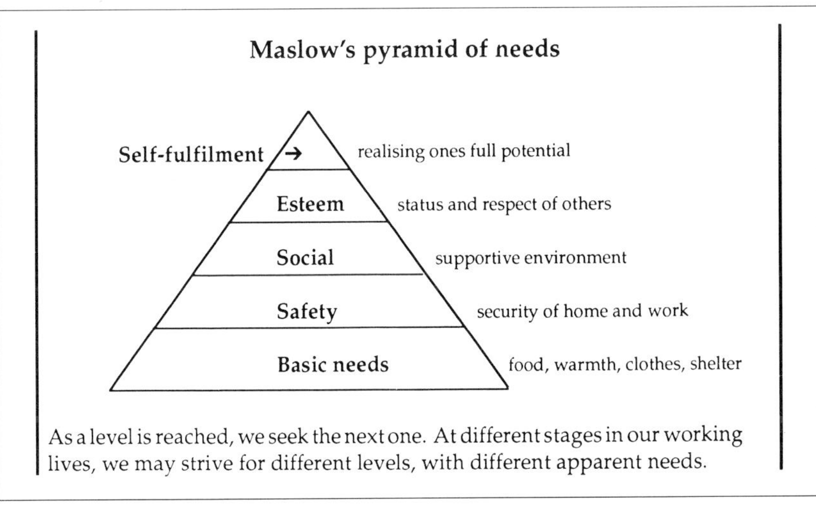

Fig 7.1 Maslow's hierarchy of needs.

This theory suggests that those at a subsistence level will be worried only by the need to survive. Their concern will be with food, warmth, clothes and shelter. Once these aspects of an individual's life are ensured, the concern becomes safety. This may be safety at home, safety at work, or indeed, safety going between the two. The third level is the social environment that the individual inhabits. Everybody has a need to belong, and a range of love needs. These come to the fore, once the lower order needs have been satisfied and we seek a supportive environment.

Many workers within industry never reach higher than this level. Indeed, work will not be expected to provide anything more than the two basic levels. Traditionally though, some have sought more. The next level leads us to seek esteem, status and the respect of others. The ultimate achievement at this level is the dominance felt over others. Finally, when all other needs are satisfied, everyone turns inwards a little, and is concerned with his own self-fulfilment. Each will assess his own potential and seek to realise it fully.

Organisational motivation

Frederick Herzberg took these ideas one step further:[9] in a publication of 1958, he introduced the idea of 'hygiene' factors. These 'hygiene' factors parallel Maslow's strata, and provide a basis for satisfaction. Whilst not necessarily being intrinsic motivational factors, their absence would lead to dissatisfaction, and eventually have the negative effect of demotivation. Thus, these factors are important as a pre-condition to motivation. They will not themselves have a lasting effect. In the long-term, they must be reinforced with other more positive motivating factors.

Herzberg identified four levels:

Level 4 Organisational policy and rules.

The emphasis here is on safety. All employees need to feel secure within a framework of policy, rules, and indeed company practice. All must feel equal within this structure. They must have the confidence that within known rules, they will be treated fairly. This could be described as 'company law and order'.

Level 3 Management style and controls.

The provision of a good working environment is essential for each employee. This echoes the contention that the management's role is to facilitate the processes of the company. Quality has to be managed. Motivation is a management concern. The provision of the ingredients for success, including job satisfaction and self-fulfilment, is a necessary prerequisite for the motivational situation.

Level 2 Retirement and sickness policies.

Future security, for all employees, their families and dependents, must be taken for granted if people are to be expected to give of their best. For many, work is seen as the bridge to future security.

Level 1 Pay and status.

Security now is the basic level of need, both in financial and social terms. The two can be balanced out, with more emphasis placed on one rather than the other if motivation is to be achieved. Without either, there is unlikely to be much personal drive or achievement.

Herzberg's 'industrial hygiene' approach

Pay and recognition of status	stemming from job security
Retirement and sickness polices	giving security in the future
Management style and controls	providing a good working environment
Organisational policy and rules	in other words, safety at work

These needs are additional to other longer term motivating factors.

Fig 7.2 Herzberg's hygiene approach.

It is easy to think of examples of poorly paid individuals who are given considerable status and public recognition, often via impressive uniforms. Hotel doormen and parish priests could fall into this category. On the other hand, there are many examples of people doing unpleasant, low-status jobs, often compensated only by high remuneration. Examples would be sewer-men and prostitutes.

This idea of 'industrial hygiene' thus provides the basis of an organisational input for the company. Clearly, the areas involved here are normally covered by the institutional arrangements of the company. These 'hygiene' factors are the responsibility of the senior management and, in some cases, the board of directors. It is for them to provide the framework within which managers, at all levels of the company, can motivate others. Without this organisational element being in place, any effective, long-term motivation of the workforce may be very difficult, if not impossible.

Motivation – a more simplistic approach

A company needs to appreciate the priority of motivational factors that are within its control. There are four basic areas that need consideration:

1. Job satisfaction.
2. Financial rewards.
3. Recognition of superiors.
4. Peer group recognition.

1. Job satisfaction

Most people need the satisfaction of making a meaningful contribution. They wish to take some ownership in the achievements, even if direct ownership of the results is not possible. This is often described as pride, and many have expressed the principle that everyone has a right to such a pride. Deming suggested that barriers are often erected dividing people from this right.[10]

'Job security' is often rated as the highest concern of working people. This may reflect the industrial climate of the 1970s and 1980s, as the industrial world first plunged into recession, and then painfully climbed out of it. Prior to this, many never gave a second thought to life-time opportunities for work. The world of redundancy, frictional unemployment and constant change, has removed this complacency. The personal involvement of the individual with the prosperity of the company, is now a vital aspect. Only successful companies can offer continued security of employment.

The concept of 'job security' is, therefore, the most important prerequisite to the motivational situation. Note the parallels with Herzberg's lower levels.

Few argue about the individual's right to job satisfaction, but many doubt that it is possible to give everyone such an opportunity. It is often thought that boring and repetitive jobs, such as those on a car assembly line or a food packing line, are bound, by their very nature, to be devoid of any job satisfaction. All jobs can be inherently satisfying.

Employees not seeking job satisfaction from their daily work will be incapable of performing satisfactorily. They will probably be unhappy at work, are almost certainly in the wrong job, and will only perform in an inefficient manner. Happiness might be an excellent measure of job satisfaction.

2. Financial rewards

It is dangerous to see straightforward *pay* as the motivational factor. Very often, it is the life style and security that stem from the level of pay that is of greater importance. The money earned by individuals is really only their means of satisfying all their other needs and expectations, and those of their dependents.

Traditionally, part payment in kind (coal for the miner), or other means to *needs satisfaction* (tied housing for the agricultural worker), accounted for a substantial part of the company's payment to the worker. Examination of the historical occurrence of such part-payments will show that they met the lower order of needs, on both the Maslow and Herzberg scales.

To a great extent, there is no definitive amount of money sought by an individual. The judgement is often based upon the concept of comparison with others similar in status, but possibly in quite unrelated jobs, and indeed on the concept of *fairness*. The sayings from the past, such as 'a labourer is worthy of his hire', and 'a fair day's pay for a fair day's work' embody these feelings. It is seen as a *right* for a worker to maintain his status vis-a-vis other workers. This leads to many anomalies. Some workers in repetitive and boring jobs, which are nevertheless perceived as having a high status, are thought to be entitled to high salaries. Others, in traditionally low status employment, have relatively low wages, despite greater responsibility and/or technical knowledge.

The transport industry gives good examples of these perceptions. The job of an air hostess could be seen as messy, repetitive and not far removed from that of a waitress in a fast food outlet, and yet the 'jet set' image maintains a high profile, and a commensurate salary. Conversely, the driver of a modern inter-city express has as much responsibility, and less technology to assist him, than the airline pilot, whose remuneration is probably several times greater.

Generalised perceptions of job status are very different, with wage/salary levels following suit. The people who seek certain types of employment differ in their expectations of remuneration. The difference in these perceptions is to do, not so much with money, as with an expected life-style. The life-style often pre-dates the career move, and monetary reward is expected to follow these social needs. Financial rewards are necessary only to satisfy these life-style needs.

The major problem that arises from this consideration is that the actual financial remuneration sought by any individual is related to factors *outside* the company or organisation. It is thus totally disconnected from the wealth-earning capacity that the individual and the company have. It is further disconnected from the market forces of supply and demand which effect recruitment possibilities in an area.

This distancing of money, as a motivational factor, from the direct wealth generating capacity of the employing firm has considerable Quality implications.

A re-education is needed within the industrial society. First, it is immoral and not very effective to exploit labour, as described in detail by Marx.[11] It is not very effective, since it removes the use of money as a motivational force to obtain Quality. In a basic situation, where job satisfaction is not seen as a possibility, people can be encouraged to work directly for money. However, they will never take a pride in such work and will never accept responsibility for the Quality of the work. Though *quantity* may be achieved, *Quality* will always be elusive.

The captains of industry, who are responsible for the organisation of people's work, should appreciate that success in the future will come from a partnership of interests. The 'new capitalism', that allows everyone involved with enterprise to share in the risk and the benefits, will prove to be the environment for Quality.

The second area for re-education is within the working relationships of each company and organisation. All employees should appreciate their relationship with the wealth generating aspects of the company, with particular respect to their own processes. Only in this way will it be possible to breed the necessary Quality environment, in which the costs of manufacturing can be minimised.

The relationship of money to employment is very interesting, and greatly underestimated. The damage arising from bonus schemes and simplistic financial incentive devices is vast. Such arrangements should only be contemplated when the implications for all the other motivational factors have been fully recognised and taken into account.

A poor motivational device can reduce the effectiveness of all the others being implemented. Bonus schemes are ruining the chances for individual managers to motivate their staff. They mitigate against any real improvement in working relationships. They overtly claim that the whole workforce is deliberately working below its potential standard. This is usually patently untrue. Poor process design and control, usually not within the capability of individual workers, contribute to poor Quality standards. Bonus schemes deny trust!

3. Recognition of superiors

It is natural for each of us to seek recognition. In many instances, the evaluation of our own achievements can only be assessed when we have synthesised the feedback from others involved with our work. Genuine praise and pleasure are always of great importance.

It is important to stress the word *genuine*, for there is a lot of bull around some organisations. There are few spectacles less distressing, and more costly, than a circle of managers undertaking a round of back-slapping. Seldom is there any justification, and the mutual appreciation societies are often set up as protective measures. The absence of any real performance indicators is the cause. This absence of real data allows praise and judgement to be given with no objective measure.

However, this internecine praise should not blind us to the value of genuine appreciation. If this praise is backed by real, objective performance criteria, we have the opportunity to assess not only our own job, but our value. The absence of genuine praise may well undermine self-appreciation, and indeed self-identity. This could lead to the alienation of the individual from the work and, thus, from the company.

Everybody needs recognition as a person, rather than just as a functionary of the job. When recognition is received, the individual will be well motivated for the next task.

4. Peer group recognition

Work is inevitably a social event, as well as a business affair. The relationship between two employees working in the same area will often be quite complex, as there will be elements of potential friendship, cooperation, competition and conflict.

In many ways, though, we only find our identity by considering our reflection in others. This will always be more true for some than others. The more confident do not have the same need for recognition by equals and friends. The less confident need a constant re-inforcement of their image.

The danger here, for the poorly organised company, will be that an individual's superiors may hold a different set of values than the individual's peer group. An individual's superiors may appreciate certain achievements that are unrecognised by the peer group. There may be a different agenda at work. It may be that the interests of the two groups are seen not only as different, but as actually in conflict. In such circumstances, the recognition of one group may well bring disapprobation from the other.

The internal energy expended on the dissonance caused by such conflicting forces is extremely expensive and damaging to the company. In motivational terms, the presence of differing value systems will probably have the negative effect of demotivating the individual. He/she will probably perceive that an equable relationship can be maintained with both groups by simply doing nothing, rather than appearing to take sides.

The aim of the Quality Culture is to reduce such differences to an irrelevance. By placing Quality at the top of the agenda, it becomes difficult to perceive different objectives, in the eyes of superiors and the group of workers. Pulling together as a team, eliminates this conflict, allowing peer group recognition to be a major motivating force. Indeed, a by-product of such achievements is that the peer group becomes the major source of industrial discipline. The potential achievements of the team can be maintained as a group motivator, thus triggering peer group discipline where necessary, in the interests of the team.

What motivates ?

1/ Job satisfaction	Most people want the satisfaction of making a meaningful contribution. We wish to take ownership and take a pride in our own achievements. (Anyone not wanting job satisfaction, is unhappy and should look for another job.)
2/ Money £	Money is important for everyone. It is the means to satisfy all our other needs and expectations, including the welfare of our family. However, a fair reward for each of us, has to be balanced against the ability of the organisation to produce wealth. We, that is, the whole company, must earn it first, before we can enjoy it.
3/ Recognition of superior	It is natural for each of us to look for praise and feedback. When our work is recognised by our supervisors and managers, it means that our value, as a person, is recognised.
4/ Recognition of peer group	Each of us values the esteem and appreciation of our friends and work-mates. In a way, we find our own identity, by considering our reflection in others.

Fig 7.3 What motivates?

Other parallel factors

There are three other motivational factors that act in parallel to those mentioned above, but on a higher plane. They only become motivational factors once the previous four have largely become satisfied.

The term parallel is used, as the circumstances inhabited by different people may give a stronger impetus to one factor, rather than another. These three are, therefore, *not* in a hierarchy.

- Advancement

The career opportunities available within the job will greatly influence the motivation of some people. Indeed, it is one of the basic concepts of this book that it is important to give everyone a way forward, to think in terms of a career, rather than just a job.[12]

For most, this advancement may be within the company or organisation, but for some, it may be providing the stepping stone to a further career elsewhere. Either way, the motivational impetus can be considerable.

- Interest

Is the job intellectually stimulating? Does it challenge the mind? Is it a learning and extending environment? All these thoughts can be very important to some people, who need daily an intellectual challenge. It would be wrong to identify such people with any particular section of the population, such as university graduates. Many people who in the past have shunned close contact with knowledge and techniques, may develop an acute interest in their work. In some cases, this can become an obsession that overrides their own interests.

An example of such a group might be young computer programmers who, though lacking in formal qualifications, become obsessed with their work. They work late, and often take work home and work all night, seemingly not noticing the passage of hours. They may design intricate programmes, equipment, control packages or computer games. They live their job.

- Responsibility

Most people find that at some stage of their life they have a need to be responsible for both themselves and others. For many this need is sublimated within family life, and they have no further need for such responsibility. Indeed, some shun responsibility, not wishing to have anyone else's future in their hands.

There is no particular age when this need to be responsible is likely to develop. There are many examples of fairly young school children, often pre-teenage, who relish and enjoy responsibility. Many adults don't have the same desire. The point being made is that this is not a static situation. There are not two types of people, but people at different stages of their lives, with different needs, self-perceptions and abilities.

No-one should be forced or even cajoled into wielding responsibility, or expected to be ambitious. Everyone has a right to choose. Everyone should be given opportunities, but have the right to take them or not.

The author recently met an honours graduate with production experience, who ran the 'post room' of a company. He shunned responsibility for other people, and sought a working life with clearly defined boundaries. Some in the company thought this a waste of talent, education and ability. However, he is a happy man who performs his role exceedingly well. It is a good post room.

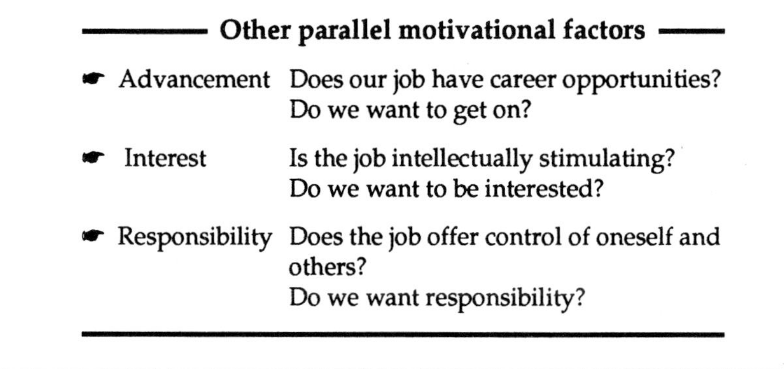
Other parallel motivational factors

☛ Advancement	Does our job have career opportunities? Do we want to get on?
☛ Interest	Is the job intellectually stimulating? Do we want to be interested?
☛ Responsibility	Does the job offer control of oneself and others? Do we want responsibility?

Fig 7.4 Additional motivation factors.

Motivation – a management tool

Motivation should be taught to every manager, in every position and in every sector of industry or commerce. This seems so trite and obvious that many will feel annoyed at the statement. My experience suggests, however, that most managers and others responsible for the output of processes involving others have little or no formal management training. Those that do are more concerned with book keeping than with people-management. Indeed, it has been said that we put far more effort into understanding our machinery and equipment than into understanding the people who use them.

Despite this, a wide understanding of each employee's relationship with his work is essential.

As a rough starting point, six areas of activity are offered that will help to define the relationship of a manager with those managed. These six points can be the basis for a motivational input to their working lives.

- Know your staff

By appreciating people as people, rather than treating them as mere extensions to the machinery, the desired aims can be achieved. All members of the staff, whatever their position, have many complex features and involvements beyond their jobs. By keeping up-to-date with each person's situation, hopes, fears, ambitions and problems, the manager will be able to direct his energy to the best advantage.

By understanding why he works, why he works for the company and why he works for him, the manager is better able to motivate him. Above all, this knowledge will enable the manager to keep a metaphorical finger on his pulse, to know when he is unhappy, and thus functioning below maximum.

The manager has no right to pry into the affairs of an employee, but he/she must be concerned with the employee's ability to perform well. This delicate balance is the hall mark of the good manager.

- Trust your staff

Everyone needs a certain *space* within which to perform. The conditions for people to flourish will be provided by allowing all individuals to be responsible adults, able to make their own decisions and motivate themselves. Some may not be able to handle this, demonstrating that their *personal space* needs restricting. They may need given expectations and requirements. Their actions will define the space needed.

As previously mentioned, the emphasis should be this way round. There should be an implicit trust in everyone, until it is shown that the trust is misplaced. Some people tend to operate in the other direction, that is to trust no-one until they demonstrate that they are worthy of trust. Many may not bother, and the opportunity to motivate and achieve the most from them will be lost.

Obviously, the manager shouldn't be gullible. There is a need for a responsible attitude. Perhaps 'mistrust', rather than 'trust', is the commodity that should be earned, and seen to be earned.

An area of particular importance is the involvement of people with finance. The manager may well remain accountable, but should treat them as responsible people. When in doubt, consider the relationship from the other side. Are you trustworthy? Do you appreciate being trusted?

- Delegate

Most managers suffer from the unfortunate habit of doing the tasks of those on the strata beneath them. Psychologically, it is understandable, since more immediate success can often be achieved at this level than within one's own tasks. Also, there is always the comforting feeling that it is easier to do it than instruct someone else. Indeed, the feeling of leading from the front, and showing an example, often persuades managers, misguidedly, to go on litter collection and machine cleaning exercises, not realising that the act of doing someone else's job is probably the biggest demotivating force in industry.

People need some control of their daily activity; they need to be responsible for the Quality of their own work. In many instances, only the actual person performing a task can be completely in control of the Quality of the output.

The manager should be attempting to stretch the ability of each of his staff, without ever giving people tasks and responsibilities that are beyond their capability. The ability to recognise potential failure situations, and thus avoid them, whilst maximising the value of each member of staff, is very much part of the art of management.

- Communicate

Most company surveys in which the author has been involved indicate that one of the greatest problems is a perceived lack of communication. In many instances, this finding has been questionable, and it has been the type of communication, rather than the quantity, that has lead to these feelings. However, as in so many 'people' situations, the *fact* is not as important as the *perceived situation*. If individuals believe themselves to be uninformed, they will base their actions on that premise.

The general sharing of information, and the principle that all information should be available unless there is a very good reason for confidentiality, leads to the sharing of departmental responsibilities. Such sharing will lead to a commitment to the company. The achievements, both of the department and the company, will all be shared. Without such joint involvement, there will be the development of a club mentality, with the subsequent feelings of inclusion and exclusion. Most people will never be fully motivated, working outside a perceived club. They will be working for an organisation that alienates them.

There is, of course, the danger of reducing everything to a boring reiteration of unwanted detail. The aim should be to tell people what they want to know. In the end it becomes responsive. Everything is available to all – what do you want to know?

Communication of information can often include appreciation of those partially responsible for achievements identified within the data. It is an excellent medium for distributing praise. Rather than, *'haven't you done well'*, it is often preferable to stress the increased performance of the department, and then give praise to those who have been responsible for this result.

- Listen

Probably the worst failing in managers at all levels is their *inability* to listen. Indeed, the typical successful manager has a forceful character. Many such managers mistakenly believe that anyone else having anything to contribute will be just as forceful.

The first step is to create a climate in which ideas are shared. Indeed, a climate where ideas and thoughts become common property. It will be a tolerant environment, in which people will look for value in any idea, and not laugh at the far fetched.

Timing is vital, and is misunderstood by managers who gather their underlings and demand their points of view by saying, 'I'm quite prepared to listen – what have you got to say?' The good managers listen when subordinates want to speak. The subordinates choose the time when they have something to say, that is when *they wish to talk*, not just when a manager wants to listen. A good manager is approachable. This approachability will motivate many that may never wish to seek advice; it is part of the secure framework that is necessary for motivation to exist.

Often listening is not enough. The speaker is looking for more than a sympathetic ear, he is seeking action. When the manager discerns this, he has a duty to perform. Exactly what that action will be will result from the manager's evaluation of what he/she is told. Indeed, the action may be to explain that the desire of the speaker is not possible, and that a different approach is necessary. This is action. No action at all, in response to such a disclosure of a problem, is frustrating and demotivating.

People have opinions about virtually everything, whether they are informed on that subject or not. Learn to ask for, and to listen to these opinions, making judgements on their veracity, but still appreciating the fact that they have been shared with you.

- Represent

Another part of the secure framework, essential for motivation to occur, is the knowledge that when necessary, one's interests are represented fairly, and with due force. It is important that the manager so represents the staff, and lets others know how well they are doing. The manager has a voice in circles not accessible to those managed, and this will have even greater importance when a grievance appears. All individuals need to feel confident that their interests will be well represented, should the need arise. For most, this will never happen, but the belief that all would be well, gives security, and increases motivation.

The manager's function is to facilitate the processes for which he/she is responsible. Representing the attitude and judgement of the individual involved with the process ensures that the Quality of the process inputs is maximised. This is an essential process control component, and a valuable motivational technique.

At times, it will be necessary to represent your staff by protecting them from unfair criticism. The knowledge that you will uphold their point of view, and safeguard their interests if necessary, again contributes to a secure framework. At times you may have to fight for their just rewards, whether in terms of money, praise or whatever. These aspects demonstrate the recognition that you give them.

There is, however, a two-way aspect to this representation. The manager often represents the main link between the workforce and the higher levels of management. The existence of a smooth transfer of information, and the confidence of knowing that everyone is pulling in the same direction, is essential. The manager needs to represent his

How to motivate your staff

☛ **Know your staff**	Keep up to date about their situation Understand why they work for you Recognise when they are unhappy	BUT Never pry into personal lives
☛ **Trust your staff**	Allow them to be responsible adults Believe they mean to do their best Involve them with finance	BUT Don't be gullible
☛ **Delegate**	Give some control of daily activity Involve your staff in new ideas Responsibility for Quality of their work	BUT Recognise potential failure
☛ **Communicate**	Keep your staff informed Share general information Give praise for good work	BUT Don't be a bore
☛ **Listen**	Encourage them to share ideas Listen when <u>they</u> want to talk Always ask for their opinion	BUT Sometimes listening is not enough
☛ **Represent your staff**	Let others know how well they do Protect them from unfair criticism Ensure they receive their rewards Facilitate their processes Represent their grievances	BUT Also represent your superiors

Fig 7.5 How to motivate your staff.

superiors with the same vigour as he represents his subordinates. This is all part of supplying the secure environment within which people can be motivated to give of their best, and achieve the highest Quality standards. It is a balancing act, as is so much of the managerial art. This is best achieved by the fair minded, who genuinely see their future, the future of the employees and the future of the company, as intertwined.

The individual approach

The relationship between oneself and a superior is always seen as an individual, personal relationship between two people. This is so with each individual person that we seek to motivate. A whole package of individual relationships, each one different, each one within the same framework of the working environment, will need to be established.

It is not easy, and indeed, the speed with which it sometimes has to be accomplished is a further complication. It has to be done, however. Motivating people is an art – practice it!

Boring situations

Before completing this chapter, the myth of boredom should be exploded. It seems to be embedded deeply in the consciousness of the nation. Many believe that the first words spoken by their offspring were

Every person is an individual

1. *Know and be interested in them*
2. *Trust and involve them*
3. *Delegate and back them*
4. *Communicate and praise them*
5. *Listen and help them*
6. *Represent and stand up for them*

Fig 7.6 Each person is an individual.

'I'm bored', to be repeated every half hour during their first two decades.

Equally, strongly held beliefs suggest that a vast number of jobs, if not the majority of work situations, are intrinsically boring. Such jobs can only be accomplished by bribery. Mindless people, totally lacking in imagination or any other recognisable human attribute, will have to be found. They will have to be offered just the right amount of money to keep them working. Too much and they will start going on holiday or just absenting themselves, not enough and we will never recruit.

This is all rubbish! Neither people nor jobs are ever boring. 'I'm bored', means that I am more interested in something else than this. The human mind is deep and wide. If individuals find that they are a mere extension of a machine, treated as a mechanical device, they will become disinterested. They will perform their job in a mindless fashion, producing poor Quality. They probably will be unaware of their poor results, since Quality control will be perceived as someone else's responsibility.

Such an approach to the management of people is inhumane, immoral and dreadfully expensive. There has to be a better way.

Henry Ford apparently contributed to this myth when, in 1935, he was attributed with the phrase 'I employ hands, not heads!' If these were Henry's words, then he has much to answer for. There are those who consider that the subsequent fifty years of poor industrial relations within Ford emanate from such attitudes.

The solutions

Where a task is purely mechanical, that is where there is no need for any decision-making on the part of the operator, a mechanical solution, using robotic and/or electronic technology, will invariably produce a better solution to the problem. Robots do not have 'off days', go drinking the night before, or produce the 'Friday afternoon car'. They give consistent, predictable results.

Where this is not the solution, the operators should be used to the best advantage. Their manipulative skills are but part of the abilities that are available to the designer. The more control of the work given to the operators, the more they can take responsibility for the performance of the process. Quality control, indeed their full responsibility for the process in every respect, is the ultimate aim. The process should always be viewed as part of the macro-process. Total customer satisfaction is the goal. Process improvement will be an on-going activity. Where possible, team work will share both the drudge aspects and the achievements involved with the processes. The team can play a major role in the organisation of the work, and receives considerable social benefit from the interaction. From this situation, in a clean and hospitable environment, the individual can gain a great deal of satisfaction. He can be motivated and happy at his work.

No work should be boring! Everyone has the right to an interesting and fulfilling job.

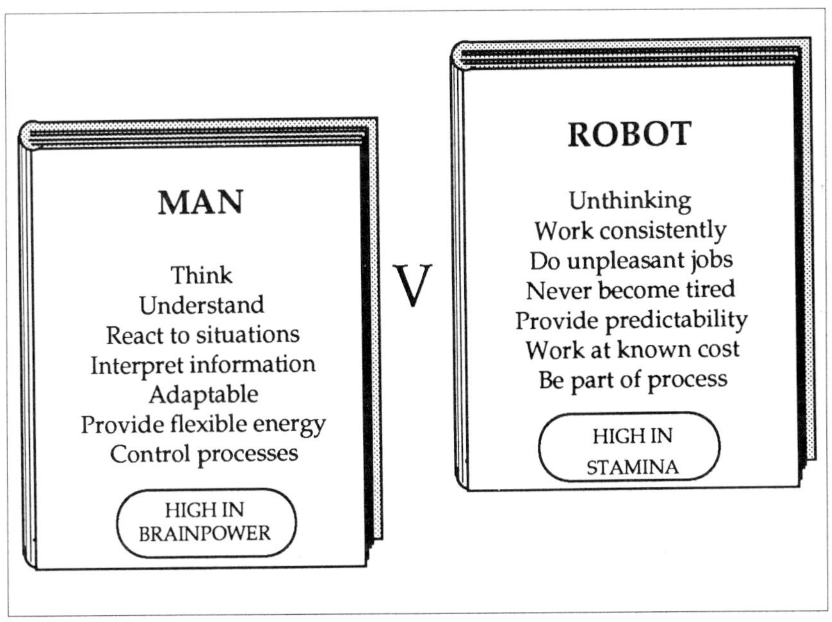

Fig 7.7 People v robots.

Summary

People's attitude to work is conditioned by general perceptions. The greatest influence in the past has come from:

- The Protestant work ethic.
- The myth of money.
- F Taylor's scientific management.

Modern theory suggests that motivation is 'needs-driven'. Hence:

- Maslow's pyramid of needs.
- Herzberg's industrial hygiene approach.

Motivation is achieved via:

1. Job satisfaction.
2. Financial reward.
3. Recognition of superiors.
4. Peer group recognition.

And then from parallel factors of advancement, interest and responsibility.

Motivation of staff:

Know your staff.
Trust your staff.
Delegate.
Communicate.
Listen.
Represent them and your superiors.

Boredom is a myth.
Everyone has the right to an interesting and fulfilling job

Last thoughts ....

Leadership is not something you do *to* people,
but something you do *with* people.

Kenneth Blanchard[13]

1. Anne Frank spent two years hiding from Nazi persecution. See *Diary of Anne Frank.*
2. Wolfgang Amadeus Mozart (1756-1791).
3. Lawrence Edward Grace Oates (1880-1912).
4. Argyle, Michael, *The Social Psychology of Work,* Penguin, 1972.
5. Taylor, F W, *Scientific Management*, 1911.
6. Story told by V H Vroom in *Work and Motivation*, John Wiley, 1964.
7. I am indebted to the idea of this conversation to Jack Nobbs *et al., Sociology*, Macmillan, 1975.
8. Maslow, A H, 'A Theory of Human Motivation', *Psychology Review*, Issue 50, 1943.
9. Herzberg, F, *Work and the Nature of Man*, 1968.
10. Edwards Deming, Dr W, *Out of the Crisis,* Cambridge University Press, 1982.
11. Marx, Karl, *The Selected Work of Marx and Engles*, 1952.
12. One More Theory, Chapter 4.
13. Blanchard, Kenneth, *Leadership and the One Minute Manager*, Collins, 1986.

Quality through People

A Blueprint for
Proactive Total Quality Management

Part
III

The Management of Process

Chapter 8

Management of Process

I must apologise to the deaf,
for the loss of sub-titles.

– Angela Rippon

Route-map

This chapter starts by comparing 'unitary thinking' with 'process thinking'.

Two levels of process are identified, the Macro level, that is the entire operation, and the Micro level that operates with individual processes.

Control and improvements are more effective, the earlier they are implemented within the macro process.

Unitary thinking

The most fundamental change to occur within society during the next 10 years will be the move to 'think process'. The author first said this in 1984. His time-scale was inaccurate. Significant change takes longer!

Western life is obsessed with numbers. We are a 'results-based' society. We don't expect to take complete control of any human affairs, but optimistically hope that the outcomes will be OK. We set things up and let them run. When the results are good, we are smugly satisfied. When they are not so good, we look for a scapegoat, and hope to make minor improvements by jiggling the details.

We often put more effort into allocating *blame* than into identifying the real causes of the failure. When the results are disastrous, we set up a 'disaster fund' for the victims, but do little to ensure that we won't have yet more victims of future disasters! Blame is a most unhelpful concept.

The root of this way of life is the results-based, 'unitary thinking' of most people in control of our affairs. The phrase 'unitary thinking' is used to describe the many situations in daily life in which decisions are based almost entirely on numbers, and often on numbers from but one unit of measure, money.

This is as true of political activity and commerce, as it is of industrial life. It leads not only to an obsessive concern with results, but to a very *slim* judgement of those results. There is little room left for other criteria to become involved with decision-making, and the time-scale for judging success or failure becomes ever shorter. Most people have a particular set of figures that dominate their thinking, and thus are involved with every decision. It may be this year's bottom-line profit, this month's sales figures or this week's production target. On such grounds, judgement is simple, quick and decisive. Success becomes synonymous with survival. 'We did it!' or 'We failed!' Either way, never mind, let's get on with tomorrow.

The involvement of politics in commercial life will always have the effect of shortening time-scales for decision-making. Ministers have a maximum of five years in which to achieve results. This time-scale is rapidly shortened as the next general election approaches. Local government is even worse, with the horizon always less than four years ahead.

Success is rarely achieved overnight, and the lesson of successful industry is the need for long-term planning, and long-term commitment. Japanese car companies, opening plants in the UK during the 1980s, expected no profit from these plants until well into the 1990s. Industry needs to plan for at least a 10 year span, and thus needs to be largely disconnected, or at least protected, from politics.

Effects of unitary thinking:

- *Static operation*

Whilst it will usually have the appearance of being quite the reverse, the company that is largely unitary thinking, will have a static organisation.

The judgements of the company, a department, and, indeed, a particular individual, will be based on a scale that remains fixed in people's minds: this years profit margin, this month's sales figures, this week's production target. The concentration on the single quantity removes others from consideration, leading to an absence of lateral thinking, and to a static approach to the company's activities. How possible is change in any organisation? Are the scales by which a department is judged fair? Can the judgements that are made on people be rewritten?

● *Undermines Quality*

The judging of activities by a single quantity leads to an undervaluing of all other facets. This will probably not be deliberate. Rather, such effects have evolved from the continual use of the particular figures, as the judgement of success. Inevitably this compromises Quality, since the definition of Quality embraces the wide spectrum of judgements that lead to customer satisfaction. Lip service will almost certainly be paid to customer satisfaction and Quality, but the day-to-day decision-making process will be largely determined by the pressure created to perform in this very restricted way, governed by the particular number criteria. What are the major pressures applied to your job or task? Are they number based? Does your company ever compromise Quality for the sake of fulfilling an order?

● *Shortens time-scales*

The meeting of the deadline, with regard to a particular numeric judgement, will lead to people's concern increasingly lying within this deadline. Always, the pressure will be to perform well now, so that the next set of figures appear the best possible. There is often a conflict between short-term aims and long-term objectives. Whilst it is obvious that in a crisis situation the long-term may have to be compromised for the sake of survival, this will only occur as the result of previous poor management. Tomorrow is important, but never as important as today. What pressures are you subject to? To whom do you have to answer? Are your shareholders mostly concerned with the next dividend? Is your boss mostly concerned with this quarter's sales figures? Have you met this week's production target? You can start to appreciate the agenda that determines priorities and actions of the company, by identifying the pressures to which you are subjected.

- *Inhibits investment*

Any investment will inevitably appear as a loss in the short-term. Where a company, department or individual is judged by a set of termly figures, the pressure is placed on the people involved, to avoid any investment that will detract from those figures. This is as true with the individual as with the organisation. Consider whether your career has always had the investment of experience, skills and knowledge at the time that would have been best for you, or has the day-to-day pressure to perform to a particular target inhibited such an investment? If you consider that you have been lucky, and have always had such an investment, spend a moment considering other areas and activities within your company, and indeed other companies known to you. Do they invest enough in the future? What inhibits their investment?

- *Compartmentalises activity*

The numbers-driven company will inevitably be closed and inward looking. The act of achieving a particular target increases the concentration on the individual, or department goal, rather than those of the company. Inevitably, people see the demands of their own smaller areas as dominant. Internal competition will grow, conflicting agendas and compromised decisions will increase, leading to a diffuse organisation. Barriers will prohibit the free interchange of ideas. Hierarchical chains of command and communication will predominate. The development of supplier/customer relationships will be impossible. A judgement of the amount of unitary thinking at play within your own organisation, can be achieved by questioning the artificial barriers between departments within your company. This is not easy, as those living with such divisions come to see them as part of the natural order of things, indeed the barriers become invisible.

- *Perverts priorities*

Unitary thinking determines the climate in which a decision is made. Inevitably, the decision will tend to benefit the parameter by which the department or individual is judged. It will often maximise the next set of figures to be produced. It will overlook a wealth of other valuable contributions to the decision, and will play a considerable part in prioritising the expenditure of resources by the company. Any overall improvement effort will be inhibited by a data-based culture. Oliver Wight, the American exponent of MRP2,[1] (see JIT) found that in a traditionally run company, most figures are questionable. The pressures are always present to exaggerate, to make optimistic forecasts and estimates and always to keep a little in reserve. People may not deliberately falsify figures, just *use* them to their advantage. These 'funny' figures are the basis for many decisions, the results of which later cause disappointment.

- *Self-perpetuating*

As with many unconscious forces at play within industry, the results-based environment produces systems and conditions that promote its own continuation. It becomes a way of industrial life. This, in fact, occurs in two ways. Since judgements are being made on a particular numerical value, those successful in achieving acceptable results become successful within the company, thus reinforcing this judgement system. At the same time, the act of unitary thinking, downgrades other judgements and qualifications, leaving only the bare numerical value as an absolute guide to performance. An example is the buyer who is judged by the price achieved on an order. The concentration on this figure limits the need for the buyer to be aware of the performance of the material through the factory. He is, therefore, unaware of any Quality aspects of the goods purchased, and does not give a high regard to this aspect when completing the next contract.

- *Diverts attention from process*

The results-based culture sees failure in terms of product failure, that is, failure is invested in things. Remedial steps are concentrated on amending the failures, or if that is not possible, on sorting the good from the bad. Such a culture very quickly becomes first inspection-orientated, putting its main efforts into appraisal, and then inspection-dependent. The devotion of resources and energy to appraisal diverts the company from the overall process, and from a deeper understanding of the individual processes. Prevention is a representation of 'thinking process' and, therefore, should invest every activity within the company.

An assessment of the Cost of Quality, described in more detail later in Chapter 12, will provide a sense of the balance of a company, between 'unitary thinking' and 'process thinking'. By moving away from the rigours of the unitary-based decision, one becomes free to consider the fuller aspects contributing to each process. It enables one to *think process!*

Think process

The act of thinking process develops into a habit that becomes part of every decision and value judgement made. It stems from the realisation, that industry is a constantly changing arena of conflicting priorities and goals that can only be controlled by the elimination of as much internal uncertainty as possible.

Since 'unitary thinking' and 'process thinking' are different parts of the same spectrum, it is possible to present good reasons for 'process thought' to match each of the areas outlined above.

- *A dynamic concept*

  Process thinking' is *dynamic*, in that it is concerned with what *will* happen, rather than what *has* happened. A results orientated company must inevitably dwell on the latest figures, which are fixed by events. The process orientated company will always be concerned with the process inputs that will lead to the process, and hence to the results occurring.

- *Centralises Quality*

  The judgement of the process will be in terms of the Quality that it provides for the customer, whether internal or external. Process improvement will be ever-present in the minds of those controlling the process.

- *Lengthens time-scales*

  The concentration on process, and process improvement, leads to a perception of the company's on-going future. Decisions are made that benefit the company long-term, rather than compromising long-term viability for the sake of short-term gains.

- *Promotes investment*

  Thinking process involves the perception that each activity and action within the company is a process. This leads to an appreciation of the importance and place of investment. The continual drive for process improvement identifies which aspects most need this investment. Impetus is given to the consideration of the long-term cost of failing to invest. The company needs to invest continually in people, machinery, better designs, better raw materials, new markets, and so on. The real task of senior management is to be responsible for an investment programme that ensures a market for the company, and its ability to fully satisfy that market. Individuals should also need to invest in themselves. Their long-term success will depend upon it.

- *Creates company culture*

  The creation of a company culture has to be one of the foremost considerations in the drive towards Total Quality. The concentration on process, and above all, the perception of an overall company process, created by effective customer/supplier relationships between interrelated processes, becomes the focus of such a company culture. Process thinking contributes to a unified company.

- *Directs effort*

  The perception of the company, as a complete process comprised of individual processes, enriches the perception of each individual. This leads to decisions that maximise the resources of the company. The concentration on process and process improvement identifies the areas in which improvements are most necessary, and directs the effort accordingly.

- *Self-perpetuating*

  Process thinking increases the exposure of all concerned to the details of the process inputs. It provides greater knowledge of the actual working of the process. Inevitably, this will lead to greater future interest in the process, leading to an ever greater concentration on the processes of the company and their improvement.

- *Concentrates on process*

  To control any activity, an understanding of what is actually occurring is needed. To have such knowledge, concentration must be on the process inputs, rather than the results. If the inputs are right, the results will be acceptable. Everyone must, at every level, and at all times, *think process*.

It is always interesting to consider any area of human activity, whether within our daily work, or in some other aspect of society. Examine exactly what control mechanisms are operating, and what information control is based on. In general, we live in a results-based environment. This is encouraged by the media: 'Thirty arrested for violence at a football match' makes a much better headline than the introduction of research to identify why people become violent at football matches. Equally, while it is good to hear that a youngster has achieved good GCSE passes, it is in fact more valuable to a parent of another child to have a greater understanding of the processes involved within the school that may contribute to their own child's success or otherwise.

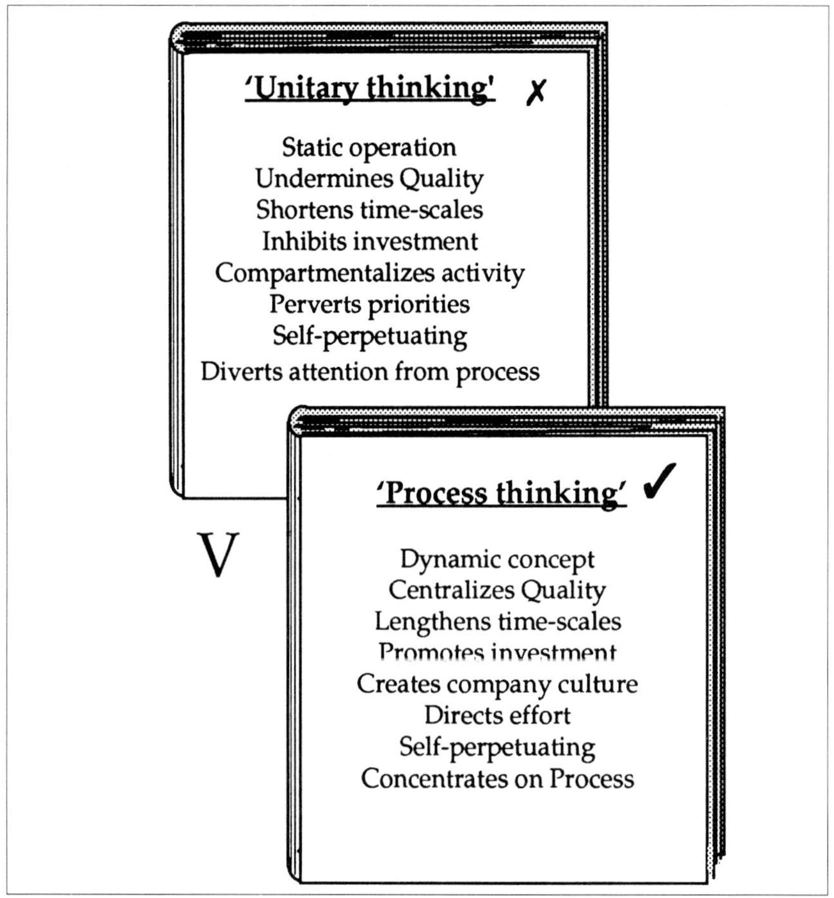

Fig 8.1 Process v Unitary thinking.

Macro level of process

There are always two levels of process for consideration. Indeed, every employee should be aware of his position and responsibility within each of the two levels.

When considering the *macro level*, the process starts from an idea or concept. To this is added a set of raw materials, basic machinery and a well-motivated set of employees. A consideration of the entire process from this point onwards, establishes a framework of customer/supplier relationships that link all the parts of this chain. It is too simplistic to consider it as a linear chain, as it will have many parallel strands, with relationships forming cross-ties back and forth.

This network may well include several companies, and operate in many different locations. Indeed, it will include contributions from virtually every activity and department, of each of these companies. The strength of the overall chain will be determined by the strength of each of these links. Indeed, it could also be said that the efficiency of the chain and its cost effectiveness will result from the effectiveness of these many links.

Consideration of process at this macro level, demonstrates:

- The need for cooperation.
- The centrality of Quality.
- The essential customer/supplier relationships.
- The need for good communication.
- The limiting of Quality costs.
- Two-way relationships.

- *The need for cooperation*

The concepts of *competition* and *cooperation* are often subject to misunderstanding and confusion in most areas of British industry. False competition is often inspired by the misguided belief that people function better in a competitive mode. Few appreciate that competition costs money, and is, in itself, a destructive element.

This sounds like heresy in the Britain of the 1990s, but the costs of competition need to be included in any consideration of the true costs of industry. It is part of the underlying belief of Western culture that organisations can only be efficient when in a competitive stance. This may or may not be so, and anyway, there is no shortage of true competition. There is no need to engineer competitive situations artificially. Indeed, true competition is a great stimulus, whereas contrived competition rarely convinces anyone, and destroys the essential cooperative relationships. It is costly. It can double the Cost of Quality.

The entire process chain competes with other similar chains, which are attempting to gain the same source of wealth. In areas of the human marketplace, where there is a recognised need for the mass provision of a product, such as soap powder, the competitor will probably be another manufacturer of soap powder. However, in many instances, the competitor may be engaged in a totally different type of business.

Are cinemas in competition with theatres, or are they part of the same leisure industry which is competing for the public's leisure resources? Might the true competition be the pub, or the garden centre? Advertisers have long appreciated that the whole of industry gains from a good advertisement, as it establishes that a particular way of life is common-place, no matter what actual brand is the subject of the advertisement.

Anyway, there is no place for *competition* within the supplier/customer relationships. These relationships will depend upon a high degree of easy, straightforward and honest cooperation.

- *The centrality of Quality*

The highest level of Quality will have to be maintained throughout the chain. The point has been made many times before, that Quality is intrinsically part of each process and product, unless allowed to drop out. It cannot be added later. Cooperation will work via the customer/supplier relationships, each of which will be informed by the provision of Quality, that is by the supplier meeting the negotiated requirements and expectations of the customer.

- *The essential customer/supplier relationships*

Quality throughout the process depends upon these customer relationships. The rigorous use of strong customer relationships within the manufacturing process can ensure that Quality reaches the end-user.

Such relationships will become integrated within every company. They will also cross from one company to another. Such Quality consideration, built upon open and trusting relationships, can lead to the least expensive form of manufacturing.

An example

Such relationships are typified by considering two imaginary companies; 'Acmé Components' and 'Bungle Ltd'.

> Acmé manufactures a component without a great deal of confidence. It devotes considerable effort to sorting good from bad, and, based on 'What can we get away with', passes the goods through final inspection to be shipped to Bungle.
>
> The past experience of Bungle leads it to suspect Acmé's Quality, and a full inspection of incoming goods takes place. The sample taken produces more than an acceptable number of items out of spec. A phone call is made to Acmé, who questions Bungle's ability to inspect the goods. After a satisfactory argument (sufficient for both Quality managers to feel that they have done their job, 'they aren't going to put this one over on me!') a compromise is reached, whereby the components are to be used, but a price discount is agreed. Honour is satisfied, but poor Quality enters Bungle, and Acmé has increased Quality costs.
>
> Soon, to compensate for its losses, Acmé negotiates a higher price. It also devotes more time to inspecting and possibly hiding any poor product. Bungle passes this price increase on to the end-user, but loses market share through poor Quality. It determines to put even more effort into goods-inward inspection.
>
> This circle turns several more times until, eventually, Bungle loses the business altogether, and ceases manufacturing. Hence it does no more business with Acmé. Acmé cannot survive without its major customer, and also closes.

- *The need for good communication*

Essential to these customer/supplier relationships, will be good communications. If daily Quality negotiations are to take place, then there must be a structure allowing horizontal communications. There must also be the physical means of communication - meetings, telephones, etc. All this has implications for the companies, departments and individuals involved. This system demands trust in the ability of people at all levels to represent their department or company in such a negotiation. Gone will be the reliance on vertical communication lines (see Fig 8.2).

- *The limiting of Quality costs*

Everyone within the supplier/customer chain will actively seek to obtain the highest Quality at the lowest cost. Assistance given freely from one part of the chain to another will become common-place. Such assistance may often cross company boundaries. Duplication of effort will be eliminated. The transfer of information will become as important as the actual goods. Lower Quality costs will mutually benefit everyone within the chain.

- *Two-way relationships*

Nearly all customer/supplier relationships are two-way, with the main supplier becoming the customer at times, and vice-versa. Often, the negotiation includes the transfer of information on how the product is to be used, from the recipient to the producer. In such circumstances, the customer/supplier relationship is reversed. Also, the payment of accounts, in effect, reverses the relationship. Companies have a mutual

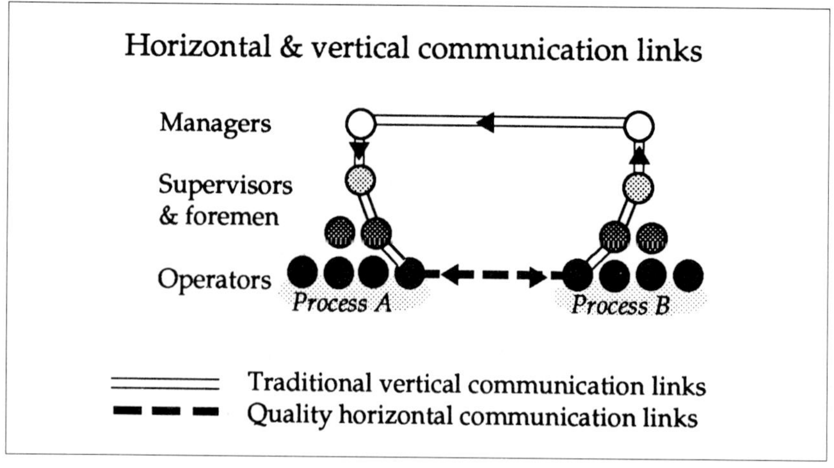

Fig 8.2 Horizontal and vertical communication lines.

need for each other, and a mutual interest in each other's welfare. Without good suppliers, the corporate customer cannot compete. Without successful corporate customers, suppliers cannot survive. They are inter-dependent, that is they should rely on each other with a spirit of mutual trust and understanding.

Acmé and Bungle, the alternative ending

The example given previously, under customer/supplier relationships, might have ended a different way. Remember that Bungle Ltd is the larger company, depending on good Quality from its supplier Acmé Components.

> Bungle Ltd is concerned about the Quality of its incoming goods. By visiting Acmé's factory, it becomes aware of the problems. Having greater training resources, it supplies the assistance Acmé needs. Acmé is now more able to manufacture and, thus, provide consistent Quality. This limits the need for final inspection.
>
> Bungle's confidence in Acmé increases. It also finds that it is able to use the product with no further inspection. The easy liaison ensures the minimum of Quality costs. This is reflected in the price and Quality, offered to the end-user. Bungle increases the business for itself and for Acmé. Both prosper!

Cost-effective accountancy practices

Research done a few years ago demonstrated that over 80% of managers in large companies considered it good business practice:

1. to collect money in as quickly as possible from customers;
2. to delay paying suppliers for as long as possible.

A true consideration of Quality quickly dispels this reasoning. Anything that temporarily inhibits straightforward, smooth business relationships, is extremely expensive. Any such additional costs will either be born by the supplying company, probably contributing to its possible eventual demise, or passed onto to the purchasing company, thus effecting its sale price, and ability to compete in the real marketplace. It must be obvious, even to the smallest-minded purchase ledger manager, that if a company regularly pays its bills late, extracting perhaps 60 to 90 days credit from the supplier, the interest costs on this money will be built into every quotation it receives. No-one gains.

Everyone loses. It is not unknown for some of the larger corporations to be brought to a standstill by such bad practice. Most large companies can tell tales similar to that of the steel plant, which found production stopped due to a burnt-out servo-motor on a valve. The engineers went to the stores, but the cupboard was bare. This surprised them, as it was

URGENT MEMO

TO: Accounts Dept.

Message to all accounts departments, in all companies:

1/ *You are **not** in competition with your customers,*

2/ *You are **not** in competition with your suppliers,*

3/ *Any costs incurred by doing business, have to be included, in **your** costs to the end-user,*

4/ *The least expensive business practice is the best,*

5/ *Cheques are expensive, use modern methods (BACS),*

6/ *Expect all accounts to be paid within the negotiated period,*

7/ *Pay all accounts within the negotiated period, (usually thirty days from delivery date).*

8/ ***Any deviation from this, is an own-goal!***

Fig 8.3 A message to company accountants.

policy to replace any such critical item as soon as one was used. The person responsible for such an order thought he remembered ordering one. They checked and found that the order had gone into their supplier, some three months previously. The supplier normally delivered within the week. Further investigation uncovered a letter, lodged in the accounts department, black-listing the plant for non-payment of an outstanding account. Following some inter-departmental arguing as to who was responsible for the non-payment, the hidden letter and the blocked order, the problem became temporarily resolved by a cheque being issued. A senior manager chased around the head office to obtain the necessary signatures, and then drove to the Midlands to present the cheque and an apology personally to the supplying company. He collected the replacement part, and returned. The round trip took five hours, which added to the several hours,that the plant had been idle. The actual cost of the stoppage was very many times greater than the unpaid bill. Such is the cost of poor Quality!

Consideration of process at this macro level demonstrates:

- The need for cooperation.
- The centrality of Quality.
- The essential customer/supplier relationships.
- The need for effective communication.
- The limiting of Quality costs.
- Two-way relationships.

The micro level of process

The second level of process to be constantly under review is that of each individual process. Most people are responsible for a multitude of processes, and it is important that they can distinguish one from another.

The definition of process has to do with change. For every process, something is changed. Anyone working, who feels that they change nothing, *beware!* You are not contributing to the overall process. You could well be surplus to requirements!

It is important to understand and appreciate all the many inputs of each process. Each must be controlled as tightly as possible. The 6Ms theory helps to identify these many facets.

As a mnemonic, it is a cheat. One word is a French word, and loosely used at that. Nevertheless, the 6Ms theory represents a good starting point for the consideration of all the aspects of any process, in whatever company or activity.

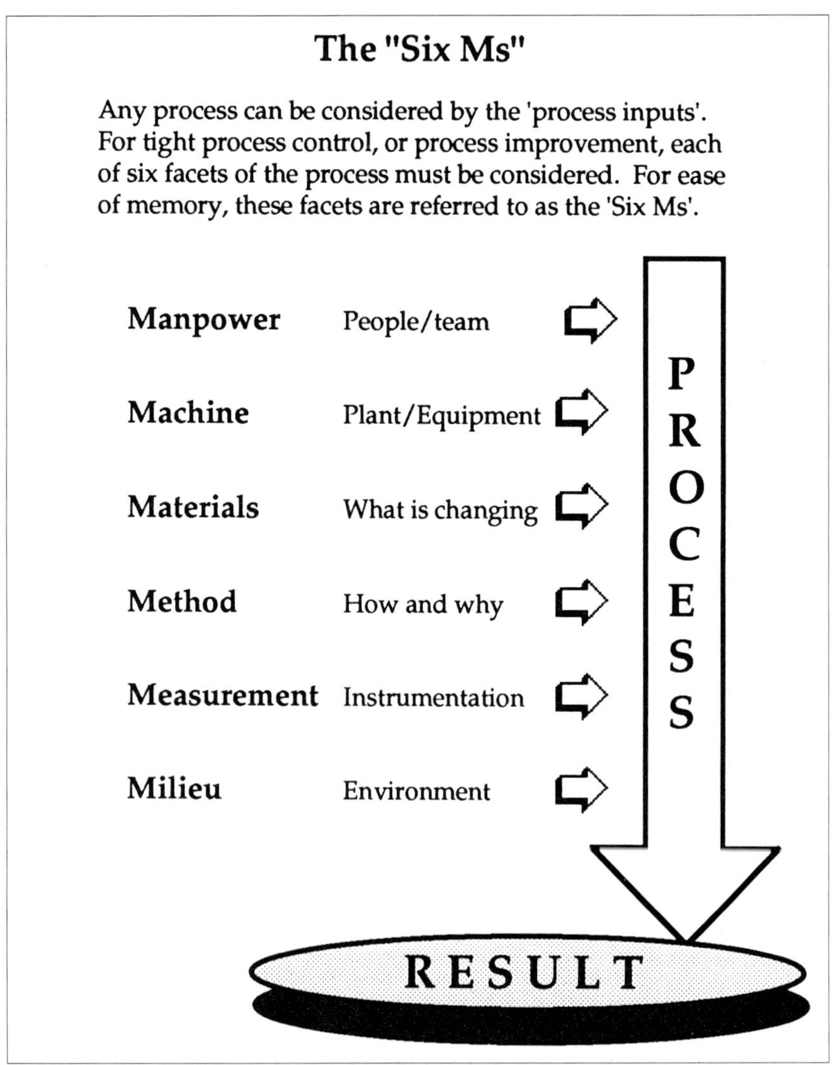

Fig 8.4 Illustration of 6Ms theory.

- *Manpower*

  Whatever the process, inevitably more than one person will be involved. There will often be several operators, a managerial input, a maintenance input, a training input, etc. The nature of this team will determine the Quality of the process input.

- *Machine*

  The plant and machinery must be the right equipment, properly maintained, to do the job. Every process will use some equipment, and even if it is but a notebook and pencil, the process will be impaired if the notebook is full and the pencil is blunt.

- *Materials*

  Clearly, the Quality of the input material, including its presentation, is of great importance. Where there is doubt in identifying the customer/supplier relationship, the consideration of the materials involved with the process defines these relationships. It is at this level that the ability to negotiate and demand Quality is at its most poignant. It will be within these relationships that the battle for Quality will be won or lost.

- *Method*

  How a process is achieved is a vital part of that process. There is always more than one method of accomplishing anything. In a repetitive situation, people have to have ownership of their activities, by building a little of themselves into the process, ie. their individual method. Whilst avoiding a value-judgement at this stage, it is important to realise the existence of this force within all processes.

- *Measurement*

  It is impossible to control any process without having some measure of its on-going performance. Some people believe that they have no process measurement with which to make process control decisions, only a measure of the results. This is doubtful. In the absence of any scientific measure, people fall back on intuitive measures, such as the sound of the machine, the look of the process, their gut-feeling; in other words, they make a judgement. Processes need process measurement.

- *Milieu*

  The environment in which the process takes place will have an effect on the outcome of the process. It is important to take all aspects of these conditions into account when considering the process inputs. The social environment is included within this area of consideration. A member of a dissatisfied workforce will have other considerations on his mind, and this will affect the operation of the process.

Obviously, there is some overlap between these areas and, as such, they cover the spectrum of process inputs necessary for an efficient and well controlled process.

The earlier the better

In considering the macro level of process, there are several modern Quality methods that have relevance. However, individually, they may not provide the improvements expected. A total approach to all aspects of the process will be necessary for tight control. Controlled conditions in each facet of the process inputs will depend on previous good management. Many companies have mistakenly and single-mindedly

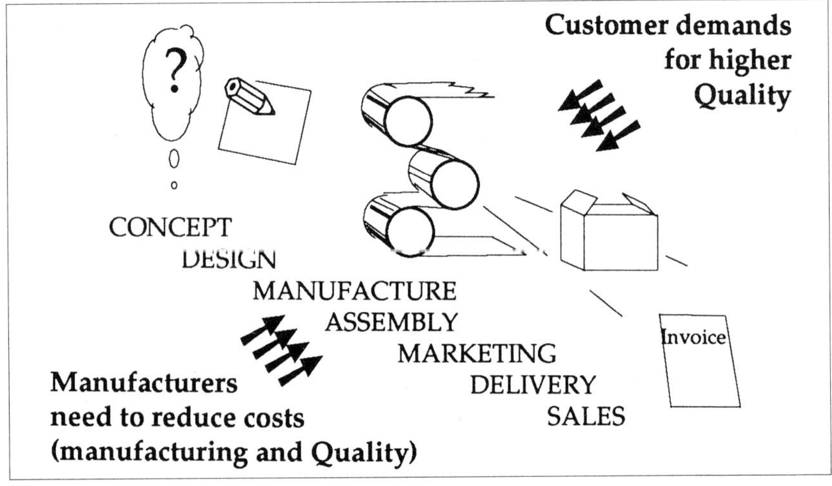

Fig 8.5 Concept to sales.

gone overboard with a particular idea, only to find little value coming from its use, because other aspects are out of control.

If the macro process is considered to be from the inception of an idea or concept, through design, planning, manufacture and marketing to sales, then there are two conflicting pressures demanding Quality improvements, one from each end of the process. The dichotomy is best seen by examining the origin of these pressures.

Usually the louder cry for Quality comes from the customer, whose ever-rising requirements, expectations, and indeed demands, keep the subject of Quality always to the front of the supplier's mind. This has led, in the past, to the Quality department being established at the end of the line, with its activities extending back into the company, against the natural flow.

The other concern that elicits instant support is the *cost* of Quality. It is obvious that the earlier improvements are be made within a process, the greater the benefits to be derived from those improvements will be.

This thought often takes the form of improvements being implemented at the 'green' end of the factory, where the first operations are performed. However, this isn't nearly early enough. Many in Japan have long since decided that the place where most manufacturing problems can be solved is the draughtsman's table. Problems can be designed out. A modification of the original idea can have more profound effects than any subsequent changes, and hence can be far more cost effective. Taguchi's ideas and methods, such as FMEA, to achieve this early process control, are explored in Chapter 9.

Idea

Designers actually design processes, rather than things. That is, they design the means of manufacturing products, rather than the result of the processes.

Summary

Unitary thinking stresses numbers and is usually results orientated (static).

Process thinking concentrates on process inputs and is 'doing' orientated (dynamic).

Two levels of process

- Macro, the entire operation.
- Micro, individual processes.

Improvements – the earlier, the better.

Unitary thinking	**Process thinking**
Static operation	Dynamic concept
Undermines Quality	Centralises Quality
Shortens time-scales	Lengthens time-scales
Inhibits investment	Promotes investment
Compartmentalises activity	Creates company culture
Perverts priorities	Directs effort
Self-perpetuating	Self-perpetuating
Diverts attention from process	Concentrates on process

Consideration of process at the macro level demonstrates:

- The need for cooperation.
- The centrality of Quality.
- The essential customer/supplier relationships.
- The need for good communication.
- The limiting of Quality costs.
- Two-way relationships.

Consideration of process at the micro level includes:

● Manpower	always plural, always a team.
● Machine	equipment must be well maintained.
● Method	individual methods.
● Materials	defines process (change). Also defines internal customers.
● Measurement	live process information.
● Milieu	physical and social environment.

Last thoughts ....

The managing director of a thriving electronics company read and was most impressed by Frank Price's book, *Right First Time*. He immediately ordered some signs to be made with the slogan 'Right First Time' painted on both sides. These he instructed to be hung in the aisles between the machinery throughout the factory. He went on his rounds, but was concerned that the signs were at ceiling level and could hardly be read. The engineer responsible was sent for and explained that the only suitable fixings available in the stores were short six inch chains. 'If its worth doing, its worth doing well', said the managing director. Longer chains were purchased and the signs were re-sited just above eye level. Everyone noticed them. Two days later, the forklift driver noticed them. He demolished an entire row with the forklift as he carried a pile of crates through the factory. They were again re-sited, this time over the machinery and well out of harms way. The workforce learnt about the necessity of doing everything right first time!

1. See Chapter 9.

Chapter 9

Modern Quality Methods

Conditions on the road are so bad, so if you are just setting off for work, leave a little earlier

– Kelvin O'Shea

Route-map

After considering the question of process improvement in general, this chapter considers the following:

Taguchi methods
Design FMEA
Process FMEA
Statistical Process Control
Just-In-Time methods

Total Quality

The three inter-related forces that combine to produce Total Quality are attitudes, actions and Quality costs (see Fig 9.1).

Changing people's attitudes leads to the possibility that their actions can be modified, thus giving improved results see (Fig 9.2).

Attitudinal change is best accomplished through education and understanding. The action that will result from a deeper understanding of Total Quality will be tighter process control. The improved results can be appreciated in lower Quality costs.

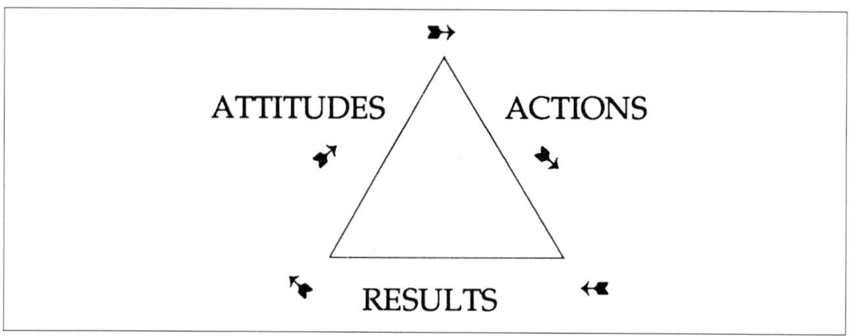

Fig 9.1 Attitudes, actions, results.

Attitudes then actions

The message the attitudinal stance of the company executive conveys, is more important than the methods employed. There are many examples of companies which have attempted to mix these modern Quality methods with a traditional 'number orientated' culture. They do not achieve very much success with the new methods.

The new attitudinal stance is needed. Tighter process control is essential. People have to be better organised and will require the tools to put these ideas into practice. In general, it is helpful to keep two basic ideas in mind when planning for production. The system should ensure

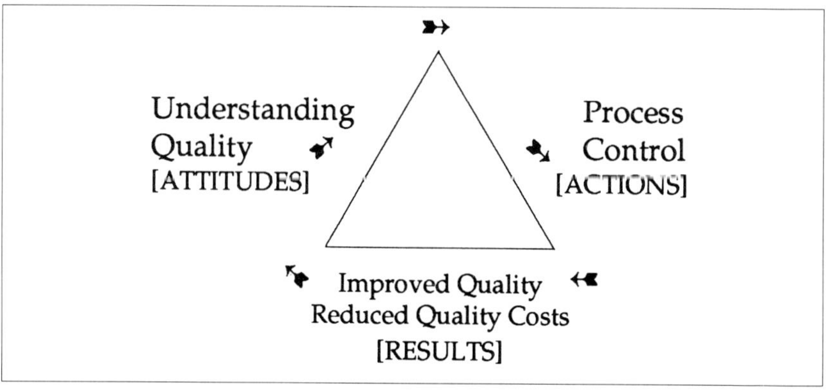

Fig 9.2 Quality understanding, process control, Quality costs.

that it is always possible to achieve satisfactory results within the normal mode of operating. It should be possible to get everything:

Right first time.

The other aspect needed to be built into the planning of any operation is the sense that perfection is never totally achievable, and yet is continually sought. As people become more practised, developing greater skill, and above all, have an ever-increasing knowledge of their processes, they must ensure that this can be put to their advantage. They will obtain:

Never ending improvement.

The earlier the better

The 'earlier the better' principle has been considered at the end of the previous chapter.

The conflicting pressures for Quality methods will always be present. The *pull* of the customer who, quite rightly, passes on his ever-rising requirements and expectations, and the *push* of Quality cost considerations that demand improvements earlier in the macro process.

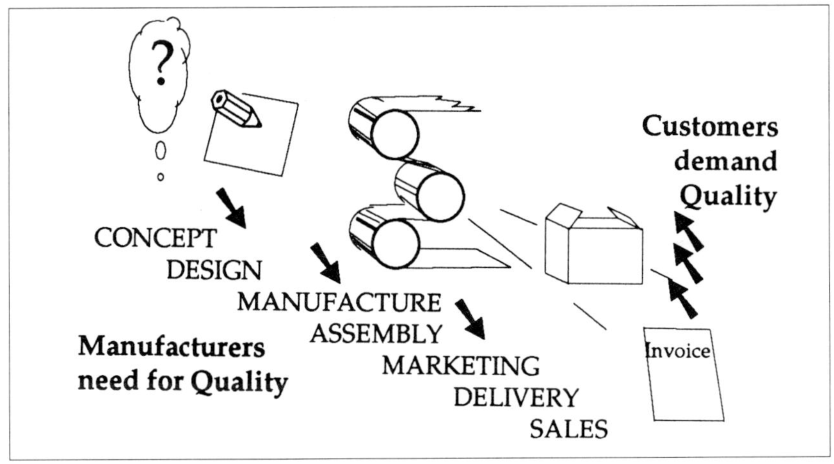

Fig 9.3 Concept to sales, with push/pull features.

Clearly, the answer lies in the total integration of these two methods, starting from the concept stage, through the design, planning, manufacturing, packaging, marketing and shipping stages. By keying the new methodology into new organisational structures, it will be possible to maximise the benefits as well as being able to give confidence to the customers.

The methods

The remainder of this chapter is devoted to identifying helpful Quality methods for use at all points of the macro process, with the intention of explaining what they are, how they can be used and what benefits will be derived (see Fig 9.4). A fuller explanation of the individual methods will have to be sought elsewhere.

Taguchi methods

Genichi Taguchi is a Japanese engineer who has specialised in Quality engineering techniques. His ideas are unique, and have the benefit of encouraging the student to examine thoroughly what is really meant by Quality, and its relationship with wealth. Most of his ideas require a higher starting point, with regard to Quality management, than is to be found in most companies, and as such, represents the next step *after* the introduction of TQM.

However, the more useful aspects of Taguchi's methods can be applied at the very beginning of the macro process. He identifies three developmental stages: product design, process design, and production – it should be noted that the same arguments apply to *service* design and production. He sees each of the three stages, whilst overlapping, determining the methods and costs of the next. Thus, there should be

Caution

Improvements are easy to achieve, but holding on to the benefits is much harder. It will be the *balance* of the methods about to be expounded that will determine the overall benefit.

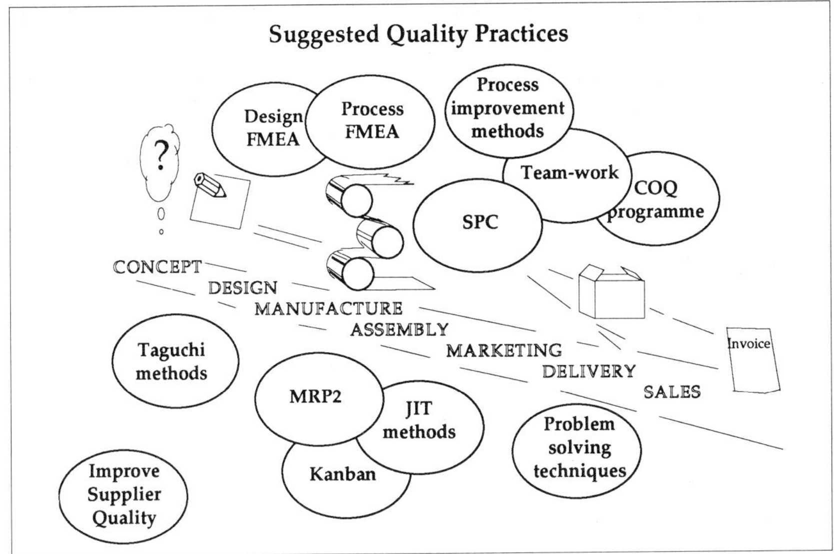

Fig 9.4 Concept to sales with suggested Quality practices.

considerable work done during the 'product design' stage to ensure that the 'process design' can be effectively and cost-efficiently achieved.

Again, the process design stage can be better accomplished by applying oneself to the methods, problems, and constraints, of daily production. In this way, problems are identified, met and resolved, before they have occurred. The solution to most potential problems can be found during this previous stage. Production problems can be reduced, if not eliminated, by careful process design. Process problems are reduced or eliminated by careful product design. Careful work at the design stage, involving production and engineering personnel, can overcome most potential problems, prior to full-scale production.

This philosophy will have different implications within various types of industrial environment. There are, however, several fundamental truths within the methods.

- Problems can be designed out

  A product can be designed to be manufactured. It is in fact the making processes that need to be designed, that is, the human actions involved. The designer should have as much knowledge of the methods, processes and people involved with the eventual production, as he does of the actual product to be designed.

- Post design problems are expensive

  Any problem occurring after the previous stage is completed will have expensive Quality costs attached. The later the problem occurs, the greater the cost. The traditional reluctance to purchase a new model of anything testifies to the assumption that not all the problems have been ironed out. 'Let's wait until it has been de-bugged by someone else'. The Quality costs involved are tremendous.

- Removes barriers

  Traditional perceptions of research and development engineers, designers, process engineers and production staff, all serve to preserve the artificial barriers between their functions. It will only be by fusing these areas, that is by cross-breeding ideas and by valuing the inputs of others, that it will be possible to design efficiently. Only in this way can Quality costs be minimised. All of this activity must occur efficiently and at the right time – *early*.

Taguchi has several other useful ideas worthy of study.[1]

Among them is his attitude to design tolerances. Any movement away from the nominal, designed value, represents a loss of Quality, incurring a loss of function for the customer. The traditional method of assigning tolerance bands to every measurement ensures that many manufacturers produce most items well away from the nominal, designed value, probably collecting most values at one end of the tolerance range. The aim, therefore, should be to reduce variation and always concentrate on the nominal value. This is best achieved via SPC, discussed later in this chapter, whereby the emphasis is on stable processes with the minimum of variation.

Taguchi has also pioneered experiments designed to reach optimum values in circumstances where there are many inter-related product and process variables. Statistics are used to minimise the number of actual experiments that are necessary to examine the inter-related effects of change within these variables. Again, no great statistical knowledge is necessary, as the application of his design of experiments is relatively straightforward.

The greatest benefit from considering Taguchi's methods may be the freshness stemming from such an open mind. The act of a highly respected 'Quality engineer', metaphorically tearing up the rule book, and considering his actions again, from first principles, has to inspire us all.

Design FMEA

Failure Mode and Effects Analysis, or FMEA for short, is a means by which a design can be tested theoretically. A small team, including those involved with planning and production, as well as the designers, considers the range of potential failure situations emanating from the design.

It must consider the purpose and possible uses of the designed item during its intended lifetime. As with all such considerations, a Quality perspective suggests a careful examination of the potential customer's requirements and expectations. An integral part of this research will be the manufacturing methods to be used. The group will keep in mind the question, 'Can it be manufactured successfully?' There are thoughts here, parallel to those of Taguchi mentioned earlier (see Fig 9.5).

The discussions centre on the FMEA chart. The purpose of this chart is to identify all possible failure modes and consider their potential effects. The group then applies a set of criteria, assessing the likelihood of each failure mode occurring, the severity of the effect, should it occur, and the chances of detection. These considerations are combined for each potential failure mode, to arrive at a Risk Priority Number (RPN). The

Idea

The Taguchi message – 'Be open-minded!'

Design FMEA

The "Design FMEA" considers three questions:

❶ What is the purpose of the design?

❷ Will it fulfil the potential customers' expectations?

❸ Can it be successfully manufactured?

Fig 9.5 Design FMEA.

group is now able to appreciate the potential effects of failure, and can identify which potential failures are the most urgent. Attention is paid to those failure modes that either produced the highest RPNs, or scored highly, usually eight to ten, in any of the three categories.

Full tables showing the criteria and their values are listed in Appendix A, at the back of this book.

FMEA "Risk Priority Numbers"

The FMEA group assess:

- Likelihood of OCCURRENCE
- The SEVERITY should failure occur
- Chance of DETECTION

The RPN is calculated by multiplying these ratings together:

$$\text{R.P.N.} = \begin{matrix}\text{Occurrence}\\ \text{Rating}\end{matrix} \times \begin{matrix}\text{Severity}\\ \text{Rating}\end{matrix} \times \begin{matrix}\text{Detection}\\ \text{Rating}\end{matrix}$$

The failure modes with the highest RPNs,receive the greatest and most immediate attention for remedial action.

Fig 9.6 RPN calculation.

It is vital that the group adopts a proactive and purposeful stance. There is little point in identifying design problems unless steps are taken to correct, or at least mitigate them. As a result of the deliberations, proposed actions are inserted on the chart. These will identify not only *what* is to be done, but *by whom* and *when*.

The resultant actions may well involve an alteration in the design, or a change of materials. Where this is not possible, it may be necessary to re-organise the intended manufacturing processes to eliminate the problem. The complete elimination of the problem has to be the aim, but where this cannot be achieved, steps must be taken to reduce the severity of the potential failure, as well as to build in adequate measures to detect the failure before it does any damage.

The FMEA chart is then revisited at regular intervals. Each failure mode is re-assessed and new RPNs calculated. The chart becomes a historical record of the design improvements involved with the particular product (see Fig 9.7).

Process FMEA

The process FMEA fulfils very much the same role as the design FMEA, except that it is concerned with potential failures emanating from the manufacturing processes. In its purest form, the full range of processes

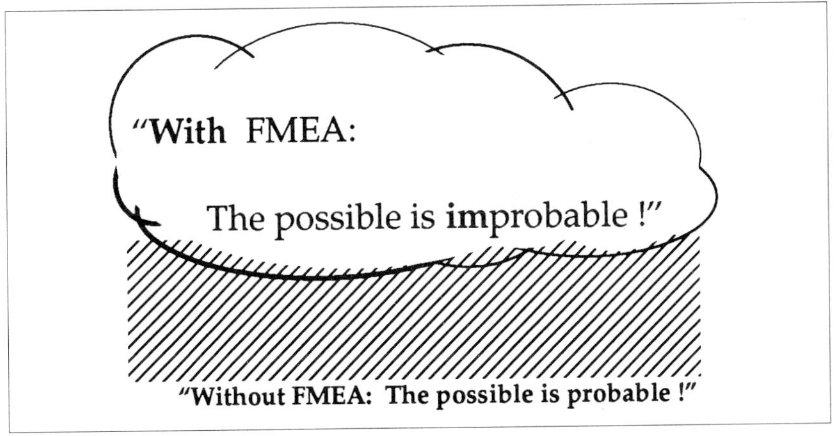

Fig 9.7 Without FMEA.

that lead from the design to a satisfied end-user customer should be considered. There is much to be gained from using these techniques on the administration process, the planning process and the handling and shipping processes.

The process FMEA often involves people from several different areas. Where the input materials come from a supplier company, it is usual for a representative of that company to take part in the FMEA. Again, a full consideration of the failure modes, and their effects, can often be enhanced by a contribution from the customer who will use the finished product.

A bi-product of these process FMEAs is the increase in contact and the spread of knowledge along the supplier/customer chain. The barriers are broken down by personal contact, and problems are shared. The realisation of joint responsibility and shared destiny develops, producing a more harmonised working environment, with reduced Quality costs.

Tribute should be paid to the Ford Motor Company, which has pioneered these FMEA techniques. It has been common practice since the mid 1980s for Ford to be working together with its major suppliers to establish both design and process improvements.

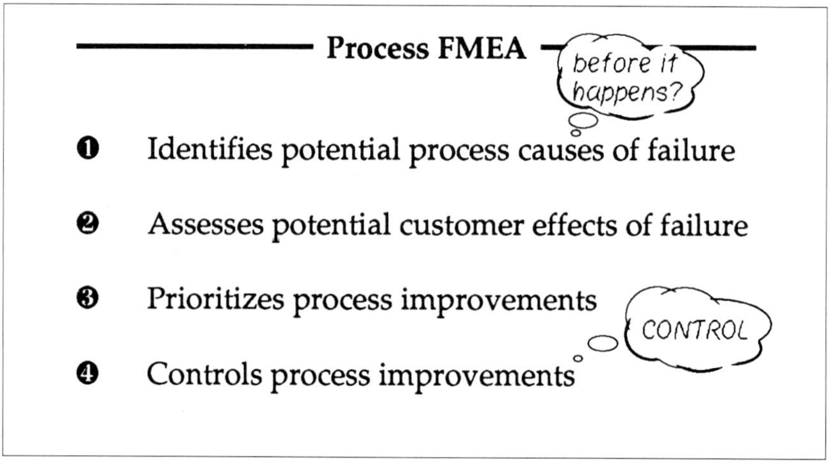

Process FMEA

1. Identifies potential process causes of failure
2. Assesses potential customer effects of failure
3. Prioritizes process improvements
4. Controls process improvements

Fig 9.8 Process FMEA.

The FMEA chart is an analytical tool. It expands the knowledge of the processes involved *before* any failure occurs. The technique ties in very well with the other modern process improvement methods suggested. All rely on an ever deepening knowledge of the actual processes necessary to achieve the desired results. The essence of the process FMEA is that it can be used to eliminate potential causes of process failure, and thus reduce product failure.

'When do we learn?' is the question for all industry. It is often said that when a failure occurs it is not all loss, provided one learns from it. With FMEA, it is not necessary to have live problems before learning from them. By considering potential failures, the problems can be removed before the failure mode ever occurs.

The FMEA chart identifies the process changes that are necessary to avoid process breakdown or product failure. As such, it is a *directive* document. The calculation of the RPNs from the consideration of the 'occurrence rating', 'severity rating' and 'detection rating', will lead the FMEA group to identify the necessary process changes.

It will be vital that representatives of all aspects of the human team concerned with the process are present. The team will need the widest possible range of knowledge, skills and experience. Not least will be the contribution of the shopfloor operatives involved. Their in-depth

Responsibilities of FMEA team

❶ Ensure the involvement of everyone who can contribute (including suppliers)

inter company co-opertaion!

❷ Conduct FMEA

❸ Ensure resultant actions are carried out

❹ Conduct a further FMEA

Keep it ALIVE

Fig 9.9 Responsibilities of FMEA team.

Benefits of FMEA

- **Better product (goods or service)**

  FMEA eliminates problems before they have occurred.

- **Higher Quality levels**

  By concentrating on the design and early processes, improvements made will increase Quality levels.

- **Increased process capability**

  Improved product and/or process design, will significantly increase the capability of the production processes.

- **Reduced re-work**

  Easier and more efficient manufacturing processes lead to reduced amounts of rectification work.

- **Scrap levels lowered**

  For those manufacturers still making scrap, FMEA can be a valuable tool to reduce it.

- **Increased customer satisfaction**

  Customers will enjoy greater reliability from your products.

- **Gradual elimination of failure conditions**

  FMEA is an on-going technique.

- **Increased profitability**

  Lower Quality costs will lead to increased profits.

- **Greater security for all**

  The elimination of failures will give a more secure future.

Fig 9.10 Benefits of FMEA.

knowledge of the process will play a vital part. Where the FMEA is being conducted prior to full scale production, personnel operating similar processes should be involved in order that the study may draw on, and benefit from, their experience.

Clearly, to maximise the effects of the FMEAs within a company, there should be considerable correlation between the design FMEA team, concerned with the initial product and process design, and the process FMEA team, responsible for the production and delivery processes. It will usually be the latter that retains the on-going responsibility for the FMEA, ensuring that both process and product benefit from never-ending improvement.

Statistical Process Control

Statistical Process Control (SPC) is the embodiment of the ideas expressed throughout this chapter. In essence, a process is controlled by keeping all of the process inputs stable. A simple form of statistics is used to establish an effective knowledge of everything that is occurring, without having to measure absolutely everything.

There are two separate strands to SPC, and both must be applied to each process. First, process stability is achieved by understanding the variation involved with each of the process inputs. The 6Ms method of assessing process inputs can help to identify the many actual process inputs. It must be appreciated that there is variation within every process, if it is examined in sufficient detail. No two things are ever exactly alike.

By collecting data from the process parameter over a period of time, and then examining the pattern of this variation, the various causes of variation can be identified. Some of these are to be expected. Indeed, they are inevitable. They will have to be 'lived with'. Many of the causes, and thus much of the variation, will be of this sort, contributing to a stable situation. Such variation, contributing to this stable situation, is said to stem from common causes.

Examples of such common causes of variation, in many manufacturing environments, are fluctuating electrical power, varying ambient temperatures and the minor differences to be found in most raw materials. Such examples can be identified within each of the 6Ms, amplified in Chapter 8, and a careful examination of each of the 'M' areas will be a useful start to understanding a particular process.

However, some of the causes of variation may not be so regular. The exceptional causes will inject instability into the process, as they are not always present in the same degree. These are called special causes of variation.

Again, it will be helpful to start looking for special causes within each of the 6Ms. Examples of possible special causes could be:

● Manpower	Erratic or unskilled operator
● Machine	Malfunctioning switch
● Method	Inconsistent methods
● Materials	Mixed source components
● Measurement	Non-calibrated gauge used
● Milieu	Extremely high humidity

SPC uses simple statistical techniques to identify and control these causes of variation. The theory is based upon the patterns of distribution, stemming from collections of process data.

The common causes will always form a bell-shaped curve, known by statisticians as a normal distribution curve. When only common causes of variation are present, a basic understanding of statistics allows a prediction of the results to be achieved.

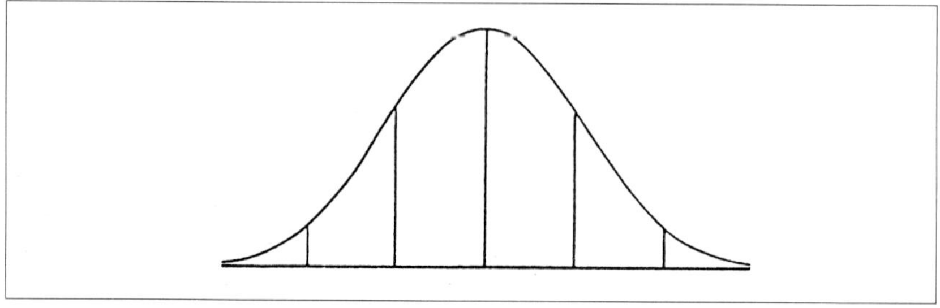

Fig 9.11 Normal distribution curve.

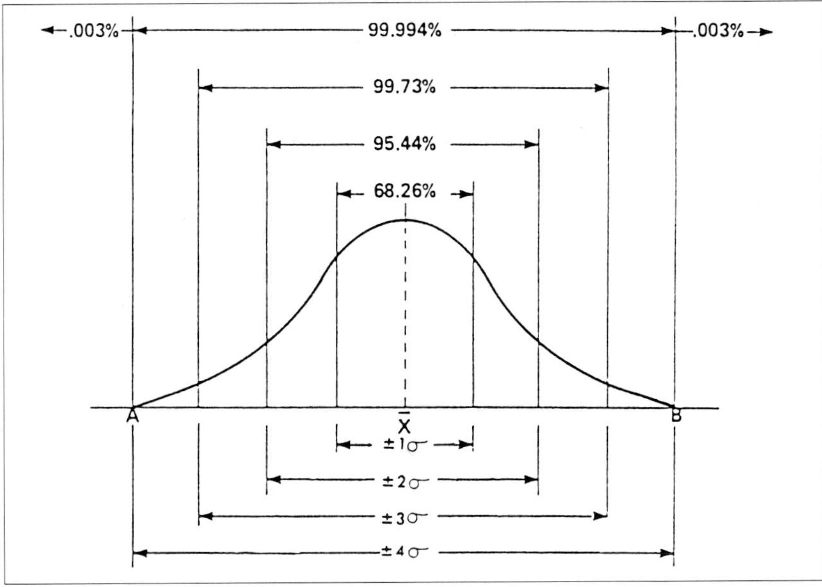

Fig 9.12 Distribution within the normal curve.

Once this is achieved, users of SPC have the task of occasionally checking a small number of samples to ensure that the process is still stable. This is done on a special chart called a Process Control Chart.

The small sample of data is usually five readings; then the operator makes two simple calculations, plots the results on the chart, and assesses the situation from the resultant pattern.

The form of the normal distribution curve represented by the data is estimated by calculating:

1. the average of the five readings;
2. the range, or spread, of the five readings.

By considering four basic rules applied to these two plots the operator can make the decision whether or not the process is still stable. In other words, these methods are used to identify the presence of a special cause of variation. Whilst the process is stable, ie. there are only common causes of variation present, the process is said to be in statistical control, and the operator knows not to take action to alter the operation of the process.

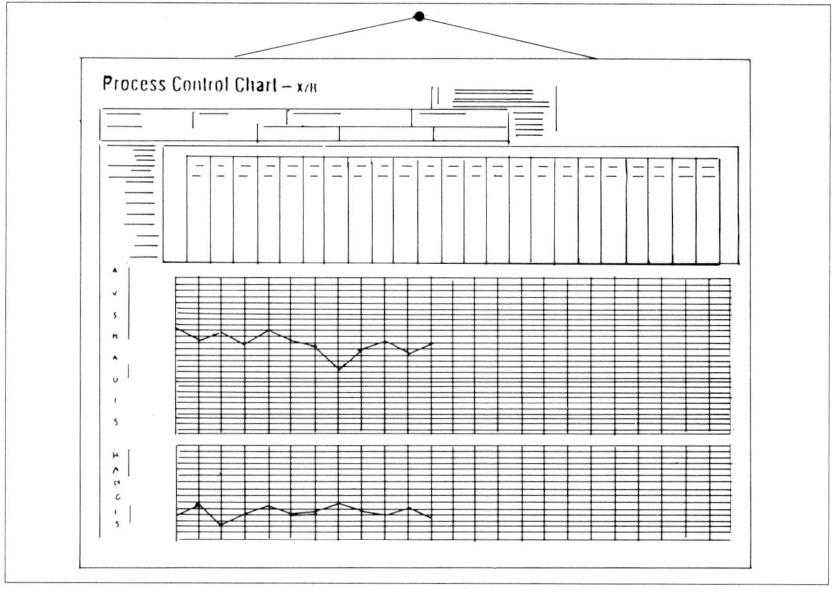

Fig 9.13 Example of SPC chart.

Experience shows that where SPC is not being used, operators make many small adjustments, often with very little justification other than their 'gut feeling', and some misguided reliance on supposed experience. This constant tinkering with the process by the operator can account for much process instability.

This explanation is of SPC in its simplest form. There are many different types of chart used to control processes in all types of circumstances. It is both possible, and necessary, to control most processes in this way. Obviously, these methods are more straightforward when applied to a repetitive process, but they have relevance to any situation in which the

Idea

Much process instability
has human origins.

actual process is repeated. This will be true when the actual outputs are in small batches, or even individually very different. It is only by keeping a tight control of the process inputs that the process itself and, hence, the results of the process can be controlled.

The other part of SPC is the matching of the stable process being achieved with its specifications. The process spread, as shown by the normal distribution curve, is compared with the tolerance spread, as defined in the customer's negotiated requirements. The result of this consideration is called *capability*. In its simplest form, a process that falls well within the tolerance spread is said to be *capable,* whereas one that doesn't, is said to be *incapable.*

In practice, of course, greater rigour produces a more sensitive measure. This is referred to as a *Capability Index*. There are several such indices, but the most useful is the Cpk.

The Cpk will normally be found by conducting a capability study. A collection of samples are taken at random, at least 50, and each one measured to give a set of data. Simple statistics are now applied to this data, easily producing the Cpk.

Many feel, quite needlessly, inhibited by this use of mathematics. There is no need to be either a mathematician, or a statistician. The use of the

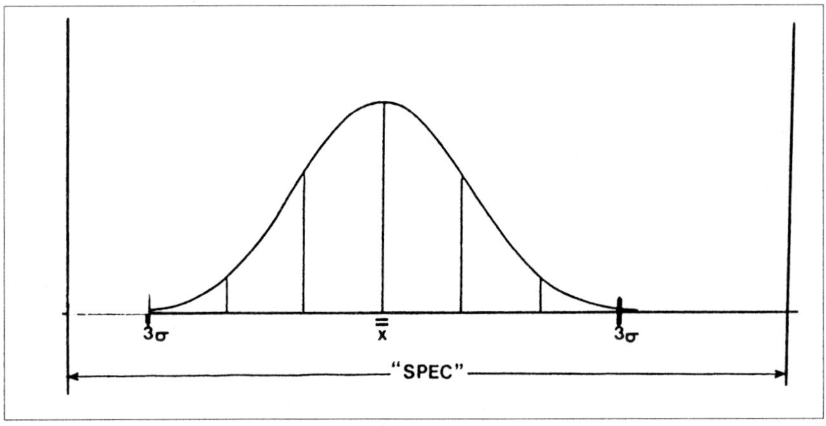

Fig 9.14 A capable process.

chart can be accomplished by anyone with a little training, indeed, SPC is much more to do with people than with statistics. Anyone with a basic competence in using a calculator will have no problems doing any of the calculations needed in any aspect of Statistical Process Control.

A full explanation of virtually all SPC techniques can be found in 'SPC-Made Easy',[2] together with worked examples of all the techniques, or in the shortened version, 'SPC-Explained'.[3] Education will be an important issue when implementing SPC. It is essential that everyone concerned has both a good understanding of the techniques, and access to the formulae and constants necessary to perform the easy calculations. These are listed in Appendix B at the back of this book.

Attributes

All the measurement data discussed above will be variable data, giving real values, whose accuracy will depend upon the capability of the measuring device. Many processes lack such variable data, and have to rely on rough checks after the process is complete.

Attribute charts are used to monitor those Quality characteristics that are countable, rather than measurable. An attribute is a characteristic that is present or absent, go or no-go, good or bad, acceptable or unacceptable. It may have different levels or grades, but not variable data.

Attribute charts are used in much the same way as variable charts, but do not actually control the process. They essentially are monitoring results, since an attribute is not known until after the process and is, in general, an undesired result. However, they are easy to use, and can quickly identify process faults and monitor improvements.

Tributes

As with FMEA, tribute should be paid to the Ford Motor Company for their efforts in pushing Statistical Process Control. In the mid 1980s it became mandatory and a condition of all its purchase agreements that all items containing a critical Quality parameter should have Statistical Process Control.

The economic push created by the fear of losing the business of the major customer, has led the supplier base to develop SPC quicker than most Ford plants. This point is made, as many people seem to enjoy relating the problems with their latest British-made car. They always find pleasure in such problems, particularly when the debt UK industry owes to the Ford Motor Company is pointed out. It was Ford which up-graded Quality to be the major concern of the 1980s in much of British industry.

Probably the best overall justification for SPC is in Frank Price's 'Right First Time'.[4] Price presents the complete scenario within which SPC is the only sensible means of control. The definitive volume on the subject is probably John Oakland's 'Statistical Process Control, a practical guide'.[5]

JIT and related philosophies

Just-In-Time (JIT) is a philosophy which, in its rarest form, means accomplishing every action or process, *Just In Time*. The processes are planned and arranged in such a way that nothing is done until it is needed. It is reliably performed. This approach can allow for smooth, on-line manufacturing, with a steady flow of materials from suppliers feeding directly into manufacturing lines, as and when needed. Indeed, the product is not manufactured until there is a known outlet for it. Storage of materials, half-finished components and the finished product are all virtually eliminated, thus greatly reducing costs.

Companies using 'Kanban' install a system whereby every process initiates an order to the previous process. No other orders are allowed, thus the entire organisation is geared to the rate of production. Indeed, the rate of production is a direct response to the rate of sales. Theoretically, nothing is made and nothing is ordered until it is needed. A total move in this direction is impossible, for there would be no leeway to account for minor variations in production times. The partial introduction of these methods can lead to a considerable reduction in the value of goods held within various inventories. Clearly, any such reduction is a potential cost saving.

In the late 1970s the initials MRP stood for Materials Resource Planning, and represented computer-based systems that planned material inputs to the process. This ensured a steady flow of materials, whilst keeping stocks to a minimum. These ideas were expanded in the early 1980s, to become MRP2, or Manufacturing Resource Planning. Basically, all the company's resources, both physical and human, were now included in the computer-based plan. The complex combination of plant, machinery and people availability is constructed into sophisticated computer programmes, in a manner which allows effective planning to be accomplished.

One big advantage of this type of programme is the theoretical running of the computer programme in advance of real-time. This allows the plans and decisions to be tested on the computer. Any possible scenario can be included, such as a stoppage from a particular supplier, an outbreak of bad weather, or a sudden increase in demand. The costs of alternative decisions can be calculated. The problems can be diagnosed and the programme amended in the light of the computer results. The eventual production costs, and use of resources, both human and material, can all thus be made more effective.

JIT is a less sophisticated and, therefore, more easily accessible approach, identifying the manufacturing process whereby each operation is performed at the last possible minute, that is 'just in time'. The implications are explored thoroughly by David Hutchins, in his book 'Just in Time'[6] He defines JIT as a term used to indicate that a process is capable of instant response to demand, without the need for any overstocking, either in expectation of the demand being forthcoming, or as a result of inefficiencies in the process.

The dangers of attempting to implement JIT in isolation from any Total Quality Management, cannot be overstated. The author recently visited a factory heralded as a leader in the JIT philosophy. Indeed, the five year old factory had been purpose-built for on-line, free flowing production. It was in trouble though. Because its processes were so out of control, it had found the need to store part-finished components emanating from part way along the line. It had no facilities to do this. No storage, no transport, no space. The subsequent packing, palletising, transporting, storing, then re-transporting and unpacking these part-finished items, absorbed a large amount of effort. The systems were there, but they didn't work. The people were there, but they were untrained. The ideas were there, but lacked understanding.

The process implications of these methods are considerable. Whilst they are outwardly involving resources, planning and communications within a company, they depend entirely on the smooth operation of each and every process. To embark on such schemes without tight process control, is to court failure. Indeed, the scale of the potential failure is greatly increased. Factories designed for such operation do not include vast storage areas. Planning of production schedules does not include buffer stocks between each operation, to protect them against breakdown and failure of parts of the production line. With JIT, it all works, or it doesn't.

There are further implications for the education of all the people involved with JIT schemes. All such schemes depend upon accuracy. Indeed, the more sophisticated the computer software involved, the more the company will become data dependent. The complete honesty of everyone involved will have to be taken for granted, and yet this is foreign to the traditional mode of operation.

Many companies have lived for years with estimated figures, half-truths, hidden stocks, partly fulfilled orders and the like. For any JIT or related scheme to have any chance of success, a company will have to take on board a major re-think in terms of its personnel.

Attitudes, understanding and working relationships will have to be carefully studied, and rigorous education programmes embarked upon. All staff must be orientated towards the honest and open relationships that are essential for these systems to operate.

Idea

Tight process control is the first essential in any overall resource planning.

Idea

Education is an essential ingredient of all successful industry.

Kanban

Kanban is the Anglicised equivalent of a Japanese word meaning 'visible record'. There are two main differences between Kanban and traditional manufacturing systems.

1. Work is only initiated *in response to* a card detailing the needs of the customer (internal or external). Work is not seen as a continuous and never-ending succession of parts moving through a particular work centre, with no apparent immediate demand, and only the generalised need of producing as many of these as possible. Rather, work is directly related to a particular customer, who clearly states the immediate need.

2. Kanban is a *pull system*, whereby the system pulls the work from the product (customer) end of the system, as opposed to the traditional push system, in which a half-finished component goes to the next operation, thus triggering more work.

No work is done at any work centre, unless there is a 'Kanban' to authorise it. The system is entirely customer-led, and driven by the pull of real need. It gives positive substance to the concept of 'the internal customer'. The system provides parts and materials only as they are needed. It avoids merely guessing how many will be needed and when. It avoids over stocking against a possible unexpected order. It avoids expensive excess inventory and stock-piling.

Clearly, to be effective the system will operate across company boundaries. Orders will be initiated to suppliers on a basis of exactly what and when the items are needed. For the full benefits to be obtained, the supplier base will have to be operating a JIT system as well.

Problem-solving techniques

It may seem churlish, but the methods outlined in this chapter are not nearly enough. They provide merely the basis for running a tightly controlled organisation.

The implementation stage will soon pass. The methods will become thought of as normal operating procedures. It will seem strange and archaic that the company ever managed to survive without tight process control. It will be the norm. It will be static.

Quality is not static. The quest for Quality means a constant never-ending search for better results, tighter control, less variation, more consistency and lower Quality costs. To achieve this, Quality improvement will become part of everyday of life. The company will need to become literate in problem-solving techniques.

Summary

Improvements – the earlier, the better

Taguchi methods –
Problems designed out
Post design problems expensive
Barriers removed
Design tolerances
Experiment design

Failure Mode and Effects Analysis

Identifying potential failure modes
Potential effects of failure modes
Potential cause of failure modes
Design FMEA
Process FMEA

Statistical Process Control

Control of variation
Stable processes
Statistical control
Capable processes

Just-In-Time methods

Process implications
Tight process control essential
Education essential
MRP = Materials Resource Planning
MRP2 = Manufacturing Resource Planning
Kanban

Last thoughts ....

During an SPC course I was running, I asked what the actual spec was for a particular item we were considering. I was told 'Well, we are supposed to aim at 110 mm ±5 mm, but we try to keep it within ±10 mm, and its really OK if we keep it within ±15 mm'.

1. Taguchi, G, *Offline Quality Control*, 1979, and *Online Quality Control During Production*, 1981.
2. Choppin, Jon, *SPC-Made Easy*, 1986.
3. Choppin, Jon, *SPC-Explained*, 1988.
4. Price, Frank, *Right First Time*, Gower, 1984.
5. Oakland, John, *Statistical Process Control: A Practical Guide*, Heinemann, 1986.
6. Hutchins, David, *Just in Time*, Gower, 1989.

Chapter 10

Problem-Solving Methods

Common sense is the most widely shared commodity in the world, for every man is convinced that he is well supplied with it.

– Descartes

Route-map

This chapter is devoted to some of the modern problem-solving techniques that are now in general use. It attempts to provide useful summaries, rather than give definitive interpretations of these methods.

It reviews:

- Aural communication methods
- Visual communication methods
- Brain-storming
- Pareto analysis
- Cause and Effect diagrams
- Quality Circles
- Process improvement groups

Problem-solving techniques

The theme of this chapter is the harnessing of the intelligence, enthusiasm and ingenuity to be found in any group of well managed people. Nearly all the resources necessary to solve problems are to be found within the people nearest and most involved with the host processes. In many companies, most of this wealth of talent and experience is left untapped. The constant pressure to perform to targets, unobtainable with processes that are 'incapable' and 'out of control', leaves little time to identify, let alone *solve* any real problems.

As with so much of industry, it is the lack of human understanding and commitment that denies the benefit of the methods. By endlessly ploughing more effort into processes not fully understood, there are no resources available to improve the situation. Thus, the processes fail to improve, calling for even greater panic measures to keep them running.

The only sensible way forward is to break this cycle. This will require investment. Sufficient human resources must be provided to enable some of the process failures to be properly investigated, the causes identified, remedial action taken, and research carried out to provide a safe means of averting any recurrence of the process failure, *ever again.*

Some Definitions

A problem	-	A process failure. It is important that the problem is seen to inhabit the active process, rather than the result of the process. As such, all problems lie within the various process inputs.
A failure	-	An inability to produce the desired Quality level. All failures should be considered either process failures or design failures.
Process failure	-	Some aspect of the process that produces unacceptable results. It is not necessarily a breakdown, or even lost work.
Design failure	-	A failure attributed to an inherent design fault. As such, its occurrence should be considered as inevitable until a design change has been accomplished.
Human failure	-	An unhelpful excuse, more concerned with re-allocating blame than with problem-solving. The human input is but one aspect of the process. The concentration on human failure by-passes any proper consideration of the whole process. Identifying human failure is an extremely expensive exercise.

A solution	-	A combination of all the following: 1. An understanding of the cause. 2. Remedial action. 3. Preventative action to ensure no recurrence of the failure.
A problem fix	-	Action sufficient to obtain a temporary solution, but not to prevent a recurrence.
A process	-	The active combination of the inputs from the six overlapping areas described as: ● Manpower – team of people involved. ● Machine – plant and equipment. ● Materials – that which is being changed. ● Methods – skills and methodology used. ● Measurement – of process performance. ● Milieu – the process environment.
Control	-	The degree to which the process inputs are known, stable and predictable.
Prevention	-	The virtual elimination of the causes of a problem.
Detection	-	Ensuring that a defect in a process will be found prior to the resultant defect leaving the process area.
A cause	-	An input to a process, ie. a cause is a condition or action that is present or takes place *prior to* or during the process.
An effect	-	The result of a process, ie. an effect is the condition resulting from the combination of a set of process inputs.

Clear thinking required

In many companies, problem-solving is considered as a peripheral area, requiring few resources and little expertise. As a result, there are many misconceptions. Many people believe that they spend a considerable proportion of their time solving problems. On closer examination, they prove to be only fixing them, indeed they claim to be constantly solving the *same* problems.

Some actually feel a pride in this activity. They are the trouble-shooters of industry. They are typified by the energetic person who always arrives early, leaves late, but never manages to keep an appointment on time. His in-tray is overflowing, since mere paper-work has a lower priority than his vital shopfloor activity. He is considered, by himself and others, as the only person who can solve production problems. He hurtles round the factory, getting it moving again. He develops great experience of all these recurrent problems, and can be relied upon to give the necessary quick fix. Unfortunately, he is usually well thought of, and promoted, to play the same game at a higher level. In reality, he is the antipathy of a problem-solver. His familiarity with the numerous problems, gives evidence that he rarely solves *any* problem. He knows nothing of the underlying causes, and has a vested interest in the continued chaos. In many ways, he is the problem!

Even more frightening is the computerised problem-solver. A recent multi-million pound investment in the steel industry purchased a horizontal caster. This new technology was born in Sheffield, starved of investment in Westminster, developed in Japan, and installed in South Wales. It arrived from Japan, complete with a computerised problem-solving ability. This appeared to be a splendid idea. In fact, it was most dangerous. It suggested that all problem-solving activities could be handled by the computer. When the process fails, the computer identifies the symptoms, and recommends a cure. The computer, though, is unable to recommend any preventative work, and so the symptoms will regularly recur.

The computer removes the essential input of the human brain, and keeps people from ever seeking the real underlying causes. They become content with the symptoms. If the work has been done to identify the potential causes of failure, it would seem logical to match it with effort in eliminating these causes. If the potential causes have not been identified, the computer can do no more than act as an alarm. As such, its recommended action will be in the realms of a fix, rather than a solution.

Essentials for problem-solving

The following list is meant to give guidance to those seriously intending to make good use of their human resources.

- People
  The solutions to problems lie only in the minds of people. Any one individual probably doesn't have the whole solution, since it would have been made public if it were that obvious. Probably the most able minds are those belonging to process experts, that is those who control the processes, all day and every day, the operators.

- Skills
  Problem-solving needs the professional input of someone trained in the techniques of inter-personal communication. Problem-solving techniques are also necessary skills for the maximisation of the time devoted to problem-solving.

- Time
  Any activity takes time. If an activity is valuable to the company, it should not be considered as additional, peripheral, a luxury or a part-time activity. Problem-solving activities are part of the production process. Time will have to be made for them during the normal organisation of the day.

Fig 10.1 Essentials for problem-solving.

- Place

  Often, work places were not designed and built with any provision for a regular interchange of ideas between people. Suitable sites for group activity will have to be established.

- Resource

  The minimum requirements for such a group meeting place will be: tables, chairs, wall/pin board, flip chart and pens, and an overhead projector and screen. These will all be well used in the future, and are but a minimal investment for the increased productive capacity resulting from process improvement.

Aural communication methods

Almost every problem-solving initiative will involve teams or groups of people sharing opinions, and discussing and developing ideas. It is of the utmost importance that such interchanges are conducted in a professional and effective manner. There are, today, many techniques that are helpful.

1. A trained discussion leader

   The usual method of conducting a meeting, with the most senior person present taking the chair, is extremely limiting. Such leaders influence unduly the type and scope of the problem as perceived by the other group members. The initial interpretation and assessment of the problem by the senior people present will define it in the eyes of the rest of the group. They are also likely to have strong opinions concerning the problem, and thus will wish to participate in the discussion. This will be difficult without any contribution appearing to be the 'company' viewpoint.

   It is impossible to lead a discussion effectively whilst taking part in it. The style is different. The leader will need to be listening for new ideas, keeping the discussion on a logical track, observing those who may have a contribution but are shy, whilst remembering points raised by others but not pursued. All of this is a full-time task, and should not be diluted by direct involvement in the discussion.

The senior person will be able to make a more significant contribution as an ordinary member of the group. The discussion is best led by a trained group leader.

2. Clearly stated objectives

   Many discussions suffer through incomplete or muddled objectives. It is vital that each member of the group appreciates the nature of the problem, the resources at hand, the objective of the group and the aim of a particular meeting. None of these can be taken for granted. All are essential.

3. The right skills present

   In most discussions concerning Quality, a range of skills and expertise is required. If the discussion is process-based, and this is generally the most productive type of discussion, it will be essential to have the process experts present. Usually, these will be the people who operate and/or control the process.

   The range of additional skills needed may include engineering, planning, design and accountancy. The latter is most important, allowing improvements to be properly costed.

Fig 10.2 Aural communications.

Visual communication methods

Probably the most significant move forward in discussion methods in recent years has been the adoption of visual methods of communication.

The most effective of these, uses cards and felt-tip pens, allowing everyone to communicate on an equal footing. Ideas thus presented can be grouped on a pin-board, moved, discussed and rearranged. Various strains of opinion, ideas and values emerge from a discussion that takes place visually before everyone's eyes. Ideas cannot be overlooked or forgotten. They come into the public domain, dissociated from the original proponent and, therefore, separated from any prejudice or animosity that may be felt between group members.

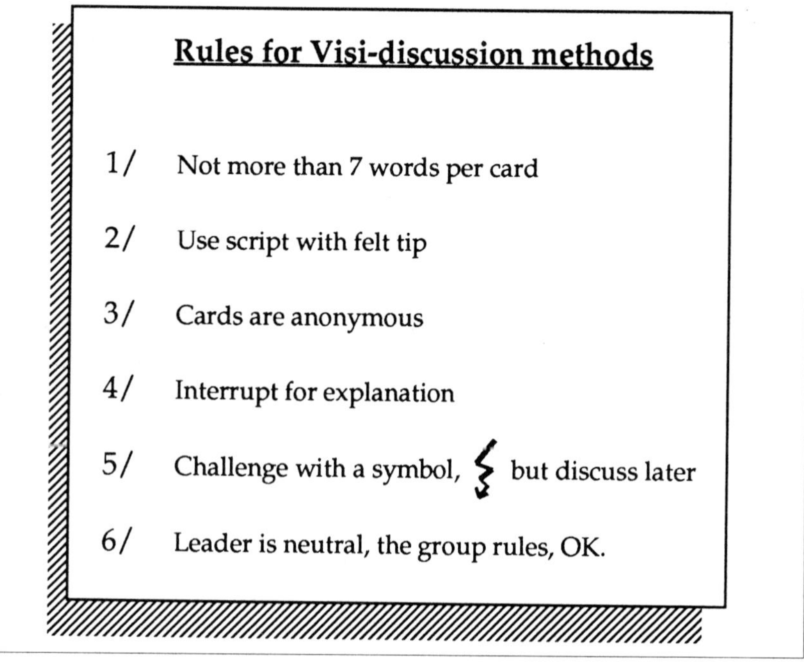

Fig 10.3 Rules for visi-discussion methods.

Flexibility is the key to this method of organising and running a discussion group. It is quick, efficient and always leads to the heart of the matter. By grouping ideas and comments, concepts appear as more than the few words in which they are written. The method promotes conciliation rather than confrontation, and leads discussions on a convergent course, rather than the divergent one followed by many discussions held in the traditional method.

Poor packaging causes damage in transit

Fig 10.4 Example of thoughts on a card.

The final state of the pin-board represents the discussion, and the cards can be glued in position on the backing sheet, which can then be retained as a record of the meeting. Alternatively, a photograph, Polaroid or otherwise, of the finished sheets, can be duplicated to provide the minutes of the meeting.

Resources

The visible characteristics of this method of problem-solving are the use of large sheets of brown paper, coloured cards, adhesive dots, felt pens and pin-boards. These tools allow individual views to be visible to everyone.

Such interactional situations need professional leadership, able to stimulate simultaneous responses in all the participants. Well led by a neutral group facilitator, the group clarifies contradictions, interprets unexpected events, formulates new questions and develops insight and a deeper awareness of the problem and potential solution.

These ideas are used widely within Europe. Possibly the best exponent is Metaplan of Quickborn, West Germany (see Fig 10.6).[2]

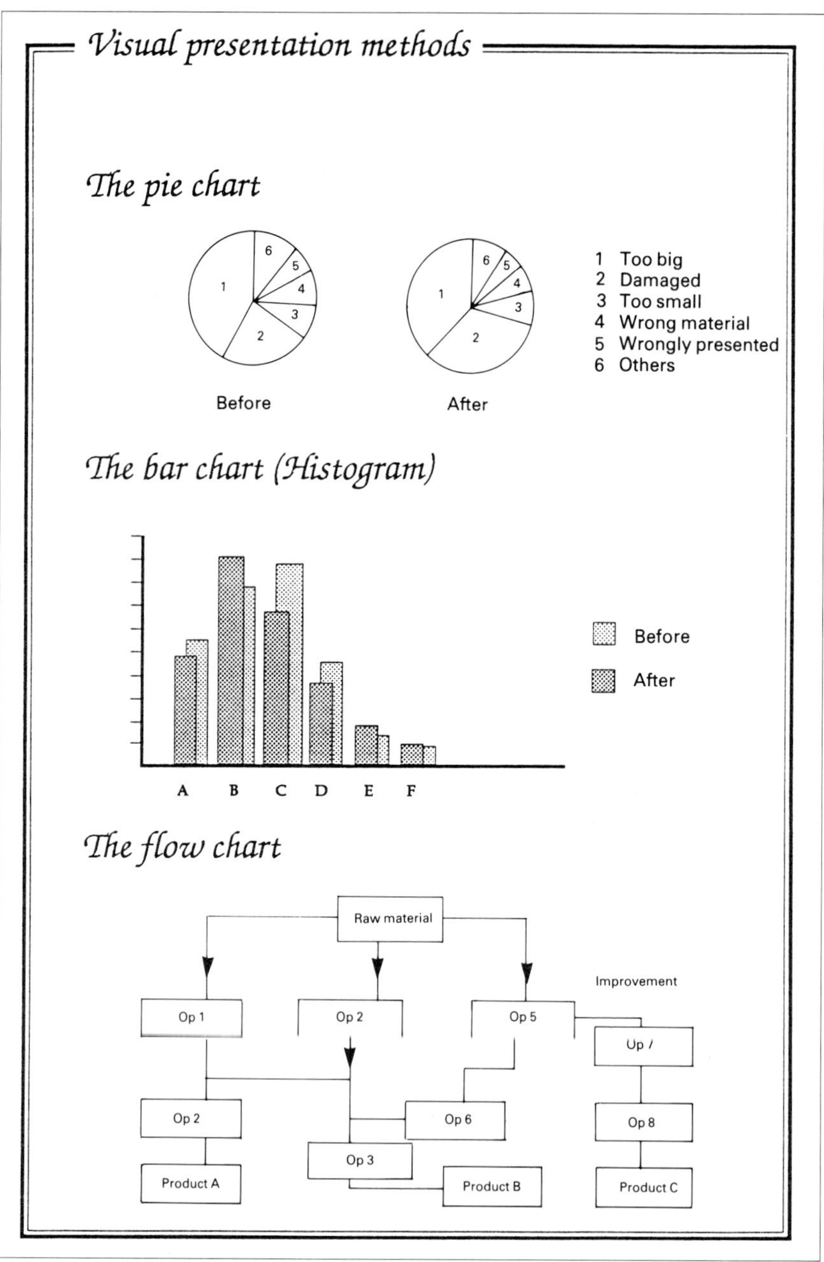

Fig 10.5 Visual presentation methods.

Fig 10.6 Example of Metaplan.

Neutral presentation

The value of all the ideas presented above can be lost if they are not presented well to the decision maker. It should not be taken for granted that the group has the skills to communicate the results of the meeting to those outside the group. Neither a verbal impression of the meeting by a representative of the group, nor a closely typed three page report, will inspire confidence and the action that the meeting deserves.

The final presentation needs to be balanced. It needs to be neutral, presenting the arguments for a certain course of action in logical steps, from the problem to the proposed solution. If it appears to be propaganda, or hiding certain aspects not favourable to the case, it will be flawed, and lack credibility.

Again, visual presentations will be easier to assimilate than those based on words. These aspects will be important even before the group meets, and should be included in the consideration of the members of the group, resources and the education of some or all of its members.

Brain-storming

There are many variations of this method of discussion in use today. Some are good, and others lack a theoretical base. Many are used by untrained and unskilled practitioners who fail to appreciate the potential value of the method.

The aim of a brain-storming session is to empty the minds of everyone in the group into a common pool. This isn't a definitive, once-and-for-all exercise – speak now or forever hold thy tongue. More, it is the starting point for a discussion. There are certain basic steps that are important if the bounds of the discussion are not to be drawn too tightly, and if some of the more unlikely and unusual thoughts are not to be lost.

1. No pre-definition of the problem

   Any words spoken about the problem before the session will limit the scope of the subsequent discussion. By talking about the problem in a particular manner, the speaker will define both the problem and the likely areas of a solution. This will prohibit some of the group from voicing thoughts, ideas and suggestions that fall outside this basic understanding. However, the optimum solution to a problem often comes from way outside the usual range of stock answers. Indeed, it is often fair to assume that the usual solutions have already been tried and found to be less than fully effectual.

   It will be impossible to create a totally neutral environment in which all ideas have equal credence, since most of the group members are likely to have experience of the problem prior to the meeting. However, the first few minutes of a meeting, whilst minds are fresh, are the most powerful. Keeping minds open, without limiting suggestions, is essential in such situations. After all, the far reaches of people's minds are sought.

2. Paper and pencil

   Any words spoken at this time may have the consequences described above. The medium for the transference of ideas must, therefore, be paper.

   A rough half sheet of paper is likely to inspire less awe than a virgin white A4 sheet and will thus produce more ideas.

   Pens and pencils need to be available so that the transfer of thoughts is not inhibited.

3. Reassurance

   Many people develop instant anxiety complexes when asked to put pen to paper publicly. They will need the constant assurance that no one will need to read the writing of others. This will overcome many people's natural fear of appearing unable to write neatly, spell correctly or even use the right words.

4. Notes only

   People should be encouraged to write down thoughts in note form, otherwise they begin to write essays. The thought that any idea can be expressed in less than seven words may help. Often, single words express the concern or idea in the mind of the group member.

5. Time pressure

   Emptying people's minds in this way takes only a few minutes. If the group is given a very short time to accomplish this, say five minutes, it will instantly start thinking and writing rapidly. Do not stick rigidly to any time-span, however, as the aim is to maximise the number of thoughts, rather than fill a certain number of minutes. The period should be kept going as long as ideas are flowing, but keep up the pressure! Indeed, the group should be asked at the end to add more ideas, should it think of any.

6. Collection

   Probably the best way of collecting the ideas is to go around the group, listening to one idea from each member. These are collected centrally, placing them in the 'public domain', disconnected from the proposer.

   When the same idea is put forward by more than one person, the group should listen to it again. The different form of words assists in defining the concept, and enlarges the perception of the idea. As the ideas peter out, group members will 'pass' their turn, until eventually everyone has contributed his maximum to the collection.

   The ideas may be grouped, as they are collected, so that an overall pattern begins to emerge.

   More and different thoughts are always welcome, even after the general collection appears complete.

Possible causes of scrap items

too small
too big
scratched
wrong material
poor finish
burrs
damaged in tray
missing parts
damaged thread
damaged in transit
scuffs
too soft
inside bore
holes not central
screws missing
missed thread
....

Fig 10.7 Ideas collected from group.

7. Discussion

   It should be explained at the start that discussion falls into two categories. Anyone not understanding what has been said, or seeking clarification, should interrupt immediately and seek clarification.

   Otherwise, all discussion should be held back until the collection stage has been completed. It will be important for the leader to maintain a flow of ideas. Discussion during the collection stage will stop such a flow. This may not be easy, and calls for the skill of a trained leader.

   This method will usually produce an average of about six ideas per group member. Obviously, the more conventional thoughts will be supplied by several people. Experience shows that for small groups, over half the overall number of ideas are original and separate. For larger groups, this usually drops to about one third. Thus, a group of six could be expected to produce over 20 separate thoughts, ideas or suggestions, whereas a group of 15 might create over 30 such ideas.

Once the collection stage has been completed, discussion can take place in the usual way. However, it will be vital to keep the collection lists, or

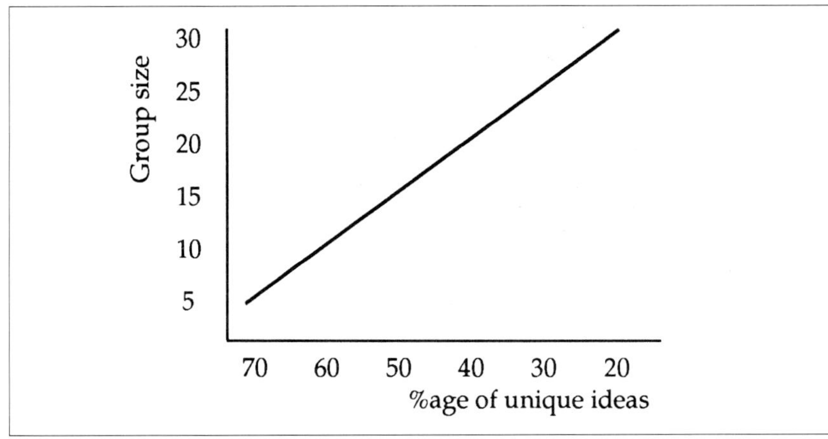

Fig 10.8 Table showing expected responses from group.

diagrams, in full display throughout the discussion. In this manner, unusual ideas and suggestions from the collection can be re-introduced to the debate.

Pareto analysis

Vilfredo Pareto was an Italian economist during the later part of the nineteenth century. He is mainly remembered for his 80/20 rule (sometimes referred to as Pareto's Law). It is said that he first discovered that over 80% of Italian wealth was in the hands of 20% of the people. He then extended this to suggest that there is an 80%/20% conjunction with many related quantities and in many situations.

80/20 rule

This rule, within industry, is usually born out by examining the Quality costs stemming from problems. Eighty percent of the costs come from 20% of the problems. Whilst this cannot always be true, it is a good starting point. It focuses the mind onto the problem areas that are costing the company the most.

Another aspect of Pareto's work was his problem analysis. The principle is quite straightforward and easy to understand.

1. Identify the areas within which problems fall.
2. Assess the frequency that they occur.
3. Calculate each frequency as a percentage of the total.
4. Order the results from the largest percentage to the smallest.
5. Draw these results as a bar-chart.

An example

Consider the situation occurring in a joinery workshop, making window frames. Of 2,378 frames made in a week, 150 were found to be unacceptable. The various reasons were examined and causes identified.

Cause	*Examples*	*Frequency*	*%age*
Material warped	///	3	2.0%
Material oversize	//////////	10	6.7%
Material undersize	////////////	12	8.0%
Material split	//////////////// //////////////// //////////////// //////////	54	36.0%
Exposed knots	//////	6	4.0%
Excess glue	//////////////// ////////////	27	18.0%
Loose joint	//////	6	4.0%
Rough surface	//////////////// ///	18	12.0%
Tight joint	///	3	2.0%
Fitment misplaced	/////////	9	6.0%
Fitment missing	//	2	1.3%

When ordered, largest to smallest, the results become:

Cause	*% occurrence*
Material split	36.0%
Excess glue	18.0%
Rough surface	12.0%
Material undersize	8.0%
Material oversize	6.7%
Fitment misplaced	6.0%
Loose joint	4.0%
Exposed knots	4.0%
Material warped	2.0%
Tight joint	2.0%
Fitment missing	1.3%

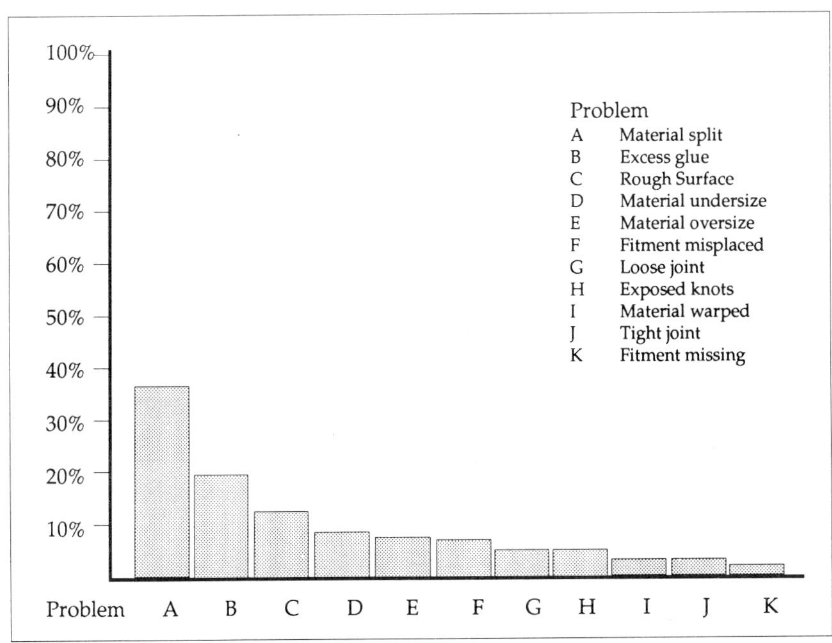

Fig 10.9 Pareto 1.

However, these figures do not represent the true cost of these failures.

Cause	*Remedial Action*	*Cost/item*	*Cost*	*%cost*
Material split	Fill and smooth	£50	£2700	20.9%
Excess glue	Clean off	£20	£540	4.2%
Rough surface	Smooth	£50	£900	7.0%
Material undersize	Scrap	£450	£5400	41.8%
Exposed knots	Fill and smooth	£50	£300	2.3%
Material oversize	Plane by hand	£75	£750	5.8%
Fitment misplaced	Realign, repair	£75	£675	5.2%
Loose joint	Reseal	£50	£300	2.3%
Material warped	Scrap	£450	£1350	10.4%
Tight joint	No action	£0	£0	0%
Fitment missing	Return to fit	£5	£10	0.1%

These results are now ordered as before. The percentages are added, to give an accumulated percentage.

Cause	*Remedial Action*	*Percentage cost*	*Accumulated %*
Material undersize	Scrap	41.8%	41.8%
Material split	Fill and smooth	20.9%	62.7%
Material warped	Scrap	10.4%	73.1%
Rough surface	Smooth	7.0%	80.1%
Material oversize	Plane by hand	5.8%	85.9%
Fitment misplaced	Realign, repair	5.2%	91.1%
Excess glue	Clean off	4.2%	95.3%
Exposed knots	Fill and smooth	2.3%	97.6%
Loose joint	Reseal	2.3%	99.9%
Fitment missing	Return to fit	0.1%	100.0%
Tight joint	No action	0%	100.0%

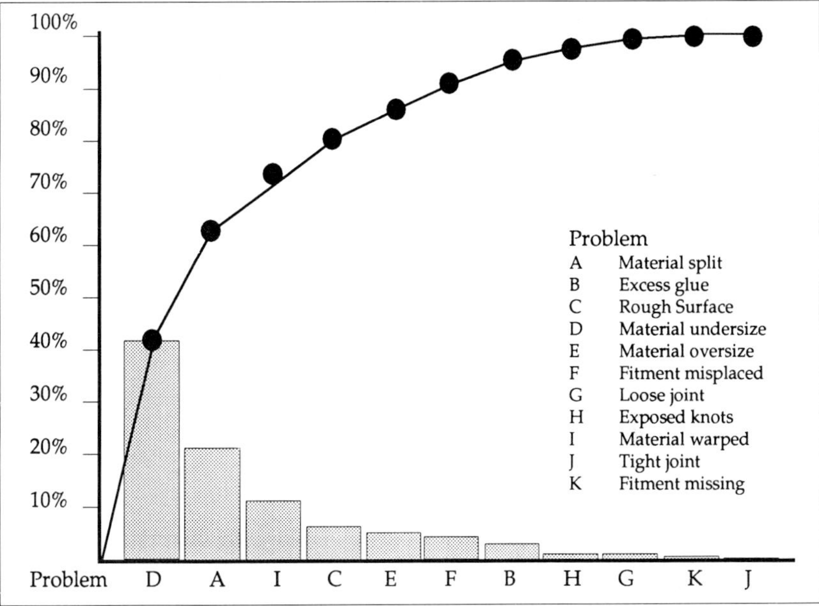

Fig 10.10 Pareto 2.

The accumulated curve allows an assessment of which problems are costing how much money. You will see that the accumulation of the four most costly causes is costing approximately 80% (78.9%) of the overall total (£13,105).

This is over £10,000 per week. Thus, it will be sensible to attempt process improvements to eliminate these causes.

- Previously, there were so few cases of warped material that no-one considered it worth while bothering. Now that the true cost can be seen, such material will be removed prior to machining and returned to the supplier at nil cost to the company. The supplying company will be asked to ensure that such material will not be supplied in future.

- All material dimensions are to be checked prior to assembly. Undersized material will be rejected, incurring a nominal cost of £5 per item.

- The splits occur during machining, and whilst inspection can remove an estimated 50% of these prior to manufacture (scrap cost of £5 per item), remedial work will have to continue on the other 50% (£50 per item).

- Careful monitoring of the tools during manufacture will change and tools will be sharpened as and when required, rather than on a time basis. It is estimated that 90% of rough work will be eliminated.

The results for a later week were different.

Cause	*Remedial Action*	*Cost/item*	*Cost*	*%cost*
Material split	Fill and smooth	£50	£1485	32.9%
Excess glue	Clean off	£20	£540	12.0%
Rough surface	Smooth	£50	£100	2.2%
Material undersize	Scrap	£5	£60	1.3%
Exposed knots	Fill and smooth	£50	£600	13.3%
Material oversize	Plane by hand	£75	£750	16.6%
Fitment misplaced	Realign, repair	£75	£675	14.9%
Loose joint	Reseal	£50	£300	6.6%
Material warped	Scrap	£450	£0	0%
Tight joint	No action	£0	£0	0%
Fitment missing	Return to fit	£5	£10	0.2%

Cause	*Remedial Action*	*Percentage cost*	*Accumulated %*
Material split	Fill and smooth	32.9%	32.9%
Material oversize	Plane by hand	16.6%	49.5%
Fitment misplaced	Realign, repair	14.9%	64.4%
Exposed knots	Fill and smooth	13.3%	77.7%
Excess glue	Clean off	12.0%	89.7%
Loose joint	Reseal	6.6%	96.3%
Rough surface	Smooth	2.2%	98.5%
Material undersize	Scrap	1.3%	99.8%
Fitment missing	Return to fit	0.2%	100.0%
Material warped	Scrap	0%	100.0%
Tight joint	No action	0%	100.0%

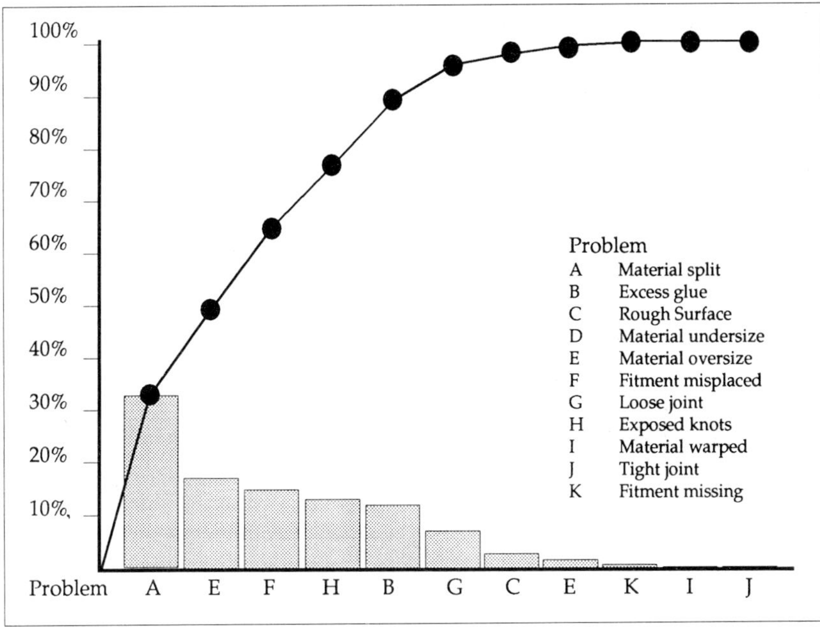

Fig 10.11 Pareto 3.

The overall costs in this example have now been reduced to £4520 per week, from £12925 (nearly a two thirds reduction). Whilst the more sceptical readers may have doubts about the ability to achieve such a large reduction, the example demonstrates that large reductions in Quality costs can be achieved by directing the resources and effort of the company to the priority areas, as defined by the Pareto analysis.

The Pareto curve in Fig 10.11 differs from that in Fig 10.10 in that it is flatter. All Pareto curves will have the same start and finishing points. The degree of curvature between these points is an indication of the control exercised in the process areas. As the major causes of Quality cost are improved, the more minor areas grow in significance. This will be demonstrated by their higher percentage values.

Constant process improvement will be demonstrated by the Pareto curve becoming nearer to a straight line (see Fig 10.12)

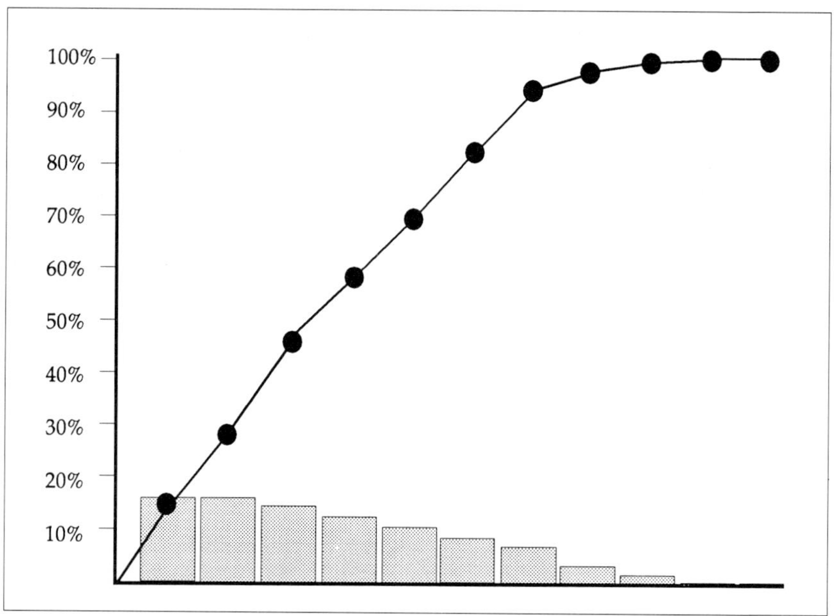

Fig 10.12 Pareto demonstrating process improvement.

The Pareto diagrams are an excellent way of presenting data. The full value of this as a standard means of communication within the company, can only be achieved through company-wide education in the techniques and interpretation of Pareto analysis.

Cause and Effect diagrams

These diagrams are also called 'Ishikawa diagrams', after Kaoru Ishikawa, and 'fishbone diagrams' after their shape (see Fig 10.15).

Whilst some people have attempted to develop the ideas behind the diagrams into a quasi-science, it is more helpful to appreciate the ideas and theories involved, and adapt them to a particular situation. In the author's view, there is not a 'right' way to use this or any other Quality theory or method. The way to make genuine improvement, in any company, is to develop the maximum understanding of the people and processes involved, so that the improvements that can and should be made, become obvious.

What is a cause? What is an effect?

The most useful idea to spring from Kaoru Ishikawa's[3] work in this area, is the identification of causes and their effects. For many people this is a very muddled area. They are far too ready to attribute the name of 'cause', to what is actually an effect. The way to clarity of thought, with regard to causes and effects, is to *think process*.

A cause is an input to a process. It is a condition or action that is present or takes place, *prior* to or during the process.

An effect is the *result* of a process. It is the condition resulting from the combination of a set of process inputs, *after* the process (see Fig 10.13).

Of course, no industrial operations are this simple. Each process will relate directly to another. Every company is a vast network of inter-related processes. The effect of one process becomes an input to another process (see Fig 10.14).

The result of one process will almost certainly become the input of another process. An effect of process A, therefore, becomes a cause of process B.

In the optimum situation, with each of these processes tightly controlled, the causes are all calculated, understood and predictable, so that the effects are all planned, desirable and within acceptable standards. The only difference between the effects that are deemed to be problems, and those that are acceptable as an everyday event, is the desirability of the result. In Quality terms, though, it is the process inputs that have changed, from the desirable to the undesirable state.

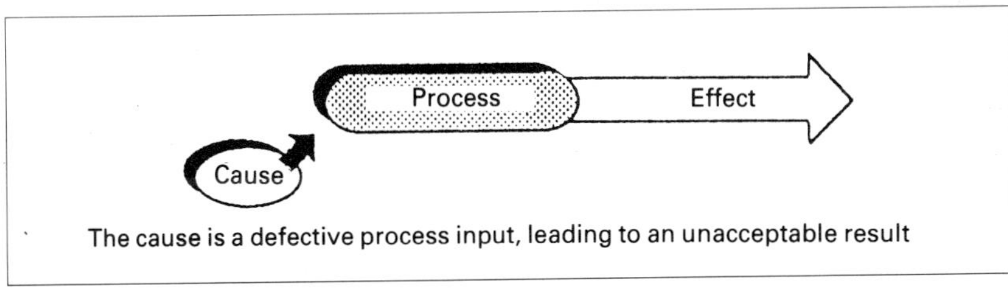

Fig 10.13 Cause – process – effect.

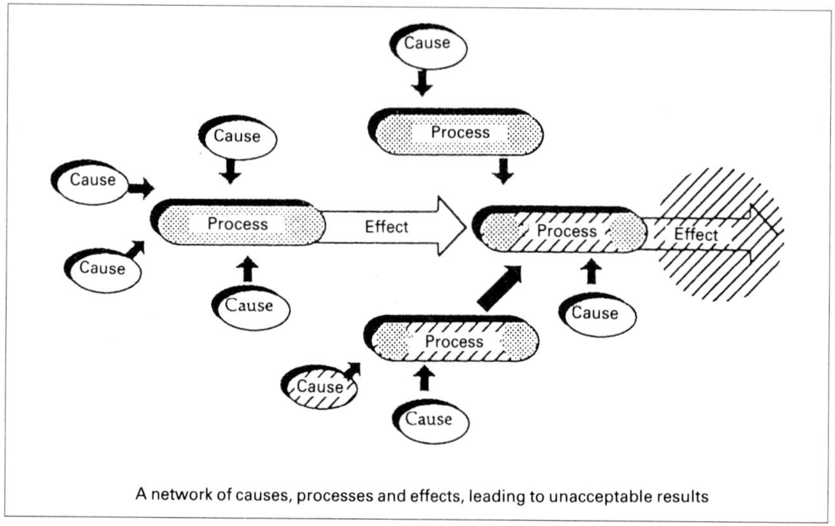

Fig 10.14 Network of cause – process – effect.

A study of the effects when the process is *in* control is useful because:

- It provides a better understanding of the operation of the process.
- It increases the knowledge of the process input, for the subsequent processes.
- It may provide the only means of on-going measurement of process performance. Note: such a measurement will always be of less value than real process input measurement.

A study of the effects when the process is *out* of control is more useful because:

- It allows remedial action to be taken to mitigate or correct the results of the problem.
- It may assist in the investigation of the cause of the problem.
- It can provide an appreciation of the cost of Quality, thus enabling resources to be provided for improvement of the process.

The most important area for investigation is always the cause. In an 'in control' situation, this can be termed 'understanding the process inputs'. It requires on-going, live measurement data, so that the abnormal situation can be identified. Such investigation should be an everyday activity.

Where this is the case, the identification and investigation of the cause of a problem will be very much easier than where such data doesn't exist.

The study of the cause of a problem will very often reveal that *cause* to be the *result,* that is the effect of a previous process. The investigation becomes one of chasing backwards through the chain of causes and effects to establish the root cause. This root cause of the problem will be the point at which an uncontrolled situation or action actually initiated the chain of events leading to the problem. In practice, this chain becomes a network of inter-related chains, with each process being influenced by the results of several others. The Cause and Effect diagram is used in an attempt to understand this network, and keep control of the cause and effect chains.

Fig 10.15 depicts the process, with several causes leading to an effect. The causes are shown as straight lines at an angle to the process.

By now considering each cause separately, and treating it as an effect, it is possible to identify further causes. This process is repeated in each area, building up the network of causes and effects. This network will reflect the process network that is in daily operation. Many are surprised by this revelation, since they had previously only considered manufacturing processes as part of the chain. There are usually more human-based processes than machine-based processes, and some of these will be occurring beyond the factory walls.

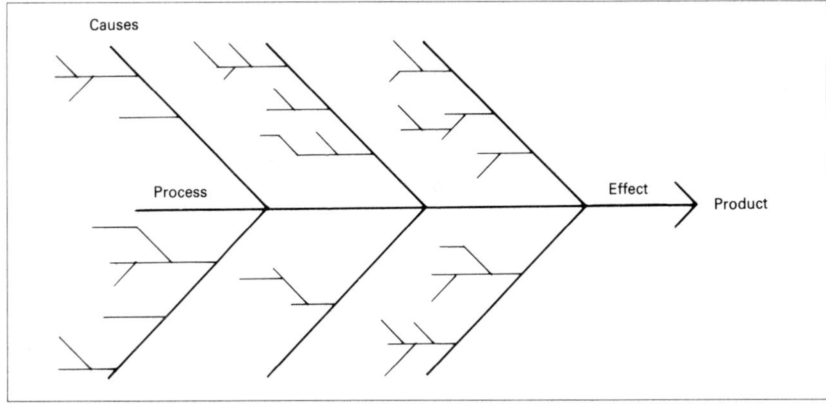

Fig 10.15 Basic Cause and Effect diagram.

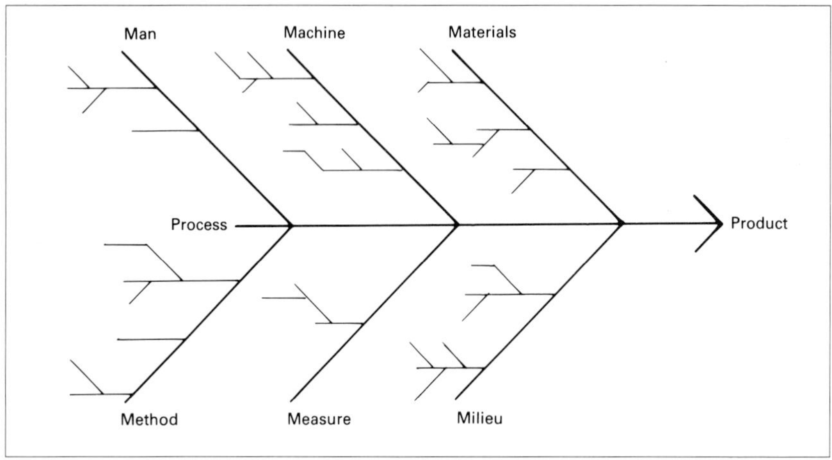

Fig 10.16 Cause and Effect diagram based on process inputs.

Each part of the network is investigated, that is each chain is pursued until:

- It becomes obvious that all the process inputs are completely in control and, therefore, not the root of the problem.
- The chain becomes circular, and leads back into an area previously investigated.
- The root cause, or causes, are identified.

The diagram can be used to identify different aspects of the problem-solving process, or to illustrate the actions being taken during a process improvement initiative. It must be remembered that there is no right way to use these diagrams. It is their very adaptability that makes them

Idea

Treat every cause as an effect, and seek other possible 'causes'.

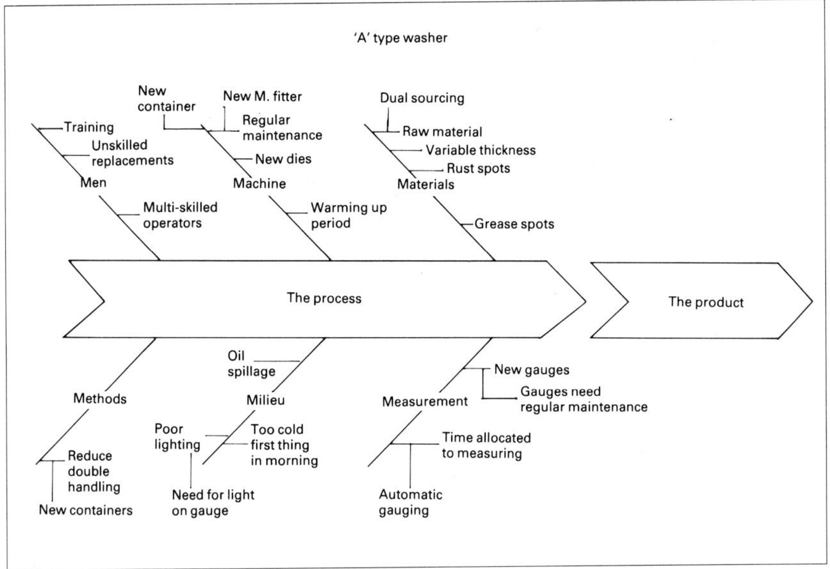

Fig 10.17 Cause and Effect diagram in use.

so useful in the commercial and industrial setting. Such use, however, will be dependent on their appreciation and interpretation being common knowledge to all areas of the company. Once again, company-wide education will be essential if the full value is to be obtained from using process improvement methods.

Quality Circles

In the words of Ishikawa,

> *'Only when foremen and line workers assume responsibility for process, can Quality Control become successful.*
> *Where there are no Quality Control Circle activities, there can be no Total Quality Control activities.'*

The use of Quality Circles was one of the most publicised aspects of Japanese management during the early 1980s. Unfortunately, in the UK many senior managers were more anxious to be *seen* to be producing Quality, than actually to develop a Quality culture. Many companies attempted Quality Circles in an isolated manner, as if Quality methods could be taken off-the-shelf. The following all led to a situation in which Quality Circles were doomed from the start:

- A lack of appreciation of the totality necessary for Quality methods to be valuable.
- The absence of any real commitment on the part of managers to change the fundamental organisation of the company.
- Too many 'out of control' processes.

There may be a rebirth of Quality Circles, however, now that Quality management is being seen as synonymous with process management, and indeed company management.

As with all Quality methods, a definitive science of Quality Circles is unhelpful. The ideas should be adapted to local need. Those involved should appreciate the common needs and circumstances that lead to the valuable contribution of such groups, whatever they are called.

What is a Quality Circle?

Simply, Quality Circles bring together those involved with a particular process to identify, analyse and solve job-related problems.[4]

In a very real sense, it is the development of 'ownership' of the problems by the people who are closest to them, that makes the Quality Circle a natural extension to the attitudes and ideas expressed throughout this book. It is the essential relationship with the process, and its results, that has identified the difference between the Japanese worker and his occidental counterpart during the last two decades.

The Quality Circle fuses the hard knowledge of the process experts, the people directly concerned with the process, with the soft knowledge in the hands of managers, engineers and designers. It represents a meeting of minds, to pursue the company objective of process improvement.

Positive or negative?

Some companies operate Quality Circles in a negative form, by introducing them only when there is a problem. Such circles tend to be concerned more with the abnormal, and concentrate on the amelioration of the undesirable effects and the detection or removal of the problem.

A more positive use of Quality Circles is to orientate them towards the process. In this way, the Quality Circle becomes a permanent group concerned to improve the process. This gives it an on-going purpose, regardless of the presence, or otherwise, of a particular problem. There is very often more to be learnt from the normal operation of the process, than from the extraordinary occurrence that may or may not lead to a problem. Indeed, by tightly controlling each process input, problems will be perceived within a process input that does not give rise, at the moment, to any unacceptable results from the process. However, by removing such problems, the process becomes more tightly controlled. More consistent results are produced more cost effectively. Through this greater consistency, the control of subsequent processes is increased.

Essentials of a Quality Circle

These are reviewed below, under the same headings identified earlier in this chapter, as being necessary for problem-solving. This is quite deliberate and aims to reinforce the normality of such groups meeting. It is far better that the Quality Circle is seen as a natural development of the drive towards Quality, rather than as a brain-child of an enlightened senior manager.

- People
  The team involved with the process, including management, engineering, and any other department that may have a bearing on the process inputs to be discussed. The usual discussion about whether membership of the circle should be voluntary or not, is irrelevant. All the people described above will be essential, and it should be assumed that they will all see such participation as an aspect of their job.

- Skills
  The leadership of the Quality Circle will require the professional input of someone trained in the techniques of inter-personal communication and the operation of Quality Circles. The provision of such skills will be an investment worth making in any company, since the time and money saved by an efficient Quality Circle operation will be considerable.

- Time

  Quality Circles should not be considered as a peripheral activity of the company. It should be seen as an essential piece of process management. Clearly, then, the Quality Circle should meet during normal working time.

- Place

  It is sometimes helpful for the Quality Circle to be in the process area. More often, though, the distractions present, outweigh any advantages. People are more at ease, both physically and mentally, in an environment designed for interaction.

- Resource

  All the resources listed under this heading in the section on communications, at the beginning of this chapter, will be needed. The circle will also need access to costing data, to allow it to assess the value of any proposed improvements.

Stages in Quality Circle organisation

Stage 1. Identification

The process to be improved needs to be identified, and the nature of the problems defined. Early in the life of a Quality Circle, there may well be a multitude of problems. Initially, then, the Quality Circle will be concerned with analysing the process, using the Pareto techniques described earlier, to prioritise the problems. All the circle should be involved with this analysis, so that they have the background to be able to evaluate all the future work of the circle.

Stage 2. Evaluation

The potential causes of the problem are investigated, and the process inputs that are out of control should be identified.

Data should be collected to extend the knowledge and understanding of the problem and its causes. If past data exists, it too should be reviewed to look for past trends.

Stage 3. Solution

Each aspect of the process (the 6Ms) should be investigated, and the optimum solution arrived at. Again, the involvement of all the circle will be essential. The best solution should be tested and costed.

Stage 4. Presentation

Plan and prepare the presentation to senior management, or whoever will be the decision-maker regarding the recommended process improvements. This presentation should include visual aids, and the full argument, complete with costings to demonstrate the benefits to be expected from the process improvements.

Stage 5. Implementation

The improvements should be implemented, and the results monitored and reviewed. The involvement of the rest of the company can be achieved by broadcasting the results of this and other process improvements.

Process improvement groups

There are now many names, acronyms and abbreviations, representing various groupings of people engaged in process improvement. This is as it should be. Such groups will thrive best where they are a natural manifestation of the company culture. They, quite rightly, should be an integrated activity within the company. They should be low key, essential, and yet unremarkable.

For many, the 'coming of age' of Quality ideals is represented by the movement away from the off-the-shelf items, the standard Quality methods, and the Japanese imitations. The movement represents an appreciation of the true nature of Quality, a deep realisation of the value of the company's personnel, and the logical progression of ideas, flowing from managers who know what they have to achieve.

Their concentration on the process is logical and profitable. It is, after all, only the active inputs to the company's activities that can be controlled, and thus improved. The widening of the Quality consideration to include the cost of Quality and the conservation of resources is, again, quite logical.

There are no rules. Each company should develop its own culture and its own methodology. Each company has to be responsible for its own future, and that of its employees.

However, the following points can be considered as guide-lines for those seriously engaged in Quality improvement schemes:

- Base all such schemes firmly in sound theory.
- Integrate improvement schemes into the everyday activity of the company.
- Cost all improvements and the benefits achieved by the improvement schemes.
- Involve everybody.
- Call in outside experience when it is needed.
- Educate all personnel, so that the full benefit of their intellect, knowledge, skills and experience can be shared.
- Review improvements at regular intervals to ensure that the benefits are maintained.
- Make constant, never-ending improvement a way of life.
- Ensure that everyone feels a sense of value and satisfaction from his involvement.

Summary

Problem-solving techniques

Aural communication methods
Visual communication methods
Brain-storming
Pareto analysis
Cause and Effect diagrams
Quality Circles
Process improvement groups

Last thoughts ....

When asked, 'What's the best way to Skelleen?', the reply was 'This is not the best place to start from!' – Traditional Irish thought.

1. Quoted from Rene Descartes (1596-1650), *Discours de la Methode*.
2. Schnelle, Wolfgang, and Stoltz, Inga, *Interactional Learning*, Metaplan GmbH, 2085 Quickborn, West Germany, 1977.
3. Ishikawa, Kaoru, *What is Total Quality Control? – The Japanese Way*, translated by David J Lu, Prentice-Hall Inc, New Jersey, 1985.
4. For UK readers, the National Society of Quality Circles is able to provide assistance. They can be contacted at: 2 Castle Street, Salisbury, Wiltshire SP1 1BB (Tel: (0722) 26667).

Quality through People

A Blueprint for
Proactive Total Quality Management

Part IV

The Management of Resources

Chapter 11

Management of Resources

Wilful waste brings woeful want.

– Thomas Fuller (1654-1734)

Route-map

This chapter considers the orientation of a company to the generation and the conservation of wealth. Company operating costs are divided into production costs and Quality costs, and 'activity costing' is examined as a means of tracking the generation and expenditure of wealth.

Wealth generation

To many it is self-evident that the only purpose of industry and commerce is to generate wealth. This truth, and sense of realism, often becomes lost when involved with the daily dramas of the company. It is all too easy for other priorities to obscure this overall objective. Local aims, personal ambitions, department objectives and company traditions can all get in the way of a clear vision.

This apparent dissonance between the company good, and the individual good of the company employees, is a recurring theme of this book. It can only be resolved by understanding how business works, and why people exchange their time and energy for money. The thoughts in this chapter should be applied directly to the reader's own experience and present work situation.

What is the company here for?

Most company directors will have no problem associating the existence of the company with its wealth creation role. They devote a good part of their activities to predicting profit margins, calculating present levels of cash flow and turnover, and accounting for past financial performance of the company. For many, this is their vision of the company; they become embedded in financial details, and can lose sight of the human factors involved with the day to day administration of the company.

For most people employed by the company, however, this world is totally foreign. Indeed, they are only slightly aware of these financial machinations. They tend only to become involved in the middle of a crisis, when a partial picture of events is given to them. They are suspicious, since the only 'facts' given to them are usually devoid of any monetary information, and are presented to demonstrate that a certain course of action is inevitable. In short, the financial side of the business is shrouded in mist, and occupies a different plane to that of most employees. Their lives revolve around the product, or some other daily commodity. The typist may be concerned with the level of work in the in-tray, the maintenance engineer with keeping the machinery going, the operator with achieving the target, and so on. All are concerned with satisfying the perceived demands of their job.

Ask most people what is the main purpose of their company, and they will tell you it is to make a product, or give a service.

This is true of all companies, but even more so for the long established company. The definition of *long established* is that it existed before we were five. When we grow up seeing factory walls, certain products, certain brand names, as part of our childhood, they become enshrined in a world that has a certain permanence. A world that exists as part of the planet and universe, the known world. It becomes inconceivable that the world could exist without Ford cars, without HP sauce, without ....? The actual names and commodities that are entered here will reflect the age and place in which the reader grew up. The actual manifestation of this phenomena is not important. It embodies our desire to find measures of stability, continuity and security.

As such, we come to work with an assumed knowledge of permanence, maybe not in our job, but in the function of the company. In this sense we would like to view the world as static. The demand for the company's products and services will always be there. Added to this is most people's static perception of their job. They are labelled and described in such a way as to identify them with a particular function. A typist, a lathe operator, a driver, or whatever: these terms are all prescriptive, all explaining the existence of the person within the company.

This sense of company purpose is daily reinforced by pressures to perform in a particular way. These pressures are again linked directly to the label and perceived function of the individual. It is small wonder that most individuals are, at best, careless of the company's wealth generation role. They are denied access to real information about the company's performance, labelled to identify them with only limited aims, and then pressurised to achieve these limited aims. At worst, they perceive themselves in conflict with this wealth production role. For many, the company is perceived to be obtaining its wealth *from* them, rather than for them.

Morals

The discussion of morals, within any company, is often fraught with problems. The company, as a capitalist institution geared to the benefit of the shareholders, is seen by many as devoid of morals. The lack of clarity of definition in such discussions, often ensures misunderstanding, frustration and suspicion.

Everyone should question the moral values of the company. If senior managers are unsure, they should take steps to identify the moral values that underpin the company.

A definition of a moral company could be a company that will share its success with each of its employees and shareholders alike. A moral company will perceive its wealth generation to be for the mutual benefit of everyone involved with the company. A moral company will have amongst its goals, its long-term survival so that it can continue to generate wealth. This will be seen as only the beginning for many, who would want to add such phrases as respect for the environment, respect for the community, and respect for the individual. Nevertheless, the morals of the company must start from the main purpose of the company, which is to generate wealth.

Question your own company

1. Is the success of the company synonymous with the success of the individuals within the company ?
2. Will increased profits mean higher rewards for the employees?
3. Would increased productivity lead to a smaller workforce?
4. Does every employee have the opportunity for a long-term relationship, career improvement and fulfilled ambition within the company ?

These are important questions. They are not questions that should either be ducked or fudged. There could be a moral situation in which a company was formed, merely to meet short-term aims, and thus the eventual demise of the company was planned from its inception. In such circumstances, each employee will be aware of the lack a long-term future, and will seek recompense accordingly. All four of the above questions tie the future of the company to that of the individual employees.

The individual's future is tied to the company's

Rarely is this the case for everyone within the company. Obviously, it is true for the directors and shareholders. Success for these people will be measured in financial return on investment, in which they will have a stake.

Senior managers may be more secure. It is usually less true that middle and lower ranking managers have an assured future with the company, and the concept often has no relevance for the non-managerial members of the company. The workforce is viewed as a commodity to be switched off when not needed.

How then do we expect these people to work well for the company? How do we expect them to feel impelled to maximise the generation of wealth? How do we expect them to give fully of themselves? This separation of those playing a considerable part in wealth generation from the company organisation, inevitably will lead to conflicting aims, diverse priorities and an impairing of the company's chances of success.

The concept of a 'cradle to grave' commitment to employment is seen as a quirk of the Japanese, and one that they will not be able to honour. For those who perceive the workforce as an expandable and contractible commodity, it seems suicidal to saddle the company with mouths to feed, forever. Common sense, though, suggests otherwise. This commitment, and only this commitment, can guarantee a similar commitment from individual employees. 'Alright in theory, but impossible in a world of changing technology', is often the response.

By venting this answer, such managers and captains of industry express the same misunderstanding of the true purpose of industry, as the misguided employees who perceive the company function as tied to a particular product line.

An alternative viewpoint might suggest that the company function is to make money, and the only resources at the company's disposal are:

1. Capital investment.
2. Ideas and concepts unique to the company.
3. Skills and abilities of the workforce.
4. Experience.
5. Customer base.
6. Plant and machinery.

In many ways, the capital investment is neutral, in that it is a product of the financial climate and world inhabited by the company. It is equally available to the company and its competitors. Also, if the company actually owns such wealth, generated from previous activities, it is as free to invest it elsewhere, as within its own activities. In reality, there is little tying investment wealth to a particular company, other than confidence in the people of that company.

The commodities listed in 2, 3 and 4 above, are all wholly invested within company personnel.

The customer base could be seen at face value to be product based, that is dependent on the continuation of product lines and Quality. In most cases, though, the personal relationships between the individuals buying and selling play a decisive role when all other factors are equal. The product Quality and image are also the outcomes of consistent work by the company personnel. It might be fair, then, to assess the value of the customer base to be at least 75% tied to the particular personnel that make up the present company.

The last component, the plant and machinery, can be seen as having a value outside any involvement with the workforce. A case could be made that no other group of people will live near the factory and possess the ability to generate wealth from the plant, but this might be spurious. The capitalisation of this last asset leads to the belief that the future of the company is not tied to the personnel of the company.

Exponents of an expendable workforce point to changing market conditions and technological innovation, as reasons for maintaining a separation between the future of the company and that of individuals within the company. These are myths.

Changing market conditions

Market conditions are always changing. They always have, and always will, change. It is the responsibility of senior management to control, or foresee, such change, and to navigate the company accordingly.

Expanding market

Be the best, become the leader, make the running, and create customer expectations that only you can meet. The company will expand with the market.

Saturated market

If a particular market sector is becoming saturated, be the best. Dominate it and make sure that it is your competitors who cut back, rather than you. There are too many examples of companies going into reverse, because of worldwide over-production of their products, whilst others, often from the Far East, continue to expand. In 1987, the British government gave over-production within the automobile industry as a reason for closing part of the UK car industry. The term *rationalisation* was used. At the same time, Japanese investment in the same industry was welcomed. Grants were provided to assist with the opening of new Japanese car plants in the UK.

This double-think is endemic within much of industry. When faced with declining or saturated markets, the tendency is to reduce production, rationalise, and collaborate with the successful companies. This is the antipathy of good management. In difficult times, the aim should be to expand and eliminate the competition, not crumble and posture before it.

To the management of Nissan, the over-production of automobiles in the world is the concern of Ford, General Motors and the European manufacturers, not theirs. Whilst there is a market, they will supply it. Where there isn't a market, they will create one.

Declining market

If fashions change and the marketplace is shrinking, do something else. Explore other outlets for the talents and abilities within the company. There will always be other markets opening up. The experience of the company, combined with the firm base of a practising and thriving company, could make an unstoppable mix. Such companies need vision. With the right management, they will start ahead in any new field. Use the resources of the company to the full. Change.

Changing market

Where technology changes the methods, equipment and operation of an industry, such as the newspaper industry, there may be difficult decisions to be made. Such technological innovation should never be shirked in order to retain jobs for the workforce. However, vision and long-term planning, combined with the belief that most individuals are capable of being educated into new methods, will ease the transformation from old to new technology.

When British Railways (later British Rail), made the decision in the early 1950s to convert from steam locomotion to diesel and other forms, it undertook rigorous training to convert the engine drivers as well. This was a major task. Drivers and firemen had to turn their backs on the oily, noisy, and idiosyncratic world in which, standing on the footplate of a vibrant steam locomotive, they constantly balanced the state of the fire, the need for steam pressure, the volume of water and the weight of coal with the traction needed for curves and inclines. Their new world was one of sitting in the cab of a diesel locomotive, surrounded by dials and switches. Power was instant. Life was sedentary, compared with the previous constant fight to maintain speed and efficiency. Equally different were the skills needed by the maintenance crews. The approach of most senior managers, at that time, was that the inherent knowledge of railways and the traditions of service made each employee valuable and worth training. New skills were learnt. The world moved on.

The unskilled labour market

It won't exist. When robots and computers take the drudge out of manual work, the manual worker must be given the chance to become the necessary technician. In Germany and other European countries, this is understood at a national level. Schools prepare the next generation of workers to be flexible and give them the learning skills necessary to be able to cope with change during their working lives. The UK has yet to learn this lesson. Many young people still move through the education system heading for the pool of unskilled labour. Such a pool is no longer needed. Many companies do not help by spending considerable resources looking for skill and expertise that is in short supply, or does not exist, rather than perceiving the intrinsic value in its own personnel. They steal from the companies which are educating their workforce, and diminish the value, prospects and motivation, of their own long-term employees.

If senior personnel within a company perceive that unskilled labour has no place in the industry, steps should be taken immediately to train all staff. Quality production, and a Total Quality culture, are both impossible with untrained and unskilled personnel. It is a management function to provide the right people to facilitate the processes, and to provide each employee with the right skills and experience to be of full value to the company in the future.

Train and retain!

History will show that redundancy only occurred as a result of bad management. Plant closure only occurred as a result of bad management. Company insolvency only occurred as a result of bad management.

A good example of such long-term planning is cited by Peter Drucker.[1] He describes the long-term planning of resources, both material and human, to exploit the need for wood pulp in the paper industry on the West coast of America. In the early 1950s, plans were drawn up to cover the 50 year period needed to grow trees. He describes this as rare, seeing most companies' planning as extremely short-sighted.

Conservation of wealth

By far the greatest problem in any company, is the active conservation of wealth. Most companies, unless in real trouble, generate sufficient wealth to remain viable. What they fail to do is to retain it.

It has to be the responsibility of each and every member of the company to actively conserve the wealth generated by the company.

Much of the wealth is unconsciously dispersed. Such expenditure results from the company using out-of-date and inefficient methods. Production costs are too high. Wrong decisions are made. The company is inspection orientated. Investment has not been made in the right areas. Those responsible probably do not appreciate that they are making poor decisions. However, such expenditure is as a direct result of other conscious decisions and actions.

There will be many other examples, though, in which wealth is dissipated quite unconsciously. Most companies have resources *leaking* from all areas and activities. Whilst each leak will probably be of little value, the combined effect will be staggering. Examples will proliferate in most companies: an open window above a radiator, a late appointment that keeps others waiting idly, over-ordering a basic commodity, so that wealth sits on shelves for months or years, sending items by courier when ordinary post would have sufficed had there been enough time. It is not so much the value of each such example, but the vast number of them, that combine to be an important loss of wealth.

Ideas

1. The main purpose of the company is to make money.
2. People will only fully participate in this enterprise if it is for their own good.
3. Only good management can assure a safe future for the company, and thus for all of the company personnel.
4. Good management *can* assure such a future.

Forms of wealth

Whilst it is easy to consider wealth in terms of visible assets, there are many overlapping forms that may not be so obvious. This is particularly so when they are seen daily, and become taken for granted. Such forms of wealth within a company could be:

Money

Clearly this is the easiest to perceive. Expenditure on un-needed commodities, or in unwise purchasing, can be identified and accurately tracked. Often, though, items are purchased at a greater cost than necessary, because no-one bothered to check the price of alternatives. It is easy to use a local supplier who responds to a quick phone call without appreciating the real cost, or use a first class stamp when a second class would be sufficient.

Petty cash, expense accounts and peripheral purchases are all subject to wastage, largely because the individual sums are small, and are considered unimportant.

Information

The acquisition of information, whether from outside the company, in terms of research, or from within the company, by means of measurement, is expensive. Rarely is such information well used. It is not uncommon for someone who needs the data to be unaware of its existence.

The concentration on achieving specified tolerances, leads to such measurement, often accurately achieved, being instantly down-graded from a variable to an attribute. The accurate and precise information is used to merely check whether or not a result is in spec.

Time

Probably, time is the area of expenditure that is least appreciated as wasted. Time management has become somewhat of a science in recent years. The company purchases time from each of its employees. It rarely gets good value. Even efficient managers of others are often poor at managing their own time. Time is wasted daily, in considerable amounts. Again, because time can be considered to be flexible, it is not valued so highly. One can always work a little harder, or do additional work at home tonight.

The more expensive the time, the more it is open to abuse. Conversely, the less expensive the time, the more it is planned and prescribed. The shopfloor worker has every minute of the day accounted for, whilst half a dozen expensive managers can be kept waiting for 20 minutes for a colleague to join them for a meeting.

Time costs mount quickly whenever there is a disturbance to normal business. Again, examples proliferate in most companies: the phone calls made because something is late or not done properly, the meeting missed because of a crisis, or the excuses necessary to explain and make amends for some problem.

Poor manpower planning, or rather poor resources planning, often leads to high overtime costs. The level of such costs can be used as a barometer to measure the effectiveness of resources planning within a company.

The real cost of overtime payments is examined in Chapter 6. In general, it has to be poor expenditure to purchase an hour of a person's time for one-and-a-half, or twice times the going rate. This is compounded by the fact that you obtain tired and 'well used' people for the money, people unable to give of their best.

Energy

Much of a company's expenditure is converted into energy of one form or another. It may be heat, light or electricity. Whatever the form, this energy has to be purchased out of the wealth created by the company. Because some such expenditure is perceived as a direct cost of production, whilst the excess is often not noticed, it is easy for energy consumption to be far greater than necessary.

Those companies that have taken such expenditure seriously, have found that they can not only considerably reduce the daily energy consumption, but that by careful planning they can moderate the peaks, giving more efficient use of equipment.

The problem for some, stems from the age when energy was thought to be cheap. It never has been, and wastage has always been expensive. Nevertheless, some factories and office buildings were built with only one lighting circuit, in an attempt to limit the cost of wiring. Often one light switch illuminates the whole floor. Heating is often simultaneously piped to every area, by the same system. This results in some being too cold and agitating for the heating to be turned up, whilst others are uncomfortable and open doors and windows to get rid of the heat.

Materials

From paper clips to consignments of the company's raw material, every item or commodity within the office or factory costs money.

Most companies have unneeded goods, wrongly ordered, or poorly made, sitting in corners, or in cupboards, or just littering up the yard. When visiting industrial sites, it is easy to believe that they are administered by kleptomaniacs. Wide ranges of bits and pieces are kept, in the vain hope that they might be useful. They haven't been used during the last 'n' years, but they might be in the future. Worse, many still purchase odd items to add to the list.

The greatest waste of materials falls into the conscious area, that of the production of scrap and imperfect goods. These are probably already assessed and understood, though the methods of reducing and eliminating them have yet to be appreciated.

Space

Storage space, made unnecessary by better purchasing policies, is but one example. In our cities, space is accounted for in small units, and the productive cost of each unit is known and appreciated. Often though, in our factories, large areas are found, often lit and heated, that are not properly utilised. The irrational use of space is expensive.

The mnemonic 'MITEMS' may be useful to orientate people in the direction of conserving wealth.

'MITEMS'

Money
Information
Time
Energy
Materials
Space

An exercise

For your own company, write down examples in which resources could be better conserved, for each of the forms of wealth mentioned above. Attempt to evaluate the potential cost of each (this might be per day, week or month).

Production costs v Quality costs

It is possible to list all the actions and activities necessary for production, that is those necessary for the company to provide its goods and services. An additional list can also be constructed that identifies all the actions and activities that exist to ensure that those in the first list are done satisfactorily, and to correct those that are not. These are the Quality costs.

The most useful format to identify these within a company, is to consider each process as separate, and break it down using the 6Ms mnemonic. Remember, that it is not only the processes in those areas traditionally referred to as 'production', but the processes in all areas, that contribute to the acquisition of wealth. The term 'production' should be applied only to the *'production of wealth'*, thus including all administrative, planning, sales and commercial areas, as well as to manufacturing.

6Ms	*Production costs*	*Quality costs*
Man	Wages/salaries	Excessive overtime bill
		Poor time-keeping
	Initial recruitment	Recurrent recruitment
	Education & training	Errors from untrained staff
	Problem-solving activities	Rework
	Scrap	
Machine	Initial purchase	Poor purchasing
		Not energy efficient
	Maintenance	Breakdown
		Lost production
	Up-dating	Inefficient working
		Rework
		Scrap

Method	Research Development Up-dating Quality methods	Poor product Inefficient methods Time-consuming methods Inspection orientated Rework Scrap
Materials	Research into best Preferred suppliers Work with suppliers	Use of poor materials Inconsistent materials Goods inwards inspection Hassle with suppliers Returned raw materials Rework
Measure	Result measurement	Lost information Wasted information Inspection orientated Rework Scrap
	Process measurement	Lost information Wasted information Inspection orientated Rework Scrap
Milieu	Provision of work space	Unpleasant to work in Incompatible with Quality Wrongly heated* Wrongly lit*
	Maintenance	Expensive to maintain Failure costs
	Provision of amenities	Wrongly positioned Inefficient
	Cleaning	Expensive to clean Inefficient Lost production

* either too much or too little

Whereas cost savings can be achieved in a piece-meal fashion, wealth conservation can only be achieved through the active participation of everyone within the company. It is for this reason that a cultural change is necessary. It is necessary to orientate everyone to identify the company's financial leaks. Much of the lost wealth occurs without anyone's conscious action or even knowledge. Only by making everyone aware of the need to conserve wealth, and of the ways in which it can be saved, can the company make significant improvements.

This will only happen when it is in the interest of each employee.

Activity costing

A useful means of tracking and controlling costs is to assess an area as a separate business.

Daily operating costs

It is possible, when considering an activity of the company, to arrive at a daily operating cost. This will be the sum of the wages involved, the nominal cost of the equipment and plant, heat, light, etc. This is the cost of maintaining this area, equipment and staff, regardless of what output is achieved.

The actual figures may be difficult to calculate exactly, but this does not invalidate the method, since real cost savings will be obtained if there is an on-going improvement, compared to past performance.

Unit value of production

It is also possible to calculate a unit value for the output of the activity. This may be achieved by considering the value added to an item, or by

Idea

Effective wealth conservation
requires a cultural change.

dividing the daily operating cost by the nominal or expected output for that day. Where several different outputs result from the work in the activity, it may be necessary to calculate a unit value for each.

Again, the exact figures are not as important as the ratio to be achieved.

Activity earnings

It is now possible to calculate the daily earnings of the activity by assessing the total output and the unit costs involved.

Additional expenditure

Any additional expenditure must be noted, this should include any lost wealth from any of the MITEMS headings that are perceived during the day. For instance, if a courier is used in preference to first class postage because of late presentation of the items required, the difference between the cost of the two should be considered as an additional expenditure.

Financial throughput

It is now possible to measure the financial throughput for the activity during the day. This can be calculated as:

Throughput = Activity earnings – Daily cost – Expenditure

This figure should never be used as a stick for beating the staff in the area, or as a comparison of one area with another. Even if such a 'carrot and stick' approach was desirable, and it is not, it is not sufficiently accurate for such purposes. Such comparisons will always have negative effects. Resentment will develop, since the unfairness will be self-evident to those involved in the activity. Next time round, the figures will be massaged effectively, to present a better comparison. People are always very good at protecting themselves when under attack.

This technique is better used as a good guide of the comparative success of a work group which desires to increase its own throughput, that is its wealth creation ability. In this way, on-going improvement can be reliably charted against past performance.

The unit of time can be taken to fit conveniently with the type of activity. Very often assessments of some of the information necessary are already made, and it will be sensible to tie in the 'activity costing' with such assessments.

Some not all

It is not necessary to chart all activities in this manner. Indeed, if just one is done, the awareness provided will give an improvement. Select the activities that are crucial to Quality, and are costing a great deal, or are potentially capable of demonstrating improvement.

Again, it is not necessary for every day to be assessed. The actual 'activity costing' will take time and, therefore, money, and as such must be carefully controlled. A method of regular sampling will provide the type of information necessary. To ensure random results that will have some significance when viewed over time, it is better to plan a pattern of sampling time periods that override any natural variation in the area activity, such as the end of the month, or half-day every Friday. One method would be to take every eighth day, to obtain a spread of results across the week. Even easier to plan, is every tenth day. If the third, thirteenth, and twenty-third of every month are taken, throughout the year, the results should even out any differences due to a particular weekday. When there is no production for that day, the costs will be different, but this is known and can be taken into account.

It is better to chart the results graphically, so that the comparison can be readily appreciated.

Adaptations to suit the circumstances

Since the aim of the activity costing is to compare like with like, the actual method of calculation can be adapted to suit the circumstances of those involved. However, the basic formula can provide a good starting point.

Financial throughput for period	=	Total activity earnings	–	Operating cost for period	–	Additional expenditure (incl. Quality cost)

Summary

Wealth generation is the main purpose of any company.
Wealth conservation does not occur naturally.
It is important to consider the morality of the company.

The company resources can be considered as:

1. Capital investment.
2. Ideas and concepts unique to the company.
3. Skills and abilities of the workforce.
4. Experience
5. Customer base.
6. Plant and machinery.

The company should consider its position in relation to:

Changing market conditions.
Expanding market.
Saturated market.
Declining market.
Changing market.
Unskilled labour.

Main ideas in this chapter

1. The main purpose of the company is to make money.
2. People will only fully participate in this enterprise if it is for their own good.
3. Only good management can assure a safe future for the company, and thus for all of the company personnel.
4. Good management *can* assure such a future.

The mnemonic 'MITEMS' may be useful to orientate people in the direction of conserving wealth:

Money
Information
Time
Energy
Materials
Space

Expenditure of resources can be considered as *process costs* and *Quality costs.*

Activity costing can provide a financial measure of performance for any activity or area of the company, via:

Throughput = Activity earnings, less Daily cost, less Expenditure

Last thoughts ....

During the 'rationalisation' of a major UK corporation during the early 1980s, mass voluntary redundancies were seen as the way to profitability. Encouraged by generous 'handshakes', many left. On one Monday morning a problem arose in the laboratory. The three technicians with the knowledge of how to conduct a certain test had all taken voluntary redundancy and left the previous Friday. Production was slowed. Emergency meetings were held. Phone calls were made. Two were recalled with the status of 'consultant' at three times the cost of their previous salaries!

1. Drucker, Peter F, *The Practice of Management,* Heinemann, 1955.

Chapter 12

The Cost of Quality

All good things are cheap:
all bad things are very dear.

– Thoreau, in his Journal, 3rd March 1841.

Route-map

This chapter explores the reasons for considering the concept of Quality cost, and the classifications that make it a useful idea.

Using a method of defining Quality Cost Priority Ratings, the various classifications are expanded.

The distribution of Quality costs for a typical company is compared to an optimum distribution.

The chapter finishes with the use of 'performance indicators' to chart improvements in Quality costs.

Money for nothing!

The rule for most people in most companies is:

Don't work harder, work smarter!

The rule also applies to each actual company. For most companies concerned with their capacity to generate wealth, (and what company isn't?), this phrase can be added:

Don't generate more, keep more!

The thrust of this chapter is *not spending money unnecessarily*. It is concerned with identifying the many small drain points in a company, through which hard-earned wealth trickles, day after day after day.

The bucket principle

A company can be considered as an imperfect bucket that is used for lifting water out of a well. A certain amount leaks. Some water slops over the top. Because of all these losses, the water carrier has to devote additional effort to lifting water. In other words, he lifts considerably more water than the value of the water achieved.

When considering the cost of the water in the well, the water spilt at the top of the well has cost us more effort than that spilt at the bottom. In the same way, value lost towards the end of the manufacturing process costs us more than that lost near the beginning.

Stopping up the holes in the bucket is not enough. The user has to understand how the holes came to be in the bucket in the first place, and take sufficient steps to ensure that they do not reappear elsewhere.

Quality costs?

It is indeed hard to chart accurately the cost of obtaining Quality within a company. So much depends on the actual definition and usage of the Quality concept. In many ways, Quality is so totally integral to each and every function of the company, that all costs become Quality costs.

Defining the Cost of Quality

The theory behind costing Quality is easier to identify than the actual cost will ever be. Within a company dedicated to Quality in the terms defined earlier, that is meeting the negotiated requirements and expectations of the customer, the Cost of Quality will be the accumulated costs of every activity concerned with this provision. In a well run company, this should account for 100% of the activities.

This is unhelpful. Perhaps the starting point is to consider the accumulated Quality cost. This will be the cost of all those activities that ensure that Quality will be in the product or service prior to manufacture or delivery, *plus* those activities that ensure that the product or service meets the customers' high Quality standards after manufacture or delivery. This assumes that all is successful, and that the customers receive what they perceive to be Quality. Real life experience suggests that not every customer is happy; not all customers feel that their requirements, not to mention their expectations, have been met.

Additionally, one must consider the costs involved when the customer is unhappy. Such costs must include the cost of recompensing the customer, plus a little bit extra, by way of a bribe to sweeten the deal. It must also include the consequential costs that will inevitably occur, following either 'an unfortunate incident' or a 'cock-up', depending upon your style of language.

So, there are many elements that combine to arrive at an overall figure for the Cost of Quality (COQ). The idea is simple, but the practice is complex!

I can't afford it!

This reaction is common among senior executives, when first faced with the ideas of assessing their COQ. Clearly, such a statement, though, is a nonsense. It is, however, understandable when faced with the extravagant COQ programmes presented by some companies. Clearly, it is important to know where the wealth that your company creates actually goes. Equally clearly, there is little future in spending £100 to save £99.

The act of investigating your COQ will cost you money. Every activity within your company costs you money. Indeed, some aspects cost you money that can't even be graced with the title 'activity', such as a pile of unused stock gathering dust on a hidden shelf.

The answer has to be to keep a careful balance between the expenditure involved with a COQ programme, and the potential and real benefits of such a programme. This is particularly true for those companies embarking on a COQ programme in isolation from other aspects of Total Quality Management. Fortunately, for those engaged in TQM, it's not that bad. The overall definition of Quality and the company's Quality Policy, should keep this balance in check.

Prestige has a value

Most companies have tales of jobs performed for prestigious reasons, rather than for profit. It might be a particularly high profile contract, such as the Thames Barrier, or the new Lloyds Building. Either way, it seems a shame that sufficient work was not done to ensure that the orders taken for such contracts were within the capability of the company, and such that a profit could be made as well. Salesmen get carried away. The overall COQ of such projects is enormous, often with as many as 10 'special' items being made for the sake of one 'good' one.

Prestige has a value though. Indeed, it would be right to assess its value as an on-going marketing cost. In many instances, the publicity value of the prestigious contract is neither calculated nor exploited. A new type of architecture, such as the Lloyds Building in London, is a tribute to the many British companies which designed it, supplied materials and built it. Whatever one's attitude to the new architecture, this is true. British Steel should bask in the success stemming from the production and use of stainless steel in this way. It broke new ground. The accolades from such innovatory work can offset the high Cost of Quality. The professional approach to business management should balance such values, prior to commencement of the project.

The ideas behind COQ

This chapter seeks to identify the areas in which Quality is costing more money than is necessary. Since nearly all such expenditure will be allied to one process or another, it is unwise to separate COQ from your process improvement initiatives.

The COQ theory does, however, provide a framework for understanding where the more significant costs are likely to be found. As with all increased demands for time, energy and money, it will be very helpful to develop a method whereby the areas, activities and processes needing improvement can be prioritised.

'We do not plan for failure!' 'We do not plan for poor Quality!' 'Yes we do', some will be saying, 'The inspection process is about sorting good from bad, the re-work line is about dealing with failure, and our complaints department is about handling poor Quality'. Most people agree that these activities exist, but those who understand Quality, question whether they should. Indeed, the whole thrust of this book is that such activities should be severely curtailed, if not eliminated.

Classification

In classifying Quality costs, the 'classification of types' idea is borrowed from scientists who, since Darwin, have found that the only way to have a deep understanding of anything, is to break the knowledge down into identifiable pieces or items.

By adopting this approach with Quality costs, not only can such costs be identified, but much more importantly, so can the areas in which effort should be concentrated to maximise improvements.

It is important to appreciate the all-encompassing logic behind the classification. Five steps are taken, separating one set of ideas and circumstances from another. In this way a logical format is defined, with which to attack the Cost of Quality.

Step 1

Separate the direct costs of achieving Quality from the indirect, or consequential costs associated with failure. The direct costs will always be easier to establish, since they are sums that you are regularly paying out. They actually exist in your balance sheets.

Since the indirect costs are the consequential costs of failure, they will be harder to predict, identify or establish. A company may not even be aware of the failure and, therefore, has no idea of the subsequent real cost.

Quality costs = direct costs + indirect costs

It is important to note here, that this distinction is not always possible to achieve. Some direct costs will inevitably incur indirect costs as well, either by shaking the confidence of a customer, or by damaging the reputation of the company. This will be particularly true when the failures occur outside the company's location, and are thus visible to customer and potential customer alike.

Step 2

Within the direct Quality costs, separate the costs of achieving satisfactory results from those that are involved with dealing with failure. The idea of 'conforming or not conforming' is used to segregate these ideas. The cost of conformance will be the sum of all the costs involved with the production of acceptable results, either goods or services, whereas the non-conformance costs will stem from the failure to produce satisfactory products, consistently.

Direct quality costs = cost of conformance + cost of non-conformance

In other words, the costs of *getting it right* are separated from the costs of *getting it wrong.*

Step 3

Identify which of the costs of conformance are incurred *before* the event. In production terms, this would be *before* manufacture, and for those concerned with a service, *before* the service is actually given. Since all products and services are the result of processes, the definition is better 'process related'. The costs of conformance incurred *before* the process occurs can be identified, thus preventing failure. These are called prevention costs.

The costs of activities that take place *during and after* the process, such as inspection and testing are called appraisal costs.

Cost of conformance = prevention costs + appraisal costs

Step 4

All the costs of non-conformance will stem from failure to produce a satisfactory product consistently. Thus, they will be the failures occurring within the factory, *plus* those that are dispatched to the customer.

The costs incurred *before* and *during* shipment are called internal failure costs.

Those failures that actually reach the customer, that is they are found *after* shipment, are called external failure costs.

Costs of non-conformance = internal failure costs + external failure costs

It should be noted that the two are always related. If internal failures are created, they will never *all* be found. Some will inevitably reach the customer, giving external failures. The only way to ensure that no failures reach the customer, is to control processes so that you never create any failures, either internally or externally.

Step 5

The separation of the various indirect Quality costs is somewhat more difficult. It will have to be in rather vague terms. It might be 'those that are known about immediately', such as a cancelled order, 'those that are discovered eventually', from comments of another customer, perhaps, or 'those that can only be guessed at', lost reputation, for example.

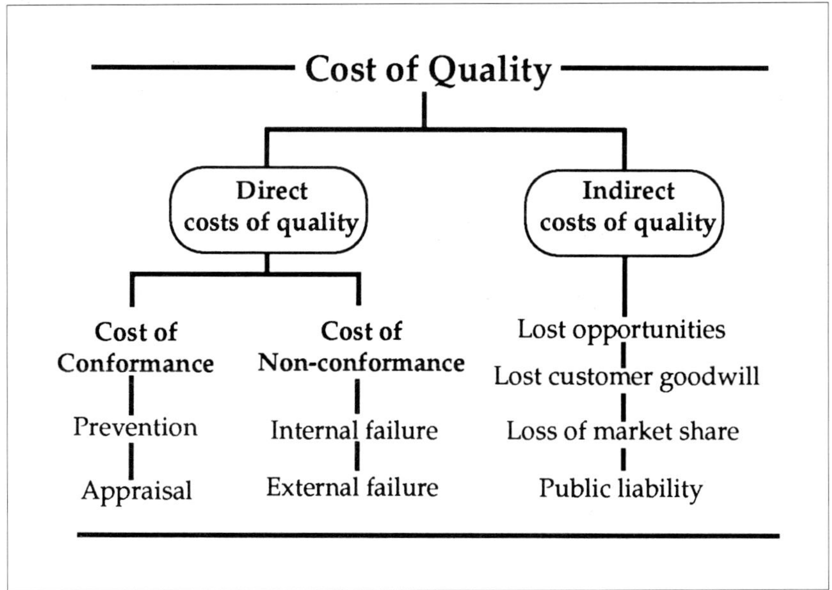

Fig 12.1 Diagram of classification tree.

Improving Quality costs

Whilst it is important to identify Quality costs, the real value comes from improving the processes. The monitoring of Quality costs can identify such areas.

The way to achieve this improvement is by focusing on a series of individual areas or processes, with comparatively high Quality costs, and then working to reduce this expenditure. In other words, a means of quickly and effectively *prioritising* the areas with huge Quality costs, is needed.

Some yardstick by which to judge any improvement that is made will also be needed. It is usually possible to identify a 'performance indicator' that is related to the area under study. Performance indicators are considered later.

It is necessary to:

1. Prioritise areas for process improvement.
2. Identify a performance indicator for each area.

Quality Cost Priority Ratings

There are several methods of assessing Quality costs, but an investigation of Quality Cost Priority Ratings (QCPRs) is probably the most useful. The basic theory and practice is explained below, but, as with all such ideas, the methods can be adapted to suit a particular organisation.

Establish the Quality cost improvement group

This may well be an existing process improvement group, Quality Circle, or the like, depending upon which process improvement activities have previously occurred.

Where a company is organised into effective teams, these teams will have responsibility for Quality within their area, and thus will be the natural group for considering the Cost of Quality of their area.

Clearly, circumstances will dictate how Cost of Quality groups are best formed, but in general, the optimum size for such a group is between four and 10. These groups, like any other process improvement group, must be well led.

The leader of the group should have:

- An understanding of the processes involved.
- The necessary communication skills.
- Some rudimentary knowledge of presenting results.
- Basic knowledge of project costing.

However, the leader should not be the most senior person, this last point is to avoid the dominance by the 'boss' of the group, and is explained in greater detail in Chapter 10, concerned with problem-solving. The group should contain a wide range of abilities and knowledge, so as to maximise the information available, and to ensure that the group has the necessary skills to deal adequately with all the ideas and proposals that may be forthcoming.

Equip the group

Each member of the group should have 'rating sheets', and a large 'rating sheet' should be available for the whole group.

Introduction to QCPR

Each area of the Quality cost classification is introduced to the group, which first considers this theoretically, and then applies the thoughts to its own processes.

Independently, each person notes down the examples, stemming from his own experience. These are listed under the appropriate heading. As the leader of the group works through the whole classification, so each member builds a list of examples and suggestions, probably each referring to a particular process. It will be important to avoid 'woolly' generalisations, such as 'more maintenance'. Rather, each comment should be specific and pragmatic, stating exactly the source of the 'Cost of Quality'.

Each entry should be: accurate, brief and clear.

A set of QCPR forms are included in Appendix C, at the end of the book.

Allocation of ratings

When their lists are complete, all the members of the group allocate ratings to each of their examples. These ratings are given in Appendix C.

A QCPR is calculated for each example.

The processes to which they have accorded the highest ratings can be identified, thus presenting sensible priorities for improvement work.

Formulate master plan.

The whole group now discuss its findings, working towards a consensus about each area and classification. These are entered together on the main QCPR sheet. Where there is discussion about a particular rating, it should be remembered that it is the balance achieved by the findings that is important, rather than the actual ratings. The group should, therefore, aim at *consistency* throughout the rating exercise. It is the responsibility of the group leader to monitor this aspect, and ensure that a sensible balance is achieved.

Action

Finally, the group considers what actions are to be taken, by whom and when. This should all be recorded and kept available by a member of the group.

The QCPR review

The COQ is the sum total of all expenditure, by any and every department or activity of a company that seeks to ensure good Quality.

Quality is defined as 'meeting the negotiated requirements and expectations of the customer'.

This definition applies to both internal and external customers, and the costs of achieving Quality will, likewise, stem from both the internal customer/supplier relationships, and the relationship of the company as a whole, to its suppliers and customers.

Notes for the group leaders presentation

Direct Costs of Quality

Cost of conformance

The cost of conformance is the sum of the costs associated with making certain that products or services meet the customer's negotiated requirements and expectations. Overall, the cost of conformance will be the accumulation of all these costs, and will be found throughout the manufacturing process. They will exist within each internal customer/supplier relationship.

Prevention

Prevention costs will include those stemming from every department and activity concerned with the prevention of poor Quality, the elimination of poor work and the subsequent increased Quality levels.

Prevention costs can be grouped into three areas:

Prevention costs associated with people

Job descriptions.
Personnel selection.
Training, etc.

Prevention costs associated with process

Machine maintenance.
Assuring good supplier Quality.
FMEAs.
Environmental improvements, etc.

Prevention costs associated with product development

Design improvements.
FMEAs.
Market research prior to manufacture, etc.

Appraisal

Appraisal costs can also be grouped into three areas:

Appraisal costs associated with product development

Testing.
Prototype manufacture.
Market research following manufacture, etc.

Appraisal costs associated with process failure

First off inspection.
On-line inspection, etc.

Appraisal costs associated with product failure

Testing.
Final inspection, etc.

Cost of non-conformance

The cost of non-conformance is the sum of the costs associated with failure to meet the negotiated requirements and expectations of the customer. Again, these costs will be the accumulation of all the costs of non-conformance. They too, will be found throughout the manufacturing process and will exist within each internal customer/supplier relationship.

Internal failure

The internal failure costs are those incurred making products that do not meet the requirements and expectations of the customer, but are discovered prior to shipping to the customer.

Scrap.
Re-work.
Re-inspection, etc.

External failure

External failure costs are those that are incurred by the company following shipment of the product, or the completion of the services supplied by the company. They almost inevitably imply the existence of non-direct Quality costs as well.

Warranty expenses.
Insurance against warranty claims.
Excessive installation costs.
Product replacement.
Complaints procedures.
Bad debts, etc.

Indirect Costs of Quality

These will take many forms. Here are some examples, but any company will be able to draw up a more significant list, based on its own type of business and business relationships.

Lost opportunity costs

These are the costs resulting from a failure to take full advantage of an existing opportunity to do business, and/or to generate wealth. This could be as a result of a lack of ability within your company to take full advantage of opportunities as they present themselves, or from a lack of information or understanding of the marketplace. It might even be that the company's energies are fully occupied with maintaining the present range of business, and thus fail to respond to the changing world outside.

Loss of customer good will

The origin of these costs usually directly effects the customer, causing him some loss, thus they are initially incurred by the customer. However, they will lead to negative opinions about the company, its products and its services, leading to a loss in reputation and subsequent loss of sales.

Reputations rarely reflect the current situation, indeed, some maintain that reputations usually run some five years behind reality. A company can live off a past good name for a number of years, but, equally, it will take a period of time to establish or re-establish a reputation. Reputations are hard won, yet easily lost.

Erosion of market share

Market share is the key to long-term business success. Loss of market share usually results in higher unit production costs, lower profitability and a greater risk of further decline in business levels. In most spheres of business, there is a reasonably finite amount of business. If you win business, it will usually be at the expense of your competitor. Conversely, if you lose it, the business is going elsewhere.

A question that should be uppermost in the consciousness of every company, is 'Why aren't we the best?' Theoretically, there is probably no good reason why you cannot do better in your sphere of business than your competitors. Being the best in any business is the net result of everyone within the company being the best at his job, be he the managing director or a process operator. Your market share is probably an indication of how good you all are at what you do.

Public liability

This heading can be extended to include any consequential loss by a customer, resulting from the failure of one of your products. At the least, this may involve loss of another company's reputation, but in its more damaging forms, could involve your company in a claim for compensation.

Most companies carry insurance against such claims, and these costs should be considered indirect Quality costs.

Where claims are pursued, the costs of actually fighting or settling such a claim, all combine to give a potentially large COQ.

Typical results

Few companies have undertaken complete studies of their Cost of Quality, but considerable research is available to establish probable figures. Whilst most of this work is in the USA, it is generally agreed that the results are applicable across Western industry.

The stage of a company's development in relation to Quality, plays a considerable part in the probable overall Cost of Quality. This may be reflected in the make-up of the constituent parts of the Cost of Quality, such as prevention, appraisal, etc. Most companies have developed from a situation in which they were unaware of the vast cost of their external failures. The have lived day-to-day with a false sense of confidence. In consequence, they spent very little on prevention or appraisal, and achieved very little internal failure. In all probability, the Quality costs of such a company are likely to be in excess of 50% of its sales revenue. This frightening figure was probably never realised, as defensive inspection methods were introduced to divert the problems before they were properly evaluated and understood.

A more typical scenario is that of the company that has progressively cut down on external failure over recent years, by becoming an *inspection orientated* company. It will now have high appraisal costs, and probably even higher internal failure costs, but a reasonable standard of Quality being shipped. In most cases, such inspection-orientated companies will have Quality costs in excess of 30% of their sales revenue, and often between 40% and 50%.

The result of operating in such circumstances is an almost total reliance on inspection. The company achieves a mind-set that cannot perceive any method of *controlling* Quality, other than more inspection. Often, this becomes self-defeating, leading to increasing, rather than diminishing Quality costs. Regrettably, the systemisation of Quality Control, via British and international standards, without the wider consideration stemming from TQM, reinforces this prejudice.

Systems are vital. Quality methods are not in conflict with any systems, particularly BS5750 and ISO9000. However, their introduction is often seen as being sufficient for salvation, rather than as an essential tool. Without such systems, little organisation for Quality can be achieved.

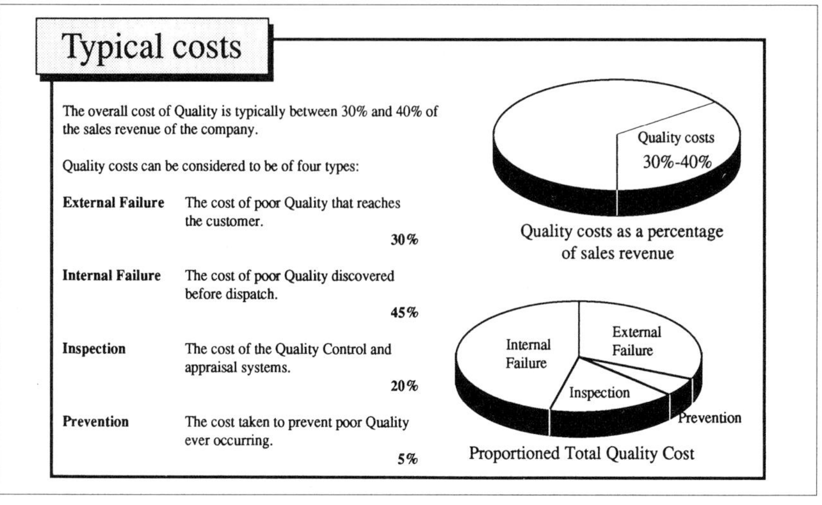

Fig 12.2 Illustration showing typical Costs of Quality.

Nevertheless, the systems are the bottom line, basic essential, and not an end in themselves. Above all, the need to move rapidly from appraisal towards a manufacturing environment must be understood. The aim is to devote most of a company's COQ to prevention.

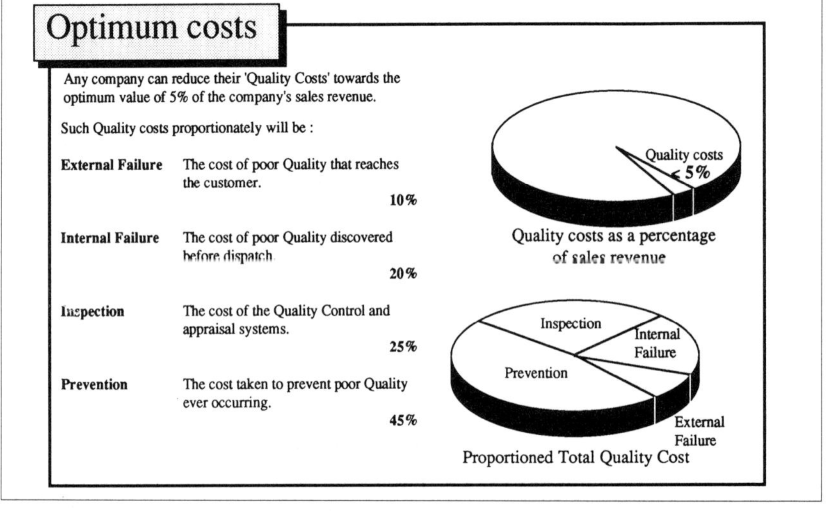

Fig 12.3 Diagram showing optimum Costs of Quality.

Some American researchers have claimed that a 2% Cost of Quality is possible, but 5% of sales revenue is a more realistic optimum figure. It should not be considered as a target, as improvement will always be possible. However, as with most improvements, earlier gains are the easiest to achieve, with subsequent improvements becoming progressively smaller and harder to achieve.

The author is indebted to Stan Bennett of the Ford Motor Company (1984) for the following developmental ideas. He suggested that there are four fundamental development stages within the mind-set of any company, which he described as 'uncertainty', 'awakening', 'enlightenment' and 'wisdom'. A fifth has been added, called 'good practice'.

Uncertainty

The first stage is typified by the muddle-headed, over confident company that is convinced that whilst it ships its products, there are no problems. Regrettably, this was all too possible during the boom years of the 1950s and early 1960s.

Awakening

The awakening stage sees the advent of the 'QC era', in which the emphasis is put on inspection, thus converting potential external failures into internal failures.

Enlightenment

The third stage sees more QC activity. However, there is the beginning of process thinking, and inspection increased from just the inspection of product and results, to the inspection of processes.

Wisdom

Wisdom creeps in with the introduction of proper process control methods, most usually SPC, and other preventative work, such as workforce education, FMEA and design modifications.

Good practice

The good practice is now possible with a company, organised and orientated towards Quality, developing a unified workforce capable of continual improvement within the processes involved. This improvement will be reflected in the overall business.

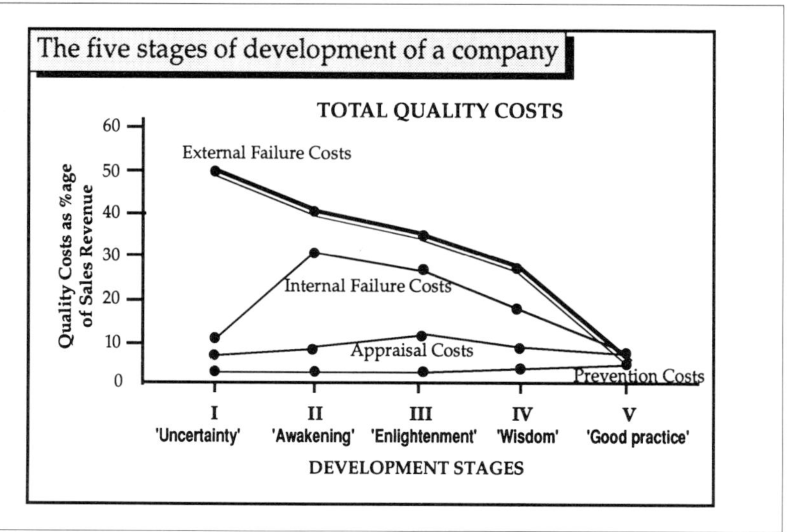

Fig 12.4 Diagram showing five stages of understanding.

Performance indicators

As previously suggested, it is seldom practical to work out and constantly monitor the *exact* COQ for the company, or indeed for a particular department or individual. Even where the simplistic nature of the business makes it possible, the cost effectiveness of such an exercise may be questionable.

It is often a better policy to identify several parameters that give a satisfactory indication of the improvements being accomplished. Local knowledge will suggest which of these parameters, and, indeed, what the units of measure should be.

A suitable performance indicator will be like monitoring a person's health with a thermometer. The actual temperature is not as important as the changes that are indicated. Perhaps an even better analogy would be the bathroom scales. The scales not only monitor the weight of a weight-watcher, but constantly seek to improve it.

Performance indicator network

However, one performance indicator is unlikely to be sufficient, and the most usual situation is the development of a network of indicators that together present an on-going indication of the state of the business.

Each and every individual within the company will need at least three indicators. All will need to be able to appreciate how the company is doing, how their department and/or group is performing, and how they match up to previous performance.

Company indicators

In many ways, this is the most difficult of the performance indicators. Often the choice of company indicators is the most controversial.

It is important that each employee of a company has a measure of the company's success. This will need to be easily understood, and to be described in terms that have a meaning to virtually everyone. Whilst many will suggest that this should be the bottom line profitability of the company, others question the wisdom of baldly presenting such a figure, that is the result of many complex financial arrangements, and indeed may be subject to a certain amount of adjustment, if not manipulation, for the sake of external considerations.

Some find an honest approach that states the value added by an individual's work dangerous. It might inspire inflated wage claims. This stems from the archaic situation of an ignorant management and workforce, struggling to find common ground within an area of difficult industrial relations. In a modern company using TQM methodology, no such problems should arise. It should be assumed that all are working in an educated fashion to the common good.

It is better to look towards indicators stemming from the stated purpose or policy of the company, and where possible, a parameter showing the extent to which Quality is being achieved. As stated before in this book, when you are in doubt about any particular decision, it is often helpful to return to the definition of Quality, and look at the question from first principles.

The definition of Quality is concerned with *customer satisfaction*, and so indicators should be sought that measure just that. Such an indicator, might be the percentage of orders fully met on time during last week. Alternatively, it might be a negative quantity, such as the number of complaints.

Whatever the indicator, it should:

- Demonstrate the performance of the company.
- Have regard to present versus past performance.
- Be significant to everyone.
- Be readily understood.
- Be presented in a chart or diagram.

Department indicators

The department, group or team, should also be able to monitor its own performance. The exact indicator may again be contentious, as it may reflect the values of someone outside the team, rather than of the team itself.

An indicator stemming from the internal customer/supplier relationships of the team has more relevance. Its measure of Quality will be the degree to which the team effectively meets the negotiated requirements and expectations of its customers. Since each team will probably have several customers, there will be plenty of scope for such indicators.

Such an indicator of performance will be a daily reminder that the definition of Quality is concerned with customer satisfaction. It is important to avoid an indicator that merely shows the volumes being achieved, as this will inevitably lead to a downward pressure on Quality levels.

Again, indicators that link the performance of one group or team with another should be avoided. The concern should always be with meeting and exceeding *its own previous performance.* Any development of false competition will prove to be counter-productive, leading to a lack of cooperation and overall company purpose.

Whatever the indicator, it should:

- Demonstrate the performance of the group.
- Register present performance against the past.
- Be significant, both within and outside the group.
- Be readily understood.
- Be presented in a chart or diagram.

Individual indicators

These will vary enormously and reflect the different tasks and jobs that people have. They may be tied into regular appraisals in which each employee, working with a superior, sets individual targets, objectives or measures. They may be informal, or written down to be regularly assessed.

However it is achieved, it will be important that each individual can measure themselves against his own personal past performance.

Summary

Cost of Quality programmes involve:

Working smarter, not harder.
Keeping more wealth, not generating more.
Defining Quality costs.
Understanding Quality costs.
Planning for success.

Quality Cost Priority Rating

1. Establish the Quality cost improvement group.
2. Equip the group.

3. Introduce QCPR.
4. QCPR review.
   Prevention costs associated with
   people
   process
   product development
   Appraisal costs associated with
   product development
   process failure
   product failure

   Internal failure costs
   External failure costs
   Indirect Quality costs
5. Allocation of ratings.
6. Discussion and formulation of a master plan.
7. Action.

Performance indicators

compare present and past performance of:

- The company.
- The department.
- The individual, group or team.

Last thoughts ....

I once conducted a senior management seminar for the most senior personnel of one of our nationalised industries. As is my custom, I arrived early, and prepared for a 2.00 pm start. At about 1.40 pm the four senior managers from an associated plant arrived and took their places. Ten minutes later, I noticed that they were looking at their watches. They had apparently been told the seminar was to start at 1.45 pm. At five minutes to two, others began to arrive and all but the three most senior personnel were present and comfortably seated. At 2.05 pm a note from the director arrived, apologising that he and his colleagues would be 10 minutes late. He eventually arrived just after twenty-five past. Unfortunately, there was an extra person; that is one more person than had been planned for. We had to find an extra chair. The actual seminar eventually got under way just over an hour after the first senior managers arrived. We discussed 'Quality – the central management issue'.

Chapter 13

Customer Satisfaction

'The Barclays Charter is our guarantee to you that a special relationship exists between you as a customer and us as your banker. We operate within a framework of honesty, loyalty, mutual trust and privacy. ..... We are committed to offering you a high quality service. We aim to meet your requirements without fault the time you ask.'

from The Barclays Charter, Barclays Bank PLC (1988)

Route-map

This chapter starts with an examination of who is the customer and then classifies the customer concept into three groups:

internal customers
external customers
end-users

It then discusses the Customer Care principles of cooperation, confidence, continuity and Quality, and concludes with the justification that for TQM to be successful, all must be good customers if they are to be good suppliers.

Who is the customer?

A question occupying many Quality commentators is 'Who is the customer?' Such a consideration is not necessary for most manufacturers, for the answer is everyone in the chain, from the designer to the end-user of the product.

As an example, consider a precision engineer whose company manufactures the core-pieces for another company, which uses the parts as the centre of electric motors. These are subsequently sold to a range of small electrical appliance manufacturers, making items such as hair-dryers. These are mainly distributed through large wholesalers, chain stores and via mail order firms. A hair-dryer may be purchased by someone as a gift for someone else.

The chain of four companies and two personal customers can be expanded by considering the four companies involved prior to the manufacture of the core. Thus, the eventual chain has at least 10 links in it:

1. Ore is taken from the earth by a mining company.
2. It is collected and shipped by an ore dealer.
3. It is smelted into billets by an aluminium works.
4. It is drawn into a bar by an extruding company.
5. This is machined by the precision engineering company.
6. It is included in an electric motor by an electrical company.
7. This is built into a hair-dryer by the appliance company.
8. It is distributed by a wholesaler.
9. It is sold by an electrical retail shop.
10. It is purchased by Frank.
11. He gives it to his daughter Mary.
    (who eventually, after two years use, gives it to Oxfam, which sells it to someone else.....etc.)

Mary has very little idea of how the hair-dryer works, and is unaware of the function, or even the existence of the aluminium core piece. She does not need to know. Her requirements and expectations are met by the smooth and efficient functioning of the apparatus. She is more concerned with the outward appearance, styling and colour, than with the intricate parts that make it work.

The Quality of the hair-dryer, when being used by Mary, is a result of all the work done by all the companies in the chain, prior to her receiving it. Indeed, even her father has made a contribution to the Quality of her hair dryer, by purchasing a particular model from a reputable dealer, by ensuring its guarantee, and by not leaving it on the train during the journey home.

This illustrates the nature of Quality as a concept that needs conserving. Quality is not an addition to the product. The high Quality of the aluminium core could have been infringed by any of those involved with its manufacture and distribution.

The definitive customer

Many see little point in closely defining the terms that are used, believing that a looseness of ideas allows initiative and enterprise. These people, however, fail to appreciate the damage done by these loose ideas. They do not attribute the lack of progress in a company to the different viewpoints often lurking beneath an apparent consensus.

The lack of communication is often cited by managers as one of the main reasons for lack of progress in their organisation. This point is discussed elsewhere, but the important aspect, for this section, is that examination usually demonstrates, not that there is a lack of communication, but that there is a lack of *effective* communication. People live by different values and principles. When they discuss an aspect of the business, the words they use are underlaid by different meanings. It is this lack of a common understanding of the everyday language used in industry, that masks the real differences. If the company is to strive in a single direction, and this is the repeated plea of this book, then adequate definition and understanding of the terms often used, is essential.

The definition of customers could be results based, that is they are in receipt of the goods and/or services resultant from a process, or series of processes. Whilst this definition is perfectly adequate to describe a customer, it lacks the dynamic input of the supplier's actions that could identify the *customer relationship*. When considering Quality, it is the customer relationship that is vital.

As with all other definitions, the explanation of the customer relationship is a tool to be of general use within industry and commerce. All definitions should be practical concepts. They are not esoteric words, used for pleasure, but industrial tools used for profit. A more useful definition of *customer* is orientated towards the supplier's involvement, or rather, the processes in which the supplier is involved.

A customer is anyone who has the benefit of the work, activity or actions of another.

It can be clearly seen that we are all customers, many times over. Within a sophisticated society, we are all dependent on the work, activity and actions of many others. In work, we also find many customer relationships that stem from us. There are many people who benefit from our work, activities and actions. Each is a customer.

A supplier can be similarly defined as any person whose work, activity or actions benefits others. 'Benefit' is used in the wide sense of assisting, influencing or making possible some aspect of the customer's life. In this way, a worker may not be obsessed with the raw materials or components being used, but without the benefit of them, the job might not exist and his employment might be curtailed. Thus, the worker does benefit from the work of others. The dustman benefits from the household rubbish that is left for collection, and the dentist has the benefit of other people's decaying teeth.

Quality underlies all these relationships. The extent to which the customer benefits is Quality dependent. Indeed, the customer's benefit depends upon the Quality of the processes involved, and it should be remembered that the process's Quality relies upon each of the process inputs, defined by the 6Ms theory. A customer relationship is dynamic. The Quality of the relationship results from the inputs to all the processes. It is these process inputs that benefit the customer.

Grouping customers

When it is difficult to decide exactly *who* is a customer of *whom*, a consideration of the material transfer involved with the process concerned will identify the customers of that process. Any process that does not change anything, and does not involve a transfer of what is changed from one point to another, achieves nothing. Such a process could be discontinued with no ill effect, and with considerable saving to the company. By considering the materials involved with the process, (one of the 6Ms), the customer relationships can be identified.

It is useful to group customers under three main headings:

Internal customers

Internal customers are people who, whilst benefiting from the process, share the company's goals and objectives. When the supplier/customer relationship is considered, both parties are in the same company.

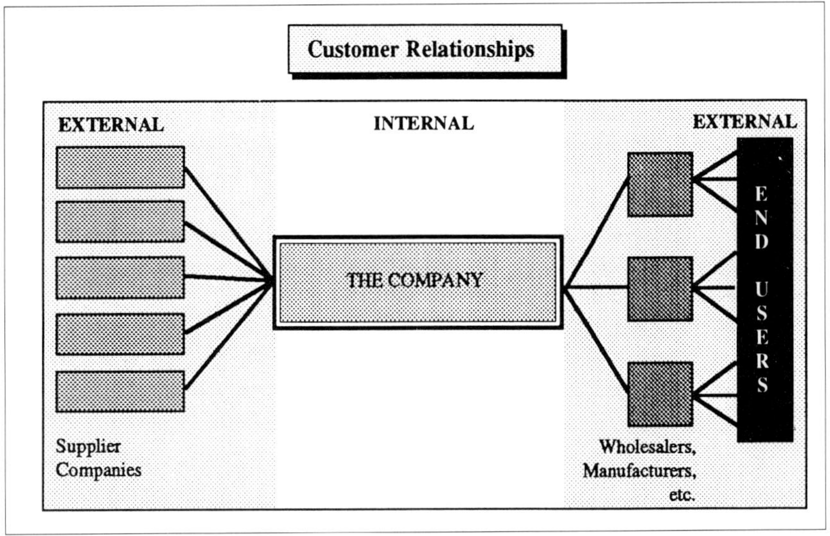

Fig 13.1 Internal and external customer relationships.

Where firms operate commercially as a group of companies, this definition may become a little obscured. The exact relationship between different companies within the same group, needs to be made explicit to all, so that the negotiated meeting of requirements and expectations can be achieved. A loose and informal structuring of such company relationships often leads to poor negotiation, unmet requirements and poor Quality.

External customers

External customers are those outside the originating company, who obtain the benefit of company processes. They may be individual members of the public but, more often, they will be other industrial or commercial enterprises. The individual members of such a corporate customer can also be considered to be external customers in their own right, provided that there is a direct relationship with them, outside the company. If they have no say in the purchasing decisions, and no power to negotiate or choose one supplier from another, they are really the internal customers of whoever makes the purchasing decisions. Such people have internal, rather than external customer relationships. The decision-makers and buyers are the partners in the external customer relationships.

The end-user

The identification of the 'end-user', or the person who will benefit from the chain of processes, is of great importance, as it allows the development of knowledge relating to the desired results and, therefore, of the processes necessary to produce these end results.

Since, by definition, when many of the earlier processes are performed, the end-user rarely exists, the consideration will often involve the *potential* end-user.

The end-user is the customer without any other customers for the commodity involved.

The internal customer

The pursuit of Quality is impossible without the active support of the internal customer. Indeed it is *within* the numerous internal customer relationships that the Quality battle is either won or lost. Since Quality is intrinsic to the processes involved, and poor Quality is the commodity allowed to creep into the process chain, active customer relationships are vital. Each internal supplier will need to be constantly aware of the Quality being passed on to the next part of the production chain, that is to the internal customer.

The Quality of the output of the supplier's process becomes the Quality of the process input for the internal customer. It is imperative that the Quality levels are kept as high as possible, thus always enabling the internal customer to achieve satisfactory results, to obtain job satisfaction, and to be able to hand on good Quality to the next customers, be they internal or external.

There are many activities within a company, all of which are geared to the satisfaction of customer needs. The organisation of a company into many departments dictates the diverse nature of the internal customer relationships. The many types of relationship involved within the company will form a spectrum that will include the following:

Regular contact between departments
These strong links will become institutionalised, and will usually be backed by paperwork and/or controlled by a computer program.

Their frequent use presents the opportunity to regularise the operational aspects of the relationships, to produce the highest Quality standards at the lowest cost. Unfortunately, though, familiarity often breeds the proverbial contempt where inefficiencies become accepted as a daily norm, low standards become the expectation, and the regular systems begin to be operated for their own sake, rather than to achieve the stated objective.

The focus on Quality can provide a new look at these regular transactions. A redefinition of the internal customer relationships can present new opportunities for internal negotiation. If backed by a Quality Policy, any customers not satisfied that they are receiving full benefit can demand that their requirements and expectations are met.

The regular use of these vital interdepartmental links has a definite advantage. Continual improvement of the operational aspects of these relationships will be vital, and can make a large contribution to the overall Quality improvement of the company, and the subsequent reduction in Quality costs.

Occasional departmental links

The occasional calling by one department on another, usually to provide a service, is often at the root of Quality problems. It may be that a manufacturing area needs occasional support by the maintenance function, or that the accounts department is in need of additional education and training. These service functions are often included in an overall budget, unrelated to the actual value of their contribution, and work semi-autonomously.

The result can be that the service provided is far from meeting the requirements, if not the expectations, of the department requesting assistance. Negotiation takes place only in a crisis. Dissatisfaction is expected, and people nobly struggle on without the desired service.

Clearly, this is unsatisfactory. The better companies have proactive service departments. Areas, such as training, planning and accounts, can take the same trouble to understand, and seek to meet, the basic needs of their customers, as the company does for its external customers. Such effort is best effectively planned, before their input has been requested. Above all, these relationships must depend upon on-going negotiation, early action (prevention is better than cure!) and a true understanding of Quality and its related costs.

Relationships between departments and individuals

Here, customer relationships tend to be less regular, and in response to a direct need, unrelated to the direct production thrust. They are typified by the individual becoming frustrated by the department involved insisting on its own codes and methods that may or may not be related to Quality.

The other important aspect here will be the two-way nature of these transactions. In most cases, the department needs something from the individual, be it information or the following of a set procedure, whilst the individual needs the input of the department to achieve the objective. With a Quality Policy, the negotiations can be kept to the point, and the expenditure of the company's resources (internal energy) in accomplishing these transactions can be minimised.

Named individual to individual

These are the real core of the productive effort, and the relationships that can respond the most quickly and strongly to the Quality call. Every company should be a mass of horizontal customer relationships between equals, often from different areas of the company. These relationships should be carried out on a personal level, where the supplier takes full responsibility to ensure the satisfaction of the internal customer's needs.

Traditionally, these links have not existed. Departments only spoke to each other at a lofty managerial level. Where a problem, Quality or otherwise, existed, the information went up the chain of command within one department, to be formalised into a report from one departmental head to another, and then to filter back down to the level concerned. This patently doesn't work, and even if it did it would be slow, cumbersome and, above all, very expensive (see Fig 13.2).

The barriers have to be broken down, and people at all levels within the organisation must feel able to communicate and negotiate freely. Only in this way can the processes be controlled. Only in this way can internal customers be satisfied. Only in this way can Quality be achieved.

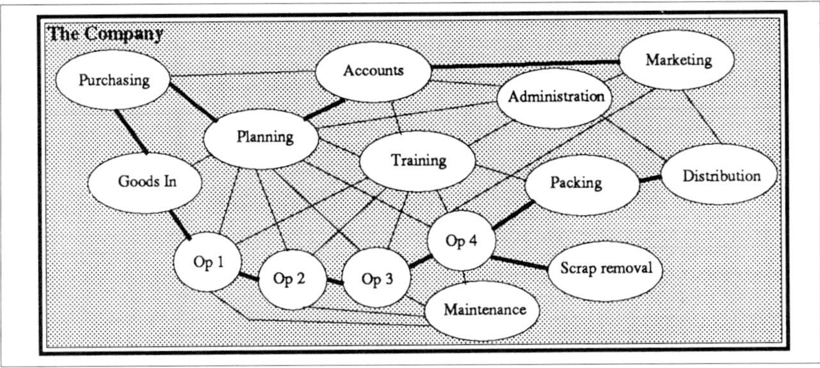

Fig 13.2 Typical internal customer relationships.

The establishment of these relationships requires new concepts of responsibility and duty to be assumed by every individual person involved. These have previously been described as industrial citizenship. Such a contribution from an individual employee will only be gained on a voluntary basis. It has to be proactive; each must demand good Quality inputs.

The lack of success from some TQM schemes possibly stems from an inability to achieve this cultural change. Indeed, many TQM protagonists speak of methods and techniques, whilst largely ignoring the human resource inputs. Without sound management motivating and orientating each to maximise their contribution, the full fruits of TQM will never be achieved.

Team work

The operation of team work brings these internal customer relationships even more tightly into focus. The aim of a well run team situation is for the team to be largely self-sufficient. The members of the team will depend on each other, as they share the overall responsibility for the team's processes. This will lead them into a very close network of supplier/customer relationships between each other. These relationships will become accepted practice, indistinguishable from the day to day operation of the team.

The team, itself, will have very strong links with other teams, and will thus be in direct customer relationships, sometimes as the customer, and often as the supplier.

Individual members of the team, or the entire team, may need the direct assistance of other areas of the company. The other half of the 'self-sufficient' scenario, is that when assistance is needed by the team, it is provided in response to its request. When the team needs the assistance of the management, it requests help. The manager is the supplier in this relationship, and the team is the customer. Thus, the team has both the right to *negotiate* its requirements and expectations, and the right to *expect* good service, that is Quality.

Similar occasional customer relationships will occur with every other part of the company. For some, this juxta-position of the senior management role with that of a supplier to the team, can bring into question doubts concerning status, position and job definitions. It is for this reason that such activities must be soundly backed on Total Quality Management theory, understanding, education and good practice. If this can be achieved, the potential of the team, and hence the company, will be maximised.

External customers

The traditional attitude in many companies is that customers are an unfortunate appendage to doing business. They are to be tolerated and humoured, but never trusted. It often appears that they think they know more about your business than you do, and usually demand tighter specifications than you think are reasonable. They become unreasonable when discussing delivery times. They invariably quibble about the price, but are usually very poor at paying their dues on time. In short, all customers want the highest possible standards from you, at the lowest possible cost to themselves.

Idea

Managers supply management.

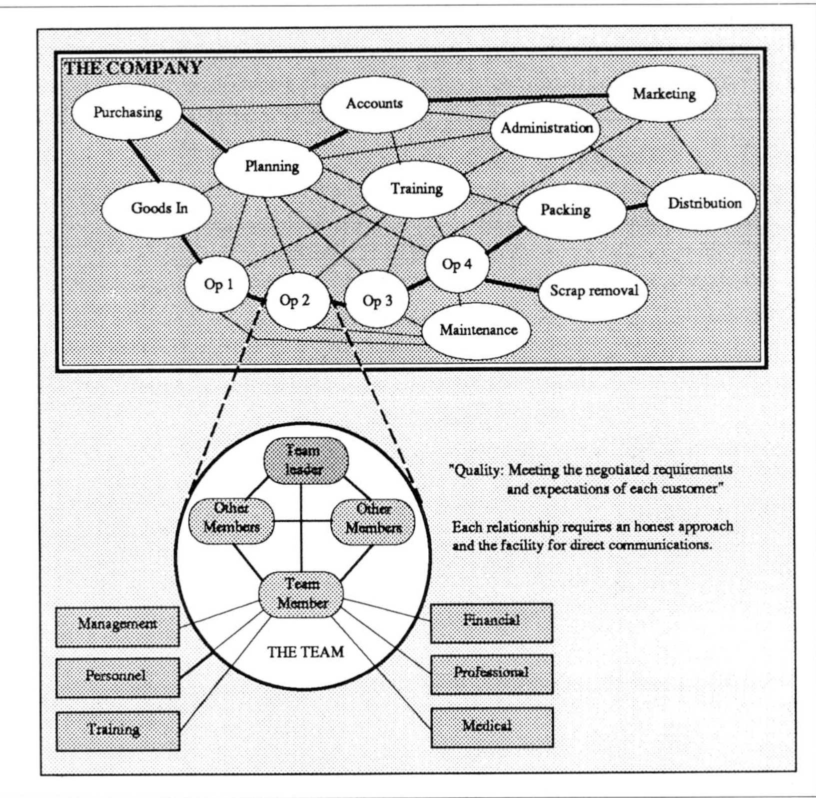

Fig 13.3 Typical internal customer relationships for a team work situation.

Regrettably, with the growth of sophisticated sales departments, most ordinary mortals within the company rarely meet customers. They tend, therefore, never to question the fundamentals of the external customer relationship. They also tend to adopt the attitude that they serve the sales department, which is probably even worse thought of than the customer. The customer is not theirs, the customer belongs to the sales department. This distancing of the production areas from the customer, contributes greatly to the inability of the company to meet the requirements and expectations of the customer.

To understand the external customer relationship, there are certain basic truths that can be pondered:

Customers are essential

Apart from the self-evident fact that the customer is the funnel through which money and resources are acquired, he is the purpose of the company's existence. He is the customer of the entire company, and we all need to perceive him as *our* customer.

The customers are not only the source of today's wealth, they are the means of success tomorrow. They are likely to be more in touch with the market sector concerned, and are thus a fount of information necessary to plan tomorrow's business.

The idea that one customer is more important than another is extremely dangerous. It is probably a myth, since the importance of tomorrow's business will be difficult to gauge with respect to individual customers. The negotiation that occurs prior to and during a contract should ensure that any differences are ironed out. The variation between size of company, research potential, and nature of the work can be resolved, so that a mutual balance of specification, price and delivery, (ie. Quality) is reached.

Once this balance is achieved, each and every customer has the right to the best possible Quality standards, and they are all equal in this right.

Customers are ignorant

If a company knows its business properly, it will be an expert in its field. Inevitably then, the company personnel know more about the processes and the finished product than the customer. Indeed, this is the main reason for the customer to bring the business to the company in the first place.

In almost every transaction today there is an element of a service. Even where people consider that they sell only objects to maximise the potential sales, they will find themselves giving advice on their use, storage, or whatever. The technical manager in modern industry is as much a salesman as the sales executive.

Don't despise customers for the ignorance that they display. It is your business opportunity.

Customers have a wide knowledge

There is, however, every chance that your customer knows more about the applications and potential uses of your product than you do. Inevitably, customers will have a wider knowledge of the industrial sectors involved than the supplier company.

This is why his view on the actual specification requirement must be respected. The customer will always carry great weight during the negotiation stage, since he does have this wider knowledge. There is an opportunity here, for the supplying company to become more knowledgeable than it was before the negotiation.

Customers need Quality

The customer's need for Quality is just as strong as that of the supplier. He is just as dependent on high Quality levels. His high demands for Quality are being made to allow him to be the best in his business sector. If he is helped to become the best, he will assist his supplier in the same direction.

He probably has a similar history with regard to management styles and priorities as the supplier company, but may not be as advanced with his Quality thinking.

The obvious sense that inhabits TQM is worth spreading to your customers.

Customers want to win

Industry is a battle field. Everyday there are winners and losers. No-one has a right to win, and there is no unwritten law that decrees that any company in particular will lose.

Success comes to those who are better than the others in the field, whilst failure will always be invested in those who are not the best. Every customer is in business to succeed: not just today, but tomorrow and in the long-term as well. Assume that your customer not only wants to win, but will win. Make sure that you go with him, sharing his drive, enthusiasm, and will to succeed.

The customers understand the marketplace better than most, and will be ideally positioned to decide on future strategy. Learn and live.

Customers have a choice

Every customer has a choice of whether to buy or not to buy.

Again, every customer can decide to do the work in-house. He chooses not to because it is in his best interests not to, but the choice is always there.

Customers and suppliers are on the same side

This simple statement is hard to believe when examining the conflicts that rage; nevertheless, it is true. What is mutually good for the supplier and customer will bring success to both (see Fig 13.4).

The end-user

The end-user is often the most ignorant person in the chain – ignorant, that is, about the product.

People don't buy products. They buy solutions to problems, or satisfactions to needs. They are more concerned with the problem, desire or need than with how it is achieved. This is why advertising and strong salesmanship works. Customers, convinced by advertising that they have a need, will purchase the item or service to satisfy a need of which they were previously unaware.

End-users buy promises!

The perceived Quality of the product will also be assessed in this manner. It might be marvellous, beautiful and work perfectly, but if the purchaser doesn't think it is needed, there will not be a sale. The Quality of the product will be judged by how well it lives up to its promise.

- Is it good value?
- Is it reliable?
- Is it fit for the desired purpose?

It must be remembered that the crude aim of industry is to part the end-users from their money. As such, the competition may not be the alternative manufacturer of like or equivalent products, but an alternative use for the end-user's funds.

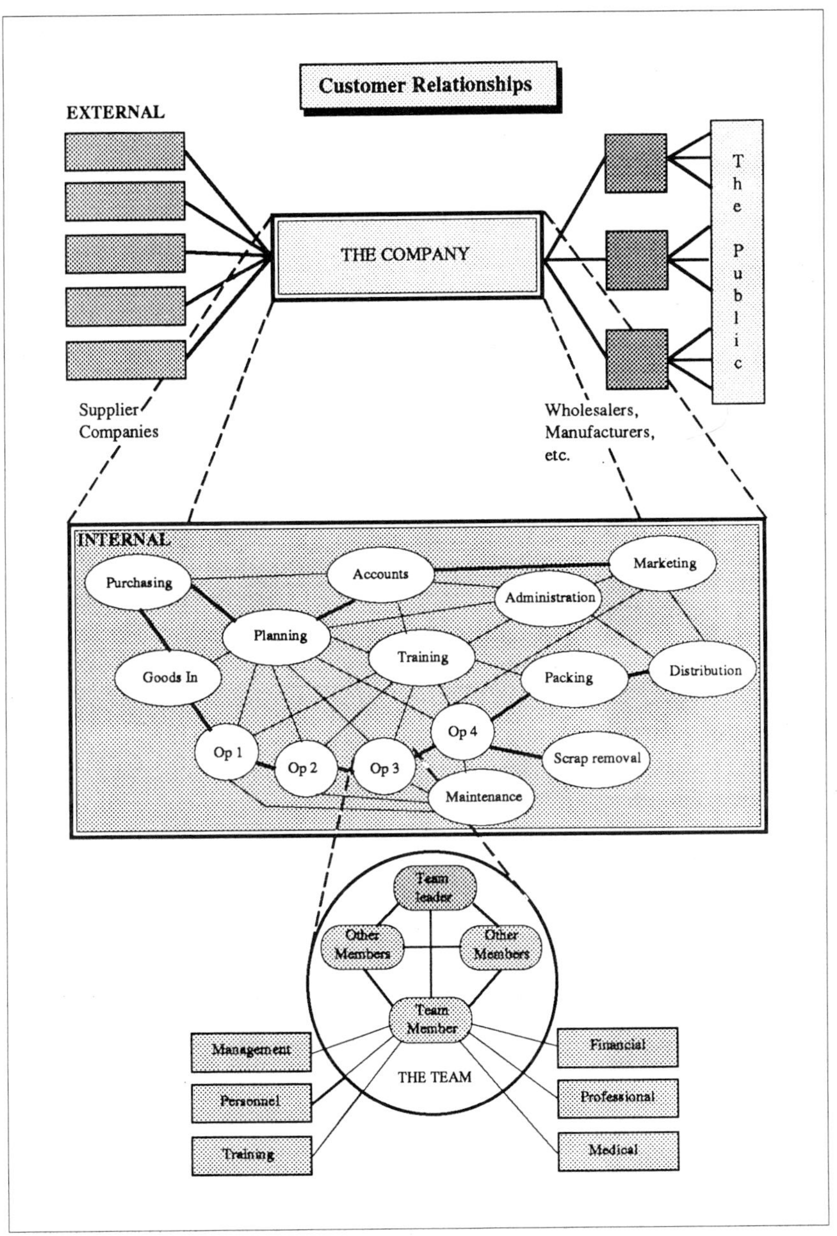

Fig 13.4 Typical customer relationships.

An example of this during the late 1980s was the decline in foreign holidays purchased by UK residents. Whilst the better summer weather in the UK was cited as one reason, the privatisation of gas, telephones and other public utilities is thought to have moved money from savings and foreign holidays, into share holdings. Time will tell whether the new share holders continue this habit, or whether some other unrelated aspect of their lives will feel the winds of change.

Partnership for satisfaction

Whichever part of the concept to user chain is considered, the customer relationships have the same underlying principles.

In each movement, first of concept, and then of materials, components and finished goods, there is a Quality transaction. Each should be subject to prior negotiation, to establish the exact requirements and expectations for the transaction. This negotiation will be on-going during the process, and will possibly have the benefit of feedback after completion.

At each stage, *customer satisfaction* is the driving force. The maintenance of high Quality standards will only be achieved by each customer being satisfied that high standards have been maintained. This is as true for internal and external customers, as it is for the end-user.

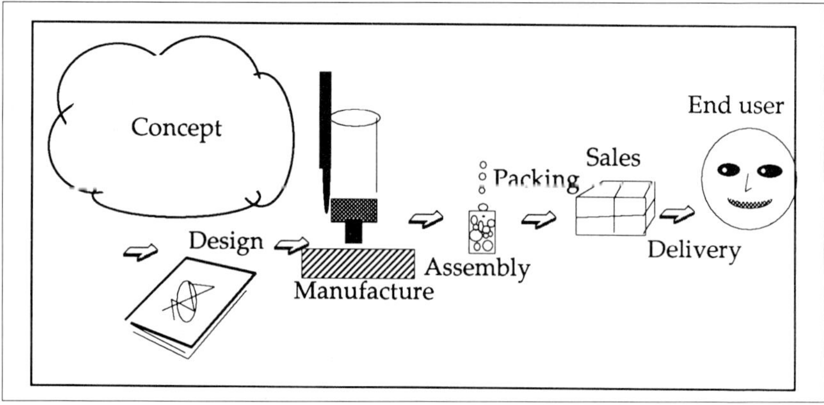

Fig 13.5 Concept to user chain.

The whole chain represents a partnership. The interests of everyone are served by the maintenance of high standards throughout the entire chain. When any one part produces less than acceptable standards, the poor Quality is transmitted onwards throughout the remainder of the chain. The end-user receives a product of questionable Quality. Future business is jeopardised, not just for the supplier to the end-user, but to everyone in the chain.

Customer Care principles

Co-operation The inter-dependent nature of all customer relationships demands that both parties, in each transaction, work together to achieve the desired result – 'customer satisfaction'.

Confidence Virtually all customers are more interested in something other than the product. The end-user is concerned with the use to which the product is to be put, whilst the internal customer seeks the temporary use of the product, until it is incorporated into his work, and moved to the next customer. They all desire peace of mind. They want the confidence of knowing that the transaction is sound, and that the product is of good Quality, and the result of tightly controlled processes. They want the confidence of customer satisfaction.

Continuity Few are involved in a one-off transaction. For nearly everyone, tomorrow's problems are an extension of today's. Successful transactions today will ease the future task of obtaining the satisfaction of tomorrow's customer.

Quality The full meaning of Quality, that is meeting all the negotiated requirements and expectations of the customer, will underlie each transaction. This will include the specifications, the timing, the presentation, the cost and all the myriad of other concerns of the customer. A smile is an essential component of most customers' satisfaction.

Total Quality approach to customer care

Many companies accept the principle of customer care in terms of meeting the needs and concerns of the end-user. Besides the general rhetoric, this is most often demonstrated by the provision of information at the point of sale, and in a substantial after-sales service.

Again, many translate the concept of internal customer relationships into in-house procedures and methods, without giving the internal customer the same status, rights and indeed, voice as the external customer.

Only a few companies attempt to take the customer care principles and build them into the day-to-day transactions in all their own departments.

And yet, this is what TQM demands. If we are to identify individuals as customers, they must be invested with the status to allow them first to negotiate, and then to demand good Quality. If this is not established, the theory will remain as rhetoric, but the practice will live as poor Quality standards.

This status as a customer with rights to negotiate and obtain high Quality standards, must be backed by knowledge and experience. The demands on education at all levels in the company, will be considerable throughout the next decade. Extended understanding and vision will be part of the new working relationships. People must be fully educated in the areas in which they deal, in order to be able to make effective judgements, conduct responsible negotiations and confidently insist on, and deliver, Quality.

Idea

Employees are internal customers who
have the right to customer status.

Duties

A duty to demand Quality from each and every supplier

A duty to give Quality to each and every customer

Fig 13.6 Customer duties.

Total Quality Management demands the active involvement of everyone, in an informed and responsible manner. All must be good customers if they are to be good suppliers.

Summary

A customer is anyone who has the benefit of the work, activity or actions of another.

A supplier is any person whose work, activity or actions, benefits others – *benefit* is used in the wide sense of assisting, influencing and making possible, some aspect of the customer's life.

Customers

Internal customers	are people who, whilst benefiting from the process, share the company's goals and objectives. Both parties in the supplier/customer relationship are in the same company. Formal and informal negotiation methods are necessary for these relationships.

External customers	are those, outside the originating company, who obtain the benefit of company processes. Customers are essential, ignorant, have a wide knowledge, need Quality, want to win, have a choice, and are on the same side as the suppliers.
End-users	are the customers without any other customers for the commodity involved. End-users buy promises, and thus question the product's good value, reliability and fitness for the desired purpose.

Customer Care principles

Co-operation
Confidence
Continuity
Quality

For TQM, all must be good customers if they are to be good suppliers.

Last thoughts ....

Words can give an impression. I well remember the amazement I felt when, as a youngster. I heard a train announced as the 'semi-fast train to London'. I had already noted from the timetable that it stopped at every station.

Chapter 14

Quality and the Supplier

If fools went not to market,
bad wares would not be sold.

– Old Spanish Proverb

Route-map

This chapter continues the study of the supplier/customer relationship, and considers that it should be a partnership.

It examines who is the friend or foe of a company, and shows how the Demand Now, Pay Later (DNPL) policy operates against this principle.

The idea of 'preferred suppliers' is developed, and the mutual benefit explored. The customer always purchases more than just the product.

The manner in which the supplier becomes a customer is examined, and the chapter is completed by linking the internal and external customer relationships.

Caveat emptor

This ancient Roman legal maxim, meaning 'Let the buyer beware', should underline all dealings with supplier companies. The good supplier relationship embodies trust, good value, cooperation, common understanding and mutual benefit. Underlying all such relationships will be the responsibility of the *buyer* to be content with the deal.

The Duchess, in Alice in Wonderland[1] said, 'If everybody minded their own business, the world would go round a great deal faster than it does'. There are two possible meanings to her tirade. Apart from the suggestion that people should take no part in other people's affairs, or as the French say, 'people should occupy themselves with their own onions', the statement could infer that the world would be more efficient if everyone could manage their own affairs better.

The supplier relationship

Within any supplier/customer chain, the introduction of poor Quality is the result of someone, somewhere, accepting a less than satisfactory product. The essence of understanding the supplier relationship is the consideration of customer assurance. That is, how can the customer be certain that all goods and services supplied are of good Quality?

Partnership

Whilst it is obvious that the supplier company is in business for its own gratification and success, that gratification and success is dependent on the gratification and success of its customer, you.

Business with the supplier company is a two-way relationship. It is conducted for the mutual benefit of both companies, both now and in the future. Indeed, any infringement of this mutual benefit will, ultimately, be to the detriment of both sides of the arrangement, and will be reflected in the goods and/or service reaching the end-user.

This attitude is in sharp contrast with the majority of supplier relationships within industry. Evidence suggests that most large companies believe themselves to be in competition with their suppliers. They view the supplier company as a business opportunity. Most chief executives would deny this, but allow their company to operate the Demand Now, Pay Later (DNPL) policy.

The supplier battleground

The supplier battleground should be one of competition. Competition between suppliers is viewed by most as entirely healthy. It ensures that companies keen to do business hone their activities to produce good

Quality. Competition is the life blood of industry. As A H Clough, the nineteenth century poet said, 'Thou shall not covet; but tradition approves all forms of competition'.[2]

Competition should be reserved for your competitors, not your customers and suppliers. As Deming says, '... he that hopes only to meet the competition is already licked'.[3] He describes an industrial society dedicated to 'all-out war to destroy a competitor, be he at home or abroad.' It is important to be able to appreciate *who is on which side.*

During the 1980s there have been several spurious deals in the UK between Japanese companies and their supposed UK competitors. Short-sighted government has often been involved in an attempt to off-load poorly managed nationalised industries. In all such deals, the Japanese appear to have been the winners.

No, it must be clearly understood that, in business, the enemy is the competition. The competition is any other company, whether at home or abroad, which can promise and/or deliver similar goods or services. There may be other enemies, such as alternative types of products, other uses for the customer's money or in the case of those concerned with education, ignorance, but this does not mitigate your direct competitor's role as an enemy.

Your friends must be all those involved with the satisfaction of the end-user – the customer.

The enemies of a company:

- All those who seek to offer the same products, as the company.
- All those who seek to offer an alternative to the products of the company.
- All those whose best interests would be served by the demise of the company.
- All those who believe or preach that the products of the company are not necessary.
- *In short,* everyone who would benefit from the loss of a sale, or any other form of business activity by the company.

The friends of a company:

- The company's shareholders.
- The company's directors.
- The company's employees.
- All the company's suppliers.
- All the company's customers.
- All the suppliers to the company's suppliers.
- All the customers of the company's customers.
- *In short,* everyone concerned to satisfy the needs, requirements and expectations of the end-user.

Our own employees are friends?

To many who have grown up amid the industrial strife of the post-war years, the description of the workforce as *friends* will appear foreign. The damaging battle between different sections of a company for resources, influence, or straightforward remuneration, has been documented elsewhere in this book. Suffice to say, that if a company cannot resolve such differences within its own gates in order to stand united against the opposition, it stands little or no chance of working efficiently together with the other members of the supplier/customer chain. The success of the entire chain will be put at risk by any dissonance anywhere within it, and can easily be jeopardised by enmity within the major company.

Idea

If the supplier/customer chain succeeds, then everyone in that chain wins*.

Even more true – if the supplier/customer chain fails, then everyone in that chain loses.

* given good management (the sharing of success may be a necessary ingredient).

The constant struggle between the management and shopfloor of the major UK automobile producers, throughout the last decades, symbolises this absurd waste of human energy, and must be a significant factor in the decline of this industrial sector.

DNPL policy

Another factor working in direct contradiction to these definitions of the company's friends and enemies is the DNPL policy. Its use within British industrial management rivals the internal conflict between management and unions as the most damaging aspect of archaic industrial practice.

This policy is assumed by so many to be good business practice that it presents one of the fundamental rethinks necessary to achieve total Quality. The DNPL policy is a myth. Far from saving money, as believed by those that use it, it is highly expensive to operate. The disturbance caused by this apparent breach of the supplier/customer contract often results in considerable extra expense to both parties. For the supplier, there are interest charges on the sum involved, plus the

The DNPL Policy

Demand Now, but	Payment for all moneys owed to the company should be demanded, as soon as it is possible
Pay Later	All payments out of the company should be retained as long as possible

Fig 14.1 DNPL.

cost of a credit controller and all the additional actions necessary to procure the payment at all. It will probably cause cashflow and on-going investment problems, and thus infect more of his business, both with the customer, and other companies.

For the customer, his accounts and/or purchase ledger department spends most of its time responding to telephone calls. A number of its payments are re-routed or rushed through, in response to fierce and justified complaints. More expensive methods of payment will often be used. Subsequent accounting will be a nightmare.

The consequences spread further. These poor business methods may lead the better supplying companies to withdraw from the fray, thus prohibiting further business. Alternatively, they may refuse to deliver any more goods or services until a particular payment has been made. At the very least, they will be reluctant to perform at their best, even though this may not be a conscious decision. Human nature dictates that people will try hardest for the customers who have played fair with them. If they know that a prompt delivery will elicit payment within 30 days, they will put themselves out to service this order. They will probably be prepared to take additional steps to look after the good customer. The bad payer loses by default. Such a company is inevitably lower in the priorities for service.

In extreme circumstances, the situation worsens. The supplying company may be carrying so much bad debt, not non-payers, but late payers, that it is robbed of needed investment. Unable to keep up to date with the competition, it may be forced to cease trading. The customer company has lost a valuable supplier.

The alternative scenario is possibly more frequent. The supplying company, finding an ever mounting debt with a particular company, needs to protect itself. It may either slow the supply of further goods, or put a stop on further dispatch until payment is made. It often imposes a ceiling on the debt that it is prepared to carry. It releases the next order only on receipt of a previously invoiced payment. The customer, usually a much larger organisation, probably remains unaware of the situation, or any awareness never leaves the accounts department. Others continue to order parts, goods or services, unaware of any commercial problem, until their failure to arrive causes plant failure, loss of production or some other highly expensive result.

Many companies can relate tales of such incidents, and production staff are well aware of both the dangers and the problems. However, it is symptomatic of the poorly run, non-total Quality, company that the production, the commercial and the accounts department all work to different agendas and with a variety of priorities. This is extremely expensive. Resultant costs should not be considered production cost since they stem from a failure of the company to be properly managed. They are Quality costs, and are quite unnecessary.

This is not the end of the process of additional costing. As so often with disturbances to smooth business practice, the circles of disturbance become ever wider. All the costs described above, to both the customer and supplier companies, have to be met. They can only be paid for from one fund, that is out of the pocket of the end-user. These additional costs will eventually find their way right through the supplier/customer chain, being reflected at each stage in higher prices. The end product is a less competitive product.

Since this practice is widespread throughout British industry, it contributes to the uncompetitive position of the UK in world markets. This has implications for the UK's balance of payments, interest rates, inflation and unemployment. The implications are so vast that it is amazing that the practice continues. It really would be so easy for every company to adopt a Quality Policy, in which they undertook to meet their contractual obligations and pay within the stated credit period. They would find it easier to adopt systems to achieve this than to continue the present messy practice of responding to those who *shout last or loudest*.

If there was one factor that could increase the productivity and competitiveness of the whole of British industry overnight, it would be to pay itself within the normal 30 days credit period. Readers from other parts of the world can relax, it is unlikely to happen, for such a seed change requires one major ingredient: education.

Preferred suppliers

It is becoming the custom to develop a preferred supplier list, from which to draw supplies. Such a list has many good effects on the business for both parties in the subsequent transactions, and can work in their mutual interest.

In preparing such a list though, the company should beware of extending it too widely. It is not a healthy practice to have several suppliers providing the same item. Multi-sourcing crept into many industries during the 1960s and 1970s. The idea was to limit the power of any individual supplier. This allowed the company to be protected from any breakdown, dispute or other stoppage within its supplier companies. It also enabled internal competition to force down prices. The effect on such blatant manipulation was the awarding of contracts solely on a price basis, and the gradual lowering of standards, particularly Quality.

The conflict between supplier and customer grew, and so the cost of Quality became greater. Business conducted in this manner is essentially short-term, and will tend to be inspection-based.

The fourth of Deming's 14 Points for Management, advises:

> *'End the practice of awarding business on the basis of price tag. Instead minimise total cost. Move toward a single supplier for any one item, on a long-term relationship of loyalty and trust'.*[4]

In many ways, the preferred supplier list embodies the long-term relationship between customer and supplier. The benefits are:

Long-term business

There will be enormous benefits for both parties, stemming from an apparent long-term commitment. Planning is easier and the supplier's resourcing can be aligned with future business prospects.

The fruits of the expertise developed by the supplier,in meeting the initial orders, can be harvested during later contracts, for the betterment of supplier and customer.

Assessment of supplier's ability

The development of a preferred supplier list allows the company to investigate and assess the ability of the supplier to meet, and exceed, the desired Quality standards.

It is unhelpful to judge the supplier on the strength of the first items delivered. They may not be typical of future production. More confidence can be gained by considering the process methods being employed. Indeed, the process control, statistically based or otherwise, will be the deciding factor for the Quality of on-going work. It will be helpful to assess the systems under which the processes operate, and the in-house ability to undertake the necessary on-going process improvement work. Repeated on-site discussions with everyone involved will be necessary to make such assessments.

Investment in expertise

It is worth considering why the assistance of a supplier is sought in the first place. There has been a tradition in both America and the UK to develop whatever skills are needed in-house, rather than use suppliers. This is the reverse of the practice in Japan, where it is believed that a company cannot have sufficient expertise to be the best at everything. They prefer to look for such expertise within specialist companies wherever possible, only keeping tasks in-house when this practice is not economically possible.

Many see economic advantages in purchasing the specialists. The specialists are employed for as much, but only as much, as are needed. Such a specialist is likely to keep up-to-date with the latest skills and technology, or even be out front breaking new ground. Such activities, inside a widely based company, have to compete for resources with many other demands, and the decisions are inevitably made by people not fully appreciating or understanding the specialisms involved.

Whilst it is often mutually advantageous for the customer to invest his expertise in the supplying company, the security of a long-term relationship is necessary to recoup the advantage.

Any joint investment, whether in skills, equipment or purely financial, will be to their mutual benefit.

Financial assistance

It is becoming the practice for major companies to invest financially in the smaller supplier companies. This may be formally, by purchasing some stock, or it may be by supplying the engineering or management expertise,necessary to upgrade the performance of the supplier.

Few smaller companies have the resources to undergo the training in modern methods needed, and again, it is in the mutual interest for this to be supplied by the customer.

Where particular work, for which the supplier lacks the plant and machinery is required, the customer can equip the supplier with that which is necessary, whilst still retaining ownership.

Cooperation

In all these ways, the companies can work for a mutually assured future. This cooperation can be extended into other areas. The smaller company's experience may well be of value in the design of the next generation of products. Its expertise can add to the marketing potential, and subsequent product confidence.

The more links there are between the two companies, the better their joint operation will be. Cooperation with friends has to be in their mutual interest. This cooperation must reflect a mutual interdependence, though, rather than developing into a one-way relationship, with the supplier totally dependent on the customer for business. Such a monopoly position can easily be abused.

Quality assurance

In the final analysis, this development of mutual goals, and their means of attainment, will be essential for Quality performance.

It will lead to ever smoother business relationships, since much of the on-going negotiation will be eased by past reference and experience. The cost of such transactions will be minimised, and the effort expended by personnel in each camp will be maximised.

Negotiation

The centre of this long-term relationship, as with every aspect of business, is *negotiation*. Indeed, it is the use of negotiation that ties Quality into the central issue. Negotiation is the discussion and meeting of minds. It involves all concerns prior to the operation of a contract. Agreement should be reached, not only on the outline, but on all the essential details. These will include price, date of delivery, and every other aspect held to be important by the customer.

It is at this point that any misgivings concerning the ability of the supplier, or indeed the veracity of the customer's requirements, are ironed out. An honest and open attitude, from both sides, is essential. The practice of obtaining sales at all costs, and worrying about meeting the exact requirements later, is bound to end in poor Quality, and in an inharmonious relationship.

The customer is purchasing more than just product. The customer purchases:

Product

The contract to purchase, or purchase order, will contain the exact requirements, stating specification, number, time of delivery, packing, price, etc.

This is the basis, and often the bulk of the written agreement. The more information that is included in the discussion, the higher the Quality of both contract and completed product. The more people included in the discussion, the greater the understanding of the customer's expectations, hence the better contract, and finished product.

Management

The customer also purchases the project management necessary for the contract. This will include the facilitation of the processes involved, by ensuring the provision of every aspect of each of the 6Ms for all the processes. It will also provide the management skills, within the supplier company, to ensure the adequate performance of the supplying company.

This is yet another reason why supplier companies can often perform better in specialised areas than the host company. Their management has a greater understanding of the complexities and implications of the processes involved.

Good examples of this can be found in any industry that depends upon artistic ability and a creative flair. The people possessing the greatest talents in these areas, often lack the necessary commercial discipline, or even self discipline, to allow these talents to be fully utilised within a business environment. It often requires particular management skills to release the full potential of such talented people.

It is in this area that the consideration of production methods is appropriate. This might be reflected in the requirement to have certain Quality control procedures, such as SPC, or even design and process FMEAs. These methods are often the only way to assure consistent Quality standards.

Peace of mind

The customer has sufficient worries of his own, without taking on board those of the supplier. He seeks hassle-free production and delivery.

If there is to be a difficulty, he wants the maximum notice of the problem. This will enable the consequential effects to be minimised.

What customers do not wish to purchase is information about problems they already knew they had, such as 'I am sorry that yesterday's delivery did not arrive.' Customers do not wish to purchase excuses, (a commodity often found in great abundance), nor do they want alternative products or services, 'I am sorry that we cannot deliver your components, but please find enclosed tickets for a holiday in Spain'!

The supplier is also a customer

No business relationship is entirely one-way. The same definitions of Quality and negotiation apply in both directions.

There may be many areas of reverse relationship, but the supplying company becomes the customer in each of these areas:

Money

Once the products have been delivered, whether goods or services, the supplier becomes a customer. He is as entitled to Quality as the original customer. The DNPL policy, discussed above, demonstrates a poor attitude to Quality.

Information before contract

Such a transfer of information will be vital if the requirements and expectations of the customer are to be met.

Full negotiation

Both sides in the negotiation are entitled to a full, honest and open approach to the negotiation. This is a necessity. This includes the prompt and proper reporting of any circumstances that alter the arrangements negotiated as part of the contract.

Live feedback

Those expanding their expertise during the course of a contract are entitled to a feedback on the effects of their work. If this feedback is live, any lessons available can be quickly learnt and implemented.

Internal and external suppliers

Every point made above concerning the relationships between suppliers and customer companies, also applies to the internal relationships.

It will only be by developing realistic and working internal customer relationships that Quality can be assured, and constant improvement achieved.

Summary

The motto for the customer is 'Caveat emptor', 'buyer beware'.

Supplier/customer relationships should be a partnership.

The friends of a company: - everyone concerned to satisfy the needs, requirements and expectations of the end-user.

The enemies of a company: - everyone who would benefit from the loss of a sale, or any other form of business activity, by the company.

DNPL Policy = Demand Now, but Pay Later

Preferred suppliers for :

- Long-term business.
- Assessment of suppliers ability.
- Investment in expertise.
- Financial assistance.
- Cooperation
- Quality assurance.

Within the Quality negotiation, a customer purchases:

- Product.
- Management.
- Peace of mind.

The supplier is a customer expecting:

- Money.
- Information prior to contract.
- Full negotiation.
- Live feedback.

All Quality theory applies to both internal and external customer relationships.

Last thoughts ....

There was a pig farmer who did not get as much for his pig at market as he expected to, but then, he didn't think he would!

1. Carroll, Lewis, *Alice's Adventures in Wonderland'*, Chapter 6.
2. Clough, Arthur, Hugh, *The latest Decalogue.*
3. Edwards, Deming, *Out of the Crisis,* University of Cambridge Press, 1982, p. 149.
4. Edwards, Deming, *Out of the Crisis,* University of Cambridge Press, 1982, quoted from p. 23 and explained in detail on pp. 31-49.

Quality through People

A Blueprint for
Proactive Total Quality Management

Part V

Q TQM

The Blueprint

Chapter 15

The Quality Culture

Remove the barriers that rob people of pride of workmanship.

– Dr W Edwards Deming, Out of the Crisis {No 12, from Deming's 14 points for Management}

No art can conquer the people alone – the people are conquered by an ideal of life upheld by authority.

– William Butler Yeats Dramatis Personae

Route-map

This chapter seeks to explore the concept of a company culture. It considers the values on which the culture is based, and identifies five steps necessary to achieve a cultural change within any company.

A company culture

Every company has a culture. Few are created deliberately. Most have evolved over years and reflect the values and priorities of those who have been in charge of the company.

Most company cultures are tolerant. They allow more than one set of values to coexist. They accept a variety of motivations and expect aberrations. These aberrations may be in the form of employees who cheat the system, are untrustworthy, or who live a different set of standards to those accepted as the norm.

The identification of 'the company' is not always easy. Some feel it has substance, above and beyond the existing people and buildings, rather like 'the regiment' or 'the school'. A more practical interpretation would be the total workforce, whereas the legal interpretation would be shareholders and/or the board of directors. The objective of a Total Quality company is to reduce these differences, by aligning the good of one group with the good of another.

The company culture is central to the ability of the company to perform efficiently and effectively. It is far too important to be left to chance. Effective TQM needs the deliberate creation of a deep culture, structured on distinct values, definitions and objectives. The ideals necessary for a harmonised and unified company must be embodied in this culture, by both custom and practice. The culture must be lived; that is Total Quality must be lived. A Quality culture must be created.

This culture is at the heart of the TQM theory and philosophy. It is entirely defined by the intrinsic values that underlie every act, decision and attitude, and is exhibited within each of the many individual personal relationships that go to make the working environment of the company.

People-centred

An evaluative understanding of people is central to understanding the Quality culture. Such an understanding will raise the crucial nature of the management of people within the organisation. Thus, essential to the construction of an effective Total Quality culture is an understanding that:

- People are the only source of creative energy (people control many other sources of energy, but it is a truism that any tool is only as good as its master).
- Delegated authority is essential for efficient production within a complex or diversified organisation (process control by the people closest to the process, will mean individuals having delegated authority throughout all levels of the organisation).
- Only educated people completely fulfil their potential (educated implies an ever-increasing knowledge of both the physical and human processes that surround each individual. Education, in this sense, is a dynamic concept).

Fig 15.1 Quality through people.

Few would argue with these three statements, yet few companies fully exploit their true significance. Tapping the human resource within a company has to be the major challenge of the 1990s.

Four levels of cultural influence

Any culture is based on a set of values and beliefs that are considered the norm within the organisation.

Society

The starting point for cultural development,will be an understanding of the 'host' culture, or cultures, that is the culture of the society in which the organisation operates. Obviously, the national culture, or Western culture is the major host culture in the UK. This is inevitably a loose cultural package, becoming more diverse as the West becomes more multi-cultural, (moving from the strictly Christian way of life) and wider as national boundaries are dropped and more people become increasingly concerned with broader issues.

The influence of the church should not be underestimated, within this consideration. The Protestant work ethic[1] still plays a strong role within the consciousness of many. It contributes to modern political theory and must contribute to the views and expectations of everyone.

Trade-based

Added to these wider, and looser issues, may be a 'trade-based' culture. Examples of this can be seen in most industries. There are accepted standards. There are expected working practices. Whether you work in a foundry, on the farm, in a city or in a car plant, certain strong influences will abound. The presence of strong trade unions may have a profound effect on this trade-based culture and, if so, should be a vital consideration when embarking on any cultural change. The trade-based cultural traits will be narrower than the societal influence, but still wider than the company culture.

Company tradition

The company culture will be the accepted norms by which the company operates. Such a set of values and beliefs is described as a 'value-system'. There is such a value-system behind every company. It will inform and direct most acts, decisions and attitudes. In most companies

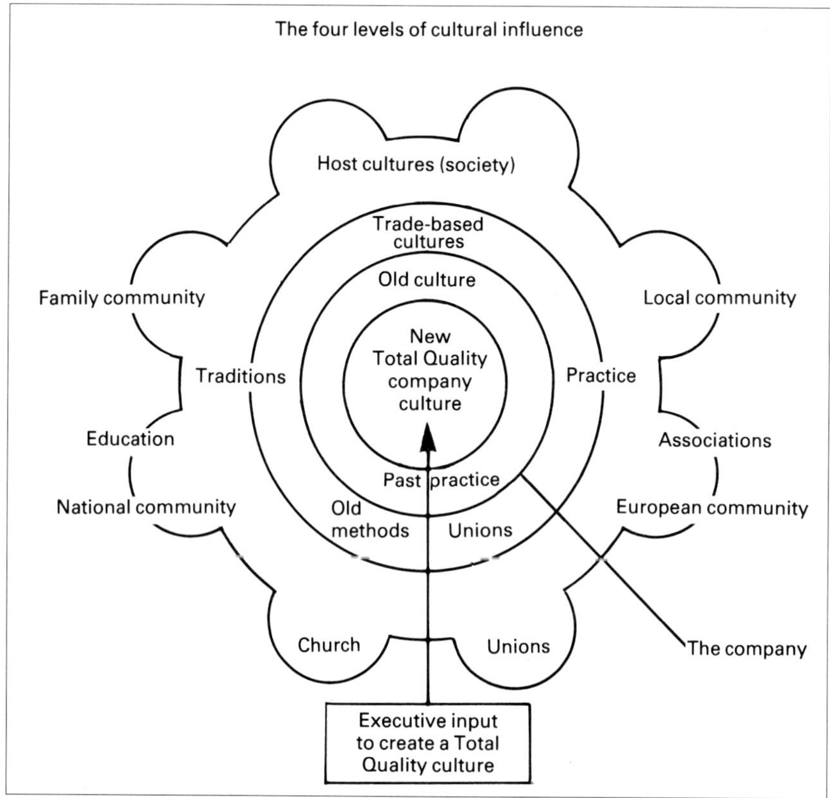

Fig 15.2 Four levels of cultural influence.

there is no single objective binding all together, and thus many acts, decisions and attitudes are in conflict.

There is an inevitable compromise between the traditional values of the company, as exhibited by the many influential people within the company, and the desired values of the executive. These desired values could form the basis of tomorrow's company culture.

Traditional values, as with traditional working practices, relationships, fears and attitudes, can be considered as the 'baggage from the past' that a company inevitably finds itself carrying into the future. It is important to appreciate that it is quite possible to gradually shrug off such baggage by changing the attitudes and practices of involved employees, or indeed, by changing some of the people. However, this is not easy, as such baggage from the past is very resilient to rhetoric, and hard to eliminate.

Total Quality input
The daily life of everyone within the company will have to change for their perceptions to change, and thus, for the culture to change. Total Quality provides such a focus, and the range of modern Quality methods become the tools that change the relationships, practices and reality of work.

Cultural values

Within what value-system should a company operate? Most people have a clear set of values and beliefs to set forth: their own! However, it is clearly unhelpful to moralise. Whilst it would be interesting to describe the author's desired value-system, it will differ from that of the reader and the reader's company, and hence will be of limited value.

Instead, questions must be asked to stimulate an understanding of exactly which fundamental beliefs *lurk* behind a company's operations. Clearly, the societal values, the morals and indeed the system of law underpin every company and are, therefore, of great importance. The aim is not to replace a culture, but to develop it, gradually narrowing it to the main company objectives.

The Total Quality company will perceive its long-term survival as dependent on the central aim of Total Quality.

Long-term objectives

Negative situations may have to be counteracted and shown to be undesirable, if viewed over time. A company operating in an illegal and immoral fashion, by stealing its raw materials and cheating its customers, may succeed economically in the short-term, but it is hard to envisage long-term success. On the other hand, many companies have found themselves disadvantaged in commercial relationships in parts of Africa and the Middle East, when they failed to understand the significance of '*baksheesh*' in some societies.

As there can be no dissonance between the definitions of Quality inside and outside the company, there should be no conflict between the value-system operated inside and outside the company. A company which openly cheats its customers, using the judgement of 'how much can we get away with?', should not be surprised when employees adopt the same attitude to the company.

Defining the cultural values

Four basic lines of questioning are relevant when trying to identify the value-system of a company. They each revolve around some aspect of *respect*, or the principle of ordered priority. This is the direction a decision will take, when those involved are faced with a conflict of interest. The counter-balance in such a situation can usually be described as some short-term expedient, usually accounted for in terms of direct money. These areas of 'respect' should be identified as superseding such instinctive management reactions.

Four areas defining the company value-system

1. Respect for humanity.
2. Respect for the individual.
3. Respect for honesty.
4. Respect for knowledge.

The identification of the company value-system can be problematic. Indeed, the clarity of the value-system could be seen as an indicator of the efficiency of the management style. These values will be embodied into every managerial act, decision, and attitude. The more closely individual managers' actions, decisions and attitudes are aligned, the more effective and successful the company management practice will be. Any dissonance between managers leads to the consumption of internal energy. Whilst the senior executives can issue statements denoting what values are important to a company, value-systems are essentially *lived*. They inhabit every human relationship throughout the company, and are communicated to suppliers and customers by every employee having such dealings.

1. Respect for humanity

Industry belongs to society. The purpose of industry is to enhance the life of people on this planet. The embodiment of Quality in industry is the Quality of Life enjoyed by all those involved with the industry, whether as suppliers, employees, shareholders, or customers. The net may be very much wider than the immediate customer list, since benefit extended to one person will often increase human activity, spreading the advantage to many others, and in many ways. The provision of fuel to a transport firm allows the distribution of foodstuffs, enhancing the lives of many people who both produce and consume the food. The acts of these people whose health, in a small way, depends upon this trade, will continue the benefit.

Regrettably, though, there are usually unfortunate consequences to this spread of the fruits of industry. The diesel fumes left by the lorry conveying the food stuffs damage the health of children living near the motorway. The respect for humanity exhibited by a company will be the balance between the beneficial and the damaging aspects of its activity.

Some state openly this commitment to 'humanity'. The late Kaoru Ishikawa wrote,

> 'Companies exist in a society for the purpose of satisfying people in that society. This is the reason for their existence and should be their primary goal'.[2]

Industry exists to enhance the life of all those who are the beneficiaries of the industrial effort. There is a moral standpoint that must gauge this value. Long-term environmental damage often has to be placed against the more immediate benefit of the company, and those in decision-making positions. The moral dilemma can be seen. Indeed, the inability of a company clearly to expound its own value-system contributes to the poor Quality outputs. In many of the dealings of the company, with either the local or global community, there must be a Quality consideration. Those who geographically share the environment with the company are also its customers. A steel works or power station justifying continued pollution by claiming that it is within certain enforceable standards, could be seen as evading an overall moral responsibility, and to be demonstrating a contempt for its own personnel, who often have to live in the polluted environment. A humanitarian approach may not be opposed to a commercial orientation. However, if it is, the executives of a company should ask themselves where they stand personally, with relation to these questions. What objective conclusions can be drawn from the past actions of the company.

Do we really care, as a company, for the world outside our business? Does the company have a relevant policy?

2. Respect for the individual

This is an extension of the respect for humanity. A large number of individuals are connected with the company: consumers, employees, shareholders, distributors, subcontractors, their subcontractors, and so on. Indeed, many of these individuals support a family, whose well-being will depend on the economic success of the company. Each of these people should feel happy with the moral stance of the company. The value-system of each individual should not be in conflict with that of the company.

This is not enough, though. Each individual will have personal needs. Each will seek a way to make use of his capabilities, skills and interests.

QUESTIONS

1/ Does your company import materials from the third world?
2/ If it does, do the workers involved receive a living wage?
3/ How does your company dispose of non-recyclable waste?
4/ Does your plant polute the atmosphere, in any way?
5/ Is your plant visually attractive, inside and out?

Fig 15.3 Respect for humanity.

Each person will wish to find satisfaction in their daily life, and realise his full potential. Theoretically, there would appear to be no conflict of interest with that of the company. If this is self-evident, there is a need to explain the apparent lack of interest in the self-fulfilment of the workforce to be found in most companies.

A well orientated and motivated individual will exhibit a degree of autonomy and spontaneity. People have the ability to exert self discipline. They have a decision-making capacity, ingenuity and a capacity for total appreciation of a situation. In short, they use their heads. They think!

Respect for the individual will not only safeguard the individual's rights and safety, but will ensure that the potential of each individual has the opportunity to blossom and develop. A major senior management responsibility is this unleashing of the human potential trapped within the workforce. No additional energy in industry is needed, merely the release of the latent energy within people. Total participation is needed.

There is a parallel with the previously stated attitude to work and wealth. We don't need more. We need to use what we already have, better.

The questions to be asked concern the value of each individual as opposed to the mass. Again, there will be no clear answers, but the questions are worth investigating. The answers will need to be embodied into the Total Quality Strategy.

Do we really care, as a company, for the people inside our business? Does the company have a relevant policy?

QUESTIONS

1/ Does your company offer secure employment?
2/ Has your company made people redundant, in recent years?
3/ Are ear/eye protectors worn by all within designated areas?
4/ Do most people consider that they have a job or a career?
5/ How are the causes of accidents analysed?

Fig 15.4 Respect for the individual.

3. Respect for honesty

Whilst in many ways this cannot be separated from respect for individual humans, there is value in the consideration of honesty as a separate issue. Honesty is not a definitive commodity. It tends to be a society-based standard. Indeed, Durkheim[3] described it as a class-based standard, with each class having its own rules for what is an acceptable standard of honesty. Perhaps openness rather than honesty, is a better description of this concept.

The lack of honesty may well be exhibited as non-information, rather than false data. It may produce false expectations, rather than directly mislead. Above all, it will lead to the allocation of blame for the outcomes, rather than to a constructive assessment of the situation.

In a closed society, people 'keep their heads down', and do not engage in activity, or even thought, that could be considered not strictly their business.

Honesty (openness) will inhabit every relationship, negotiation and dealing, both within the company and between individuals in different companies. It is suggested that the standards accepted, encouraged, tolerated, condoned or expected in one area, will gradually be transferred to other areas. In a well managed company, there will be a common view of what is accepted and expected. Otherwise, individuals will exhibit a different behaviour on different occasions, and two results will be a total lack of consistency, and an absence of confidence in any particular outcome. The subject of honesty is returned to at the end of this chapter, when its relationship with 'blame' is considered.

QUESTIONS

1/ Does your company make information generally available?
2/ Are people too 'optimistic' when judging future performance?
3/ Is there an open management style?
4/ Is there an attitude problem within the company?
5/ Could the company be described as having a blame culture?

Fig 15.5 Respect for honesty.

David Hutchins, in his book 'Just in Time', identifies, *Trust* and *responsibility* as essential features in the development of homogeneous working relationships.[4]

This theme is repeated time and time again by those responsible for developing Total Quality within their organisation. To question the respect for honesty within an organisation, examine the passage of relevant knowledge about the company. Look for the *hidden agendas* present within meetings: 'What is the real purpose?' Identify the strength actually lying behind statistics. How 'funny' are the numbers. To what extent are people prepared to express exactly what they feel? How much feeling, opinion and thought, is kept back, for fear that it may not be accepted in the spirit given. The opposite force can be described as power. In a closed society, knowledge is power.

It has been said that in business, as in war, success is all that counts. Do we, as a company, really have any integrity?

4. Respect for knowledge

This aspect may be more difficult to come to terms with than the others. Clearly, our sophisticated society is based upon a great deal of scientific exploration and discovery. It could be said that all societies are based on, and distinguished by, their accumulated sum of knowledge. The problem would seem to be more concerned with the individual than with society in general. Knowledge has become very specialised. No-one could be expected to understand every aspect of our complicated solar system and its contents. Because of this, many appear to shrug off any general desire to expand their knowledge.

Much of industry today, is based on tried and tested principles, that is, it is static. Our relationship to change may play a part in our attitude to education. It is a 'good thing' for others, but not for me.

The company's stance needs to be questioned in relation to:

- Its own technology.
- Its understanding of business.
- Its appreciation of change, new ideas, etc.
- Its expectation of individual self development.

The opposite to a respect for knowledge is probably nearer to laziness than ignorance. Everyone has undergone a degree of education, and many consider that the acquisition of academic knowledge belongs only with the formative years. Yet the total knowledge within the company is merely the sum of knowledge of individual employees. Theoretically, we need to learn every waking hour of every day of our lives.

There is considerable 'bad baggage' to contend with in this area. The British culture has traditionally linked 'education' with 'class'. Many consider that schools reinforce this perception by giving rise to as much failure as success. Thus, many individuals feel excluded from the benefits of knowledge, and develop counter-cultural ideals that belittle academicism. This is by no means limited to the lesser achievers, though the vast majority of the workforce may not expect to advance their theoretical or academic knowledge by any significant amount. Learning is considered to be an activity largely undertaken early in life, at school and during an apprenticeship. Work is expected to be something essentially practical: skills may be learnt, but not theory.

Whilst recent pressures have contributed to a breakdown of this stance, not least the retraining following mass unemployment and the various government inspired training schemes, the emphasis is still on skills training, rather than on wider and deeper education.

Does the company wish to expand its knowledge? Do individuals enjoy academic study? Are opportunities provided for individual self development? Does the company have a relevant policy?

QUESTIONS

1/ Have you undergone any education this year?
2/ Does your company circulate books/articles for staff to read?
3/ Have you kept fully up to date with knowledge in your field?
4/ Do you employ unskilled labour?
5/ Does your company meet the cost of additional education?

Fig 15.6 Respect for knowledge.

Changing the culture

Few companies have attempted openly to change the company culture to a prescribed set of values. Inevitably, therefore, their progress in this direction is slower than desired. Also, the eventual culture, whilst changed, may not be exactly in line with the Total Quality image they seek to expound.

By considering the social implications of these changes, and by examining and understanding the present cultural climate of the company, much wasted effort can be saved. An additional bonus will be the opportunity for more people to have an impact on the eventual practices that will govern the company.

Step 1 Examine the present

This is best achieved via a series of presentations by influential members of the company, jointly representing all departments and areas of activity.

If there is a strong trade union influence within the company, this is the moment at which to involve its members, so that their view of reality can be matched with others to present an overall collection of perspectives.

Differences in emphasis and interpretation should be expected, and it should be emphasised that no one perception or opinion is necessarily more important than another. The aim is to present the spectrum of views that represent the present situation. Differences here don't matter. Differences in the future perception will. It is thus important to understand the various standpoints from which individuals are coming, hopefully to arrive at the same point, or at least to move in the same direction.

Step 2 Identify desired value-system

By addressing each of the four areas of 'respect', it will be possible to highlight areas of importance. Indeed, since the need within a Total Quality environment for the four areas of respect is self-evident, there will be little disagreement at this point. The unanimity will be strained by the next exercise.

Step 3 Develop policies to embody value-system

Policies are needed to embody the practical methods that will lead to the creation of a Total Quality company. What aspects does the company hold most dear? It is better to work with the present set of declared policies in mind, if not actually on the table. In this way, the executive group will be aware of the radical departures from previous policy and, indeed, where the existing policy is being restated, strengthened or reinforced.

Step 4 The Total Quality Strategy

This is best achieved by a strategy group, that is by one other than the executive group. In this way, the strategy group can incorporate the modern Quality methods applicable to individual areas of the company, as well as represent the interests of all.

The group will report directly to the executive, which takes the responsibility for implementing the strategy.

Step 5 Implement Total Quality Management

It now becomes the task of everyone within the company to work to improve the performance of every process, with the aim of total customer satisfaction. Central to this drive will be the cascading of education, clarifying the Quality Policy and Strategy, and teaching the understanding and methods necessary for its achievement.

Blame v honesty

There are many facets to the culture of a company, and they will be found within every relationship and interaction between company personnel. Many aspects reflect the type of people involved, but others are created by the management style operating within the company. Two cultural aspects found in every organisation are *blame* and *honesty*. They are directly related, and are interwoven in every part of the company.

Blame

The allocation of blame leads to the perception of human failure. This blame will inhibit any real research into the cause of the failure, indeed the cause is thought to be known – the person.

The alternative approach questions why people fail and considers the whole range of inputs to the process. The root causes of the failure can be identified. Improvements are then possible.

Blame is results-based. Such criticism is seen as personal, rather than concentrating on the task in hand. Many now maintain that no-one has the right to criticise the person, only the task for which the individual is responsible.

The use of blame is common in areas in which very little control by the people involved is possible. They are made to feel responsible for results that are often, partially or completely, beyond their control. Thus, blame is often an irrational emotion. It is, nonetheless, deeply felt by the people who give it, and by the people who receive it. Resentment is nearly always the outcome.

As a commodity, it is self-perpetuating. The blamed will usually look around for someone else to blame. Blame is pushed up through an organisation, just as much as it is handed down. Senior managers are held, within most organisations, to be guilty of all manner of crimes. Once given reign, it will spread throughout the organisation in a most unhelpful and expensive way. Blame is probably the biggest inhibitor of process improvement, since it diverts and consumes all the internal energy available to deal with a process failure.

- Results seen as 'Human failure' rather than 'Process failure'.
- Allocation of responsibility, without control.
- Criticism is seen as 'personal', rather than 'task' orientated.
- Often irrational, yet deeply felt.
- Self-perpetuating, two way and endemic.

Fig 15.7 Blame.

Honesty

Everyone is honest. All sane people can justify their actions to themselves. People are honest to the group with whom they have affinity. Therefore, the personal definition of honesty will refer to this perceived group. For the loner, this may be a group of one, whilst in a diffuse company it will be the group of work-mates, or the department. Only in a unified company, where there is no dissonance between the company and the individual, can it be assumed that everyone is honest within the company as a whole. Where there are divided loyalties, people are loyal to the closest, and usually the smallest, perceived group. The company can only expect loyalty, and thus honesty, if there are no forces questioning the individual's loyalty to the company.

Where differences in goals lead to pressures, there is a growth of 'funny' numbers. These were mentioned in the section on MRP2, in Chapter 9, as having a catastrophic effect on the planning of activities. Loyalty to the department or group produces optimistic forecasts, or numbers that keep a little back for a rainy day. Again, this is a symptom of the diffuse company.

In general, people are more likely to be honest and open in situations in which they feel they have some control. Such honest relationships are bred by free communications and a general openness throughout the organisation.

Honesty, rather than dishonesty, is proactive. Dishonesty is seldom deliberate, but occurs by default. Wrong conclusions may be drawn

Honesty

- Defined as honest within one's perceived group.
- 'Funny' numbers .
- Stems from responsible situations with a degreee of control.
- Jeapodised by divided loyalties.
- Honest relationships bred by communication and information.
- Proactive, that is, dishonesty occurs by default.
- Self-perpetuating, two way and endemic.

Fig 15.8 Honesty.

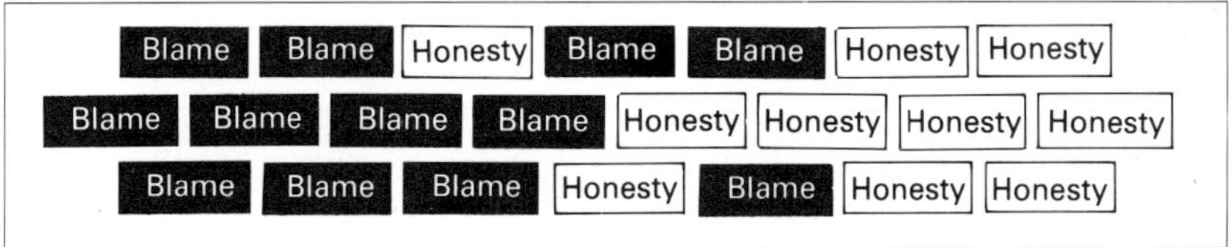

Fig 15.9 Honesty/blame wall.

because nothing was said, rather than because a deliberate attempt to mislead was made. As with blame, honesty is self-perpetuating and, given a chance, can be endemic within the organisation. It is a good indicator of the culture of the company.

The blame/honesty spectrum

Both honesty and blame inhabit every company. It is the proportions which are important. An environment in which people expect to be blamed will lead to a lessening in honest relationships. Conversely, an open environment, free of blame, will produce honest information and involvement.

Many feel trapped by the environment in which they work. But there is nothing stopping anyone from opting out of the blame culture. Readers may like to question where they and their company fall within the spectrum. If they are unhappy with the results of such introspection, they should identify methods to redress the balance.

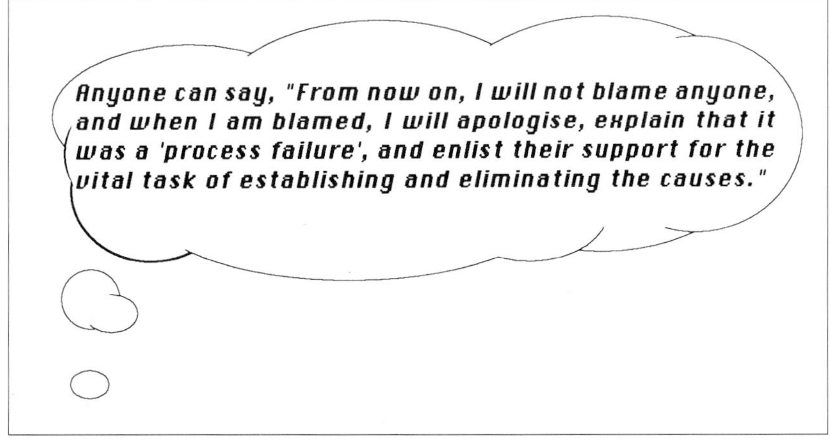

Fig 15.10 Opt out of blame.

Summary

A company culture

- People-centred.
- Incorporating the director's value-systems.
- Four levels of cultural influence:
  Society
  Trade-based
  Company tradition
  Total Quality input

Cultural values:

- Respect for humanity.
- Respect for the individual.
- Respect for honesty.
- Respect for knowledge.

Changing the culture

Step 1 Examine the present.
Step 2 Identify desired value-system.
Step 3 Develop policies to embody value-system.
Step 4 The Total Quality Strategy.
Step 5 Implement Total Quality Management.

The blame/honesty spectrum

Last thoughts ....

When considering the use of slogans, I am reminded of the time when, as an impressionable teenager, I visited our local US Air-Force base. We went to see their basketball team in action. We arrived at the base and entered the guard-house to get passes. This was the first time I had met a military policeman, of any sort, and I was confronted by two bright shiny US Servicemen, covered in white belts, gloves, highly bulled guns, lanyards, badges, arm-bands and peaked caps, polished so that we spoke to our reflections. Across the back of the room, below the giant crest of the 257th Red Horse Brigade (or something like that, my memory has lost the detail), was a vast notice headed 'Charter of the US Air Police'. Below it detailed the duties of the Air Police, 'As a United States Air Policeman, I will honour the President, protect the Nation, serve my fellow countrymen,......'I confess that I don't remember the details, but I have never since viewed slogans in quite the same way.

1. Weber, M, *The Protestant Work Ethic and the Spirit of Capitalism,* Allen & Unwin, London, 1930.
2. Ishikawa, *What is Total Quality Control? The Japanese Way,* translated by David J Lu, 1985.
3. Durkheim, Emile, *L' Evolution pedagogique en France,* Alcan, Paris, 1938.
4. Hutchins, David, *Just in Time,* Gower, 1989.

Chapter 16

A Total Quality Commitment

The heart of Quality is not technique. It is a commitment by management to people and product – stretching over a period of decades and lived with persistence and passion – that is unknown in most organisations today.

– Tom Peters[1]

Route-map

Justification and explanation is given for the concept of change being driven from the top. Commitment and understanding are needed to create a living Quality culture.

The chapter continues by considering the development of a Quality Strategy, and shows how the phased introduction of the Quality Strategy can be accomplished.

Commitment means total belief, with a total understanding and vision. The chapter concludes by assessing the meaning of 'Total' in Total Quality Management.

Commitment

People who are committed, live!
People who are committed, believe!
People who are committed, understand!
People who are committed, care!
People who are committed, *succeed!*

Glib but true. A commitment to Total Quality involves living Total Quality, through a total belief in the world that Total Quality will create. Such people understand that it is a better world, where not only are the profit margins larger, but people are happier, more cooperative and give much more of themselves to their work. They understand from very obvious basic principles that this is a better life. They understand their business and they understand people. They care passionately for the people they work with; they care passionately for the company, for the product, for the customer, for the whole way of life they are helping to create. They care about success, and they succeed!

Commitment means a total belief

Simply, without this total belief in what is happening and what can be achieved, nothing comes true. Belief is not difficult, since, when the method of doing business is looked at objectively, and through the new, questioning eyes of someone who believes in change, Total Quality makes sense and the benefits are self-evident.

Commitment will breed a lack of tolerance. Others must believe, others must be convinced. This will be particularly true of those who occupy a higher seat at the table of decision-making. They must believe, they must not be allowed just to follow the trend, fashion or apparent whim. Commitment needs this total belief, and total belief needs a thorough understanding.

Commitment means a total understanding

Commitment must be approached through knowledge and experience. Commitment is an academic exercise in which the enquiring mind ascertains the truth. A commitment to Total Quality is a commitment to education and, above all, to self-education. It is a commitment to logic and common sense.

Total understanding will never be achieved in one mind among many. Total understanding requires a spread of knowledge, a widening of belief and the full use of logic and common sense by everyone. To widen the commitment, spread the dream.

Commitment needs total vision

The dream is centred on the total vision of the dreamer. The total vision must be able to include the role that everyone must play: each relationship, every decision, always. Total Quality is this vision. It provides a total set of priorities, decisions and actions. It dictates attitudes and relationships. It gives purpose to everyone's working life.

Total

Simply everyone, everywhere, always!

Total means 'from the top'

TQM not only needs to have the full commitment at the top of the company, it needs to be driven from the top. It needs living, believing, understanding, caring and succeeding, from the top.

Total means 'from the bottom'

TQM requires the full participation of everyone, and most of the people that need to be unshackled from dreary, poor Quality work are at the bottom. With encouragement, motivation, and education, they can be the standard-bearers.

Total Quality needs everyone, at all levels, and in all departments of the company.

Total means 'in every decision'

Total Quality theory can form every priority, and thus influence every decision. Simple, yet vital yardsticks are placed in everyone's hands to enable everyone in the company to be able to make the same decision for the very first time.

The judgement, in any case, is the same. To what extent does this meet the negotiated requirements and expectations of the customer? Where there is doubt, find out more, and learn. When a decision proves, with hindsight, to have been the wrong one, say a prayer. Be grateful. An opportunity to learn and expand the knowledge and experience of the company has been presented. It re-emphasises the need for Total Quality, and outlines the route to its achievement.

Total means 'in every activity'

The company needs the unifying force of an ideal or aim that supersedes those found in different departments and activities. This ideal will stem from the basic values of the company, and will embody Total Quality.

It will operate in every activity, enabling each individual, within each activity, to develop customer relationships with others. Total Quality as a direction, unifies the company.

Total means 'a total commitment'

Clearly, if the company is to actively pursue Total Quality, the total commitment of everyone will be necessary. This commitment must be sufficiently strong to supersede other commitments and, therefore, must be firmly based upon an acceptance of logic and theory. There must be a strong belief in Total Quality as a way of life, not just because it makes sense and is morally right, but because it is seen as the way to succeed in business – the only way.

Commitment and education

Most companies declare a commitment to particular ideals and concepts. However, it is by no means easy to assess the effective commitment of a company to any particular idea. A company is a collection of individual people, each with their own sense of commitment. Even when a particular individual, such as the managing director, is considered, commitment is still difficult to assess.

In some ways, it is a 'chicken and egg' situation. It is impossible to be fully committed to an ideal that is not fully understood, whilst it is hard to devote time and energy to educating oneself in an area or direction without a full commitment.

To create change, both *commitment* and *understanding* are needed.

Education is the way to success. Commitment grows from the knowledge and understanding of basic ideas, developed during the education process. Whilst this is obvious, it has yet to become the norm.

Most companies claim to be committed to Quality. Unfortunately though, commitment without understanding is commonplace. Commitment without understanding is fickle. It is here today and gone tomorrow. Individuals within companies are committed to all manner of ideals, but only the most dominant are ever implemented. Commitment without understanding is very dangerous. It leads to all types of decisions and actions being taken, in the name of the cause, which *conflict* with the ideal.

Disagreement and unresolved conflict between individuals, followed by disillusionment and cynicism, all become inevitable. Rather than being a unifying force, such ideals aggravate the diffuse nature of the company. Human history is littered with the results of half-understood ideas, poorly implemented. Historians usually look for the resultant back-lash, which swings the pendulum in the opposite direction to that intended by the original advocates of the idea.

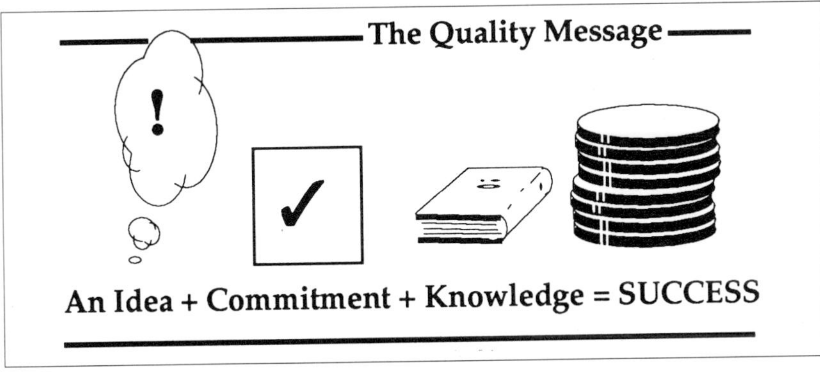

Fig 16.1 The message.

A living culture

With Quality, as with most important ideals, it is not so much rhetoric and faith that are sought, but individual perceptions. These individual perceptions will form and direct every decision and action. For success, they must all be in line, sympathetic to each other, and part of a common understanding. They are not conscious individual perceptions, but are a reflection of the generalised view of reality. As such, the ideals are rarely questioned. The truth of the perception is rarely tested; it all becomes just a 'way of life'.

This situation is often described as a Quality culture, but people are seldom aware of the nature of the culture in which they live. It is a mass of thoughts, values and ideals, all generally understood and accepted as inevitable. We cannot spend too long here ruminating on the nature of a culture but in order to understand the real meaning of a cultural force, we might ponder the place of honesty in a family situation. If it has to be questioned and examined, it isn't really part of the culture. When it has become unquestioningly assumed to be omnipresent, it is a feature of the culture.

All manner of ideals are incorporated into every company, and become taken for granted. A group of process workers of a small component manufacturer were asked if the company treated the employees well. 'No,' they replied, 'The company never gives us anything!' The question 'What about at Christmas?' brought a prompt reply, 'Well yes, they do give each of us a bottle of sherry or whisky.' 'What about the Christmas 'do'?' 'Well, yes, we do have an afternoon off to have a party, all expenses paid by the company', put in another operator. 'And there is the day trip to France for our families every summer', said a third. 'But I don't drink whisky, and anyway these things have always happened. I don't go to France, we have to buy our own lunch', put in the original complainant, obviously convinced that the company never really gave them anything out of the ordinary.

Idea

Total Quality should become part of life's furniture.

The aim – living Quality

Quality, or rather the overriding belief that Quality, customer satisfaction, on-going negotiation, and meeting requirements and expectations are all the reason for industrial life, becomes quietly accepted as part of life's furniture. This is the direction. It will take time. It will need careful nurturing, tolerance and understanding, in the same way as an offspring of a deprived family might need care and attention. Consider the care needed to bring a youngster from a home built on theft into an honest mode of living. It is possible, but the first step will be believing; believing that it is not only possible, but essential.

Living is believing. Living a culture is believing in that culture. Believing is living. Believing in the culture is living the culture.

But who should believe first? Where should the commitment originate?

Commitment from the top

It is trite, but commitment from the top is absolutely necessary. So many believe that Quality is something for someone else to do, not appreciating that they personally will have to live it daily.

Commitment *from* the top, rather than the commitment *of* the top, is essential. The latter implies that the executive has rubber stamped the Quality ideas for others to implement. Let's throw away human rubber stamps. The senior group should delegate the decision-making process to those who will implement it, wherever possible. Where they too will need to be involved, the executive should be an active part of the decision-making, thus again, not needing a rubber stamp. A rubber stamp is not necessary. Quality demands commitment *from*, not *of*, the top!

Moreover, a real Quality culture demands an educated commitment from the top. The executive, or senior management team, must be the first group of people to develop a complete understanding of what the Quality culture is, what it will produce, and the implications and benefits of the focus on Quality.

The word 'executive' is used to describe that strata of senior management which controls and manipulates the macro direction of the company. As is pointed out to managing directors from time to time, this may be an executive team of one, if none of the executive power has been delegated. Nevertheless, it is important that this executive, whatever the size, appreciates the fullness of such a responsibility. It must educate itself to be fully committed to the direction of the company. The ship must have senior officers, educated in navigational techniques and with up-to-date charts.

Consider this conversation, and its encapsulation of the idea of commitment, or rather lack of commitment from the top.

Mother calling upstairs, 'Jimmy, its time to get up!'

No reply.

'You'll be late for school.'

After a few minutes, 'I don't want to go to school!'

'You've got to go to school, get up.'

'But I get shouted at, and bullied by the teachers, I don't understand what goes on there, half the time, I don't want to go!'

'But, you've got to go.'

'Why have I got to go?'

'Because you're the headmaster!'

While the author was actually writing this chapter, he received a phone call from a production manager, asking for training for his *blokes* on TQM. When it was pointed out that Total Quality must start from the top of the company, he replied, 'Yes, yes, yes, we are committed to Quality and all that, but I want some training for my blokes, so they know what they must do!'

The author would welcome suggestions of suitable answers.

Realisation, dream to reality

When attempting to direct change, whether in a small company or in a major corporation, there is a chain of concerns that have to be met, in order to create the required changes. Fairly quickly, ideals have to be converted to ideas, statements of belief, etc. Ideas need translating into personal attitudes, throughout the organisation. These attitudes need developing into deliberate actions, to ensure that the attitudes produce the required effect. The deliberate actions will gradually become automatic reactions, as the original ideals become the culture of the organisation.

This process, once started, should move forward gradually but remorselessly. The speed of implementation will be a reflection of the size and culture of the company, but the momentum of change must be maintained.

Rome wasn't built in a day, though Nero did manage to burn it down in a night! The vast enthusiasm generated by 'seeing the Quality light' must be held in check. Bill Dolan, an old friend and mentor, who inspired *proper Quality* in the UK Ford Tractor organisation, had a habit of muttering 'There's no instant pudding!' It will take time to accomplish the in-depth changes necessary to ensure the wondrously successful future.

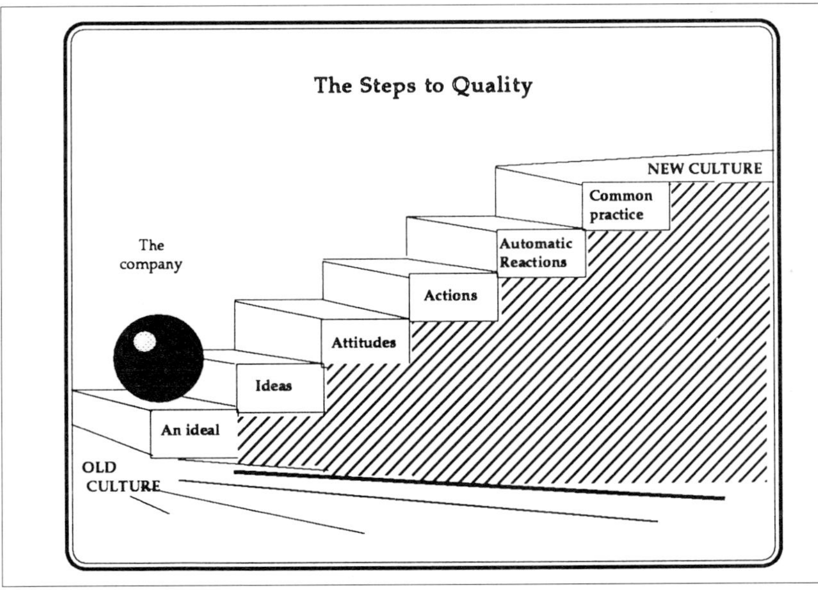

Fig 16.2 Steps to Quality.

Equally though, it will be important to maintain a constant momentum. This momentum will become a way of life, forever. There will never again be a static time of no change. The company will become dynamic.

However, there are too many examples of companies starting this journey without appreciating the remorseless nature of change. Many have started on this road only to stop very soon. They find themselves still concentrating on older concerns, such as this week's production figures.

Beware, the rhetoric/action gap! Those afflicted find that the slowing up occurs *after* the apparent achievement of attitudinal change. It is much easier to talk 'Quality' than to do things that ensure it.

Many larger organisations measure the commitment of the institution to a particular idea by the expenditure on it. Series of seminars, training courses and cascaded education, costs money. They can be organised outside production time, and can happily roll along, daily presenting the image of a company committed to Quality. The crunch comes when everyone has been told how important Quality is, and can recite the definition of Quality and the company Quality slogan, but has no idea *what to do.*

Quality is a direction, and whilst there are no eventual 'happy hunting grounds' for the completely Quality orientated company, it is essential that the next steps are calculated and known before the start of the Quality journey. There must be a plan.

The direction

It is clearly impossible to produce a plan suitable for all organisations. As previously mentioned, it is vital that the first steps of change involve an understanding of the present.

The generalised idea that follows should be used only as an example, allowing the important ideas to be developed. It presents an order of thoughts and inputs to the *Quality Improvement Process*, rather than describing the actual activities to be undertaken.

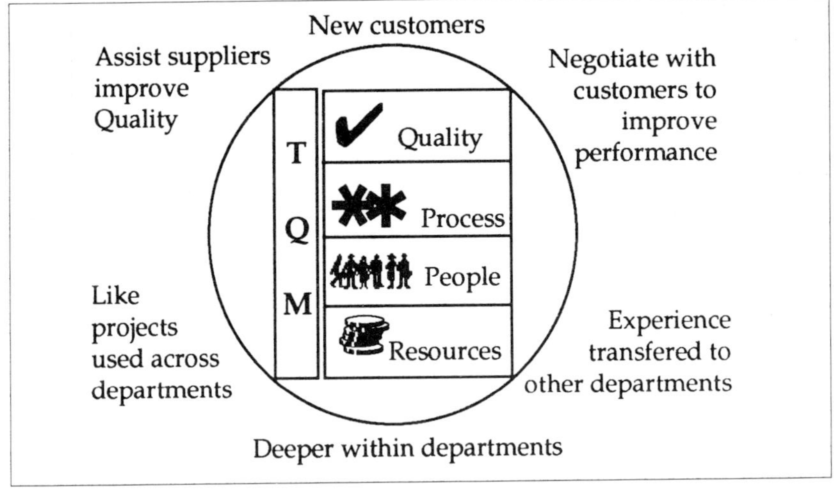

Fig 16.3 Quality ever outward.

The development of Total Quality will inevitably have a small starting point, limited to the executive, or even to a few individuals within it. The influence of the concentration on Quality will grow ever wider, as the ideas will spread, develop, and turn into action. They eventually become the cultural norm for the whole company, and a good part of both the supplier base and customer base of the company.

The Total Quality implementation plan can be considered in seven phases, moving from the acceptance of the Total Quality philosophy by the executive, to the automatic use of Quality concepts and methods by everyone within the company.

The Implementation of TQM

Phase 1 The executive dream.
Phase 2 Appointment of strategy team.
Phase 3 Development of strategy
Phase 4 Spreading the dream.
Phase 5 Implementation of strategy.
Phase 6 Review and adjustment.
Phase 7 On-going improvement.

Phase 1 The executive dream

Behind any real advance is an ideal or dream. Finding time to lift the eyes from the daily grind to look beyond the horizon, indeed to dream, may be difficult, but it is essential. This is the realm of the executive of the company. If the long-term planning and organisation have been completed properly, the executive will have time for this activity.

Stable companies may have a problem in seeing the necessity for change, whilst those that already perceive the seeds of the eventual demise of their company will need no persuading that there has to be a better way. They, however, will be hampered with the problems of keeping their head above water, whilst constructing the better future. The basic knowledge of poor Quality standards, high Quality costs, dissatisfied customers and loss of business, is probably readily to hand. For them, the main impetus can be the need for survival.

The most difficult area of industry in which to achieve change may be the major corporation. The sheer size of many companies creates a multitude of problems. Not least will be the diffuse nature of their culture. In some, arrogance has become a way of life. Many senior executives have spent many years telling each other, and themselves, just how wonderful they are. They have often failed to convince the public, but they do at least believe it themselves. The consequent layers of self-satisfaction and arrogance will need to be peeled back. This will need evidence. The evidence will be perceived as bad news, and the 'difficult person' who insists that the company examines its own drawbacks, will be liable to the same treatment as the messenger bringing news of the military defeats at Thermopylae.[2]

Idea

Every company needs a dreamer!

(Primitive South Sea societies always employ a dreamer as an integral part of the social fabric).

Idea

Every company needs messengers!

It is not unknown to hire a messenger in the form of an outside consultant, able to withstand the slings and arrows.

However it is achieved, the message must be infiltrated into the busy, daily minds of the executive. They must be convinced of the need for Total Quality. The dream will be born in the mind of each member. He will believe, not only that it can happen, but that it should. Each member of the executive becomes a dreamer too, concerned, not just with today, but with tomorrow too.

Phase 2 Appointment of strategy team

The formation of this strategy is best achieved by the Quality Strategy team.

This team should:

- Be composed of about five people.
- Have sufficient experience to command general respect.
- Represent all major areas of the company.
- Be led by a senior manager.

The tasks of the team are:

- To formulate a set of stated intentions or objectives that together will achieve the stated aim of maximising the company's Quality performance.
- To ensure that the means, as well as the objectives, are enshrined within the strategy.
- To present the strategy to the executive group, with recommendations that include costs, a time-scale, and responsibilities.

- To be a monitoring group during the implementation stages, and after it. (This 'watch-dog' function, responsible to the executive, will indicate when and where the practice of the company strays from the stated strategy).
- To review the strategy at regular intervals, and make recommendations to the executive, amending the strategy in the light of experience and changing circumstances.

Phase 3 Development of strategy

The strategy must be based on the intrinsic values of the company, and on such attributes as honesty and fairness, together with beliefs in the value of human resources. The Total Quality Strategy, combines these to achieve the desired aim: a prosperous company in which Quality is the central concern.

Fig 3.4 in Chapter 3 provides an example of a Total Quality Strategy.

Each company's strategy will be entirely different, reflecting the very different circumstances under which it is created. This example is just that, an example designed to give an impression of the types of activities that can be delineated.

The essential elements of this strategy will be:

- Each point is a statement of intention or action that can be clearly understood, appreciated and achieved. It must be a springboard for clearly perceived action.
- The strategy is a management tool. Thus, each point of the strategy will indicate which aspect of the business will be managed and in what ways. It must be relevant to each and every manager. Change must be managed. Quality must be managed. People must be managed.
- The strategy must embody the underlying principles of the company. It should, therefore, address each and every major concern of the company. It must be perceived as the supremely important document of the company, and not open to subversion.
- All the points of the strategy should be perceivable as separate facets of a whole. There must be no implied or overt conflicts within the strategy. The overall aim is to produce one company, moving in one

direction. The traditionally different viewpoints of various departments should be considered, and the actual wording of the strategy modified to ensure that it means the same thing to all readers.

- Quality will be the central issue of all points within the strategy, and each should be under-pinned by the same basic understanding of Quality, related to customer satisfaction.
- The four over-lapping areas that need addressing are:

  Management of Quality
  Management of People
  Management of Process
  Management of Resources

Without any one of these aspects, the Quality initiative is likely to misfire, and fail to produce the expected benefits.

Phase 4 Spreading the dream

Clearly, the mere formulation of the strategy will not be sufficient: the dream behind it must be spread throughout the organisation. The strategy will identify what needs doing, but it will have difficulty in encapsulating the excitement stemming from *why* the company must move in this direction.

Total Quality Strategy Development

1 Executive acceptance of Total Quality Philosophy
2 Appointment of Total Quality Strategy Group
3 Development of Total Quality Strategy
4 Presentation of Strategy to executive
5 Amendment and acceptance of Strategy
6 Implementation of Total Quality Strategy

Fig 16.4 Total Quality Strategy development.

The easiest vehicle for the dream is a clear-cut idea that will have relevance to every employee. It will be up to the individual company to determine what best meets the circumstances. Here are three examples of possible *dream-wagons*:

We are going to be the BEST!

It is hard to find any convincing arguments, in most companies, why they cannot be the best in their field. Whatever the advantages of the competitor, there will also be drawbacks. The route to being the best is by each individual being the best at his job. Excellence is a good word to use, meaning each person excelling. Barry Popplewell in his book Becoming the Best,[3] describes a company moving down this track, complete with all the stereotype management figures to be expected in most companies.

We are going to SURVIVE!

Where this is in question, survival is the most vital issue of the day, for all employees. If doubts have been expressed about the on-going security of the company, these will have been translated into many homes and families. Survival is like war: the rules can be changed, people can be rallied to exceptional effort, and the company can pull together. Each person is working, not just for the company, but for their family and friends.

We are joining the BIG BOYS!

To move a company from its stupefying, run-of-the-mill, ordinary business, to start competing against the big companies for the 'market leader' business, can lift the entire operation and give new purpose to everybody. The first step is to convince people, both inside and outside the company, that this is possible; the next step is to show how! The answer is Quality – giving the major customers exactly what they want. You may find that many of the larger companies fail to achieve this, just because they are larger than you.

Creativity will be needed, to construct an approach that is different and unique to the company. A company needs a phrase that means as much to its employees, as it does to its customers. The Avis slogan 'We try harder', being worn by every employee, meant that most actually did.

A certain structure will be needed to spread the dream. Posters will not be enough. Rhetoric will not be enough. Hope will not be enough.

Education is the answer

Each employee needs to feel that he has been taken into the confidence of the company. He needs to share the dream. An understanding of the centrality of Quality will be essential, together with an appreciation of internal and external customer relationships and the responsibilities involved. Each needs to know the direction, and the means by which the company will move. Each needs to know what contribution he can make and what part he can play.

Phase 5 Implementation of strategy

The implementation of the strategy will involve everyone. Planning will be essential, so that people's daily work changes to meet the new challenges, responsibilities and direction.

Exactly what is to be done and when, can only be established from *within* the company. Clear cut responsibilities will assist the effective changes that will be required. It is vital that all know their role in the procedures.

- Outside assistance: – Suggestions from outside can be presented to stimulate thoughts and discussion.

Idea

Everyone needs to know how he can best help the company!

- The strategy team: – This group will have the task of planning the overall strategy, but cannot be expected to determine exactly how each department implements change.
- Senior managers: – Senior managers must have the accountability for the overall company direction and be responsible for the ultimate success of the Quality initiatives being embarked upon.
- All other managers: – Everyone else in the company must have a part to play. Managers must be prepared to undergo considerable self-development. At the same time, they must be orientated to manage with the right spirit, taking on board the need to amend the attitudes of those working with them.
- Every employee: – Each individual needs to understand where the improvements will take the company and, indeed, the personal possibilities open to everyone within the company. Change means changing each individual person, and personal development should become part of the everyday language and expectation of each employee. The individual employee will often be the customer in this regard, and will need to negotiate inputs to maximise the potential for the company, and for himself.

Phase 6 Review and adjustment

Whilst constant review would be useful, it would probably inhibit the daily workings of the company. A timetable of assessment, review and

Total Quality Management

✔ Quality	Process	People	Resources
Management of Quality	**Management of Process**	**Management of People**	**Management of Resources**
?	?	?	?

Development of these four overlapping areas of management must be co-ordinated within an overall Total Quality Strategy

Fig 16.5 Elements of TQ Strategy.

amendment will be of considerable value, from the outset. A typical time-scale for such activities would be:

Activity	*Time*	*Period between activities*
Development of TQ Strategy	2 months	
Presentation/amendment	1 month	
Implementation of strategy		3 months
Initial assessment and review	1 week	3 months
Second assessment and review	1 week	6 months
On-going assessment and review		every 6 months

The Total Quality Strategy team will gradually be transformed from the group who proposed the original strategy, to the group to assess and review the performance of the strategy. This may require a change of personnel, to ensure that the right questioning skills are always present. It might be the type of group on which each member serves a year or eighteen months, allowing others to become more involved with the Total Quality Strategy.

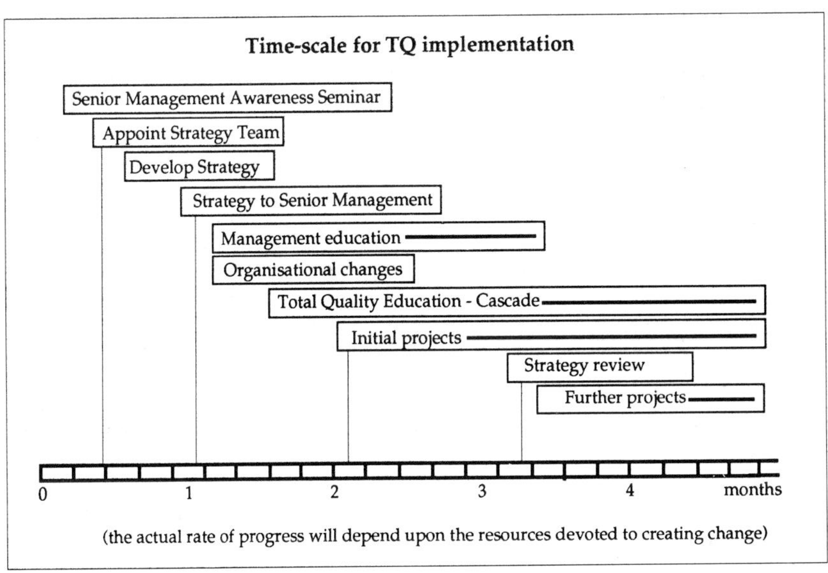

Fig 16.6 Time-scale for TQ implementation.

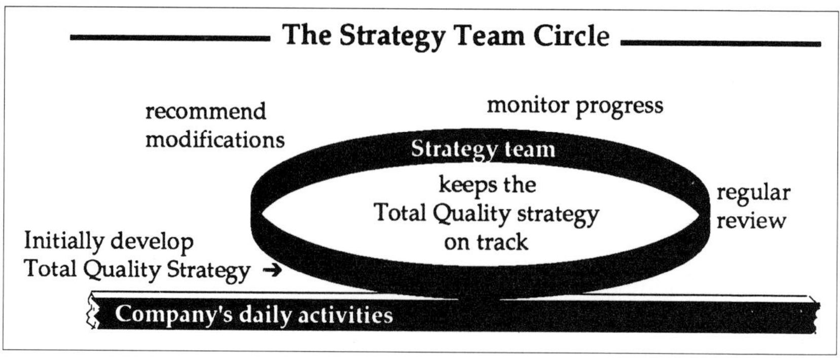

Fig 16.7 Strategy circle.

Like the original strategy team, it should be composed of about five people with sufficient experience to command general respect. They should be drawn from all the major areas of the company and be led by a senior manager.

As previously suggested, the team has a 'watch-dog' function to assess the effect of the strategy, and indicate when and where the practice of the company strays from the stated strategy. It will act as an executive conscience, keeping the ship on course.

Phase 7 On-going improvement

If phases one to six have been successful, the company will have taken on board the need for on-going improvement. This emphasis on improvement will always have several facets.

- Improvement of the company, relative to the competition. It is very easy to become complacent, particularly following success. The dream must be kept alive, or even replaced with an even yet more *fanciful* dream.
- Improvement of the department/team. It will remain important to keep customer satisfaction, as the team objective. Beware the false competition engendered by comparisons between one activity, shift or team and another. Quality will remain the direction for the team. There will always be room for improvement.
- Improvement of the process. Ever more consistency and ever greater capability will be the two measures of process improvement, and

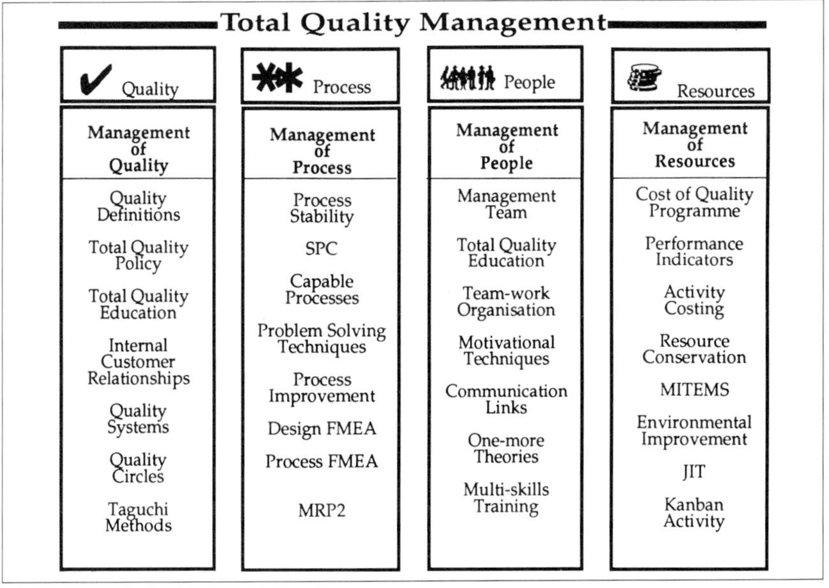

Fig 16.8 TQ implementation plan.

will apply to every process, in every activity, throughout the company.

- Personal improvement. Each individual employee, whether the managing director, or an operator, should perceive his future in terms of doing his present job better, and indeed furthering his career. The development of human resources, by engendering a sense of career, rather than job, is one of the challenges of the 1990s.

McDonald's, the well known fast food chain, is one of the very best examples of the development of a corporate identity. Its motto, 'Quality, Service, Cleanliness and Value', is backed by precise instructions on the McDonald's view of QSC & V. All employees are encouraged to find a

Idea

Every employee has a career in the company,
rather than just a job!

long-term career within the company. Virtually all recruiting for middle and senior posts is done internally, with education and training freely available to all those who wish to develop their own potential.

The result is thousands of successful outlets, with a relatively small number of corporate managers. Employee commitment comes not from a system of management controls, but from a shared value-system.

Summary

- Change must be driven from the top.
- Commitment and understanding are needed.

  Idea + commitment + knowledge = success

- Create a living Quality culture

  Step 1 Thoughts – ideals.
  Step 2 Ideals – workable ideas.
  Step 3 Ideas – personal attitudes.
  Step 4 Attitudes – deliberate actions.
  Step 5 Deliberate actions – automatic reactions.
  Step 6 Cultural change.

Implementing Total Quality Management

Phase 1 The executive dream.
Phase 2 Appointment of strategy team.
Phase 3 Development of strategy.
Phase 4 Spreading the dream.
Phase 5 Implementation of strategy.
Phase 6 Review and adjustment.
Phase 7 On-going improvement.

Last thoughts ....

Confucius didn't say, 'If you change a pebble, you change the beach', but he might have!

1. Peters, Tom, and Austin, Nancy, *A Passion for Excellence,* Collins, 1985.
2. Not liking the news, the Spartans killed the messenger.
3. Popplewell, Barry, and Wildsmith, Alan, 1988.

Chapter 17

A Total Quality Blueprint

The improvement of the understanding
is for two ends: first, for our own increase
of knowledge; secondly, to enable us to
deliver and make out that knowledge to others.

– John Locke

Route-map

This chapter sets out a blueprint for the introduction of Total Quality Management into any organisation. It is, in fact, a matrix of five inputs, addressed to each of the four management areas identified in this book, namely:

Management of Quality
Management of People
Management of Process
Management of Resources

The five inputs applied to each of these management areas are:

Basic concept
Statement of principle
Prerequisite for action
Suggested action
On-going activity

In the 16 concepts, there are 53 principles, with over three hundred suggested actions.

Author's health warning for a yet more difficult task

This chapter encapsulates the theory and practice highlighted in the rest of this book into a complete blueprint for TQM. It is therefore, of necessity, a concentrated mixture of principle, theory and methodology.

The dichotomy for the reader is that, within the confines of the printed page, the blueprint may appear fragmented, whereas success requires a totality of concept and action. The blueprint represents a matrix of concepts, principles and actions, which should serve as an example, rather than a plan. The serious seekers of TQM will create their own blueprint, to turn their dreams into living reality.

The principles are easy; the width of vision is harder, and the generation of action, a longer and yet more difficult task.

The blueprint

Whilst the following is presented in management areas and sections, it should be appreciated that it represents a whole. As such, there must be an overlap between adjacent parts of the matrix.

The order in which any organisation tackles its transformation to a TQM company or institution, will be dependent on its existing culture and managerial strengths. Indeed, perhaps the hardest tasks will be finding the starting point, and the determination of the order of Total Quality activities.

The principles set out below refer to the *organisation,* since the blueprint is valid for any working group of people, be they a manufacturing company, a commercial house, a hospital, or even a boy-scout troop. For those in industry, the reader may wish to substitute the word *company,* in each statement, should this reflect the working environment.

Each principle is drawn from ideas and concepts widely distributed throughout chapters, 1 to 16. To assist clarification, the main chapter from which each principle is drawn, is indicated in brackets, in the form: [Ch1]

Basic concepts and principles

Management of Quality

Concepts	Principles
1 Quality definitions	1.1 The organisation must identify the concepts, such as Quality, that are vital to its existence. [Ch1]
	1.2 The definitions and meaning of these concepts must be available to everyone. [Ch2]
2 Total Quality Policy	2.1 The organisation should have a Total Quality Policy, stating the centrality of Total Quality within its activity. [Ch4]
	2.2 The Total Quality Policy should identify the Quality relationships of all those who work for or with the organisation. [Ch3]
	2.3 The Total Quality Policy should be published to all who have dealings in or with the organisation. [Ch3]
3 Total Quality Strategy	3.1 Develop and maintain a strategy, indicating how the Total Quality Policy is to be achieved. [Ch3]

4 Total Quality culture

4.1 Quality should be a prime consideration within every decision and every action. [Ch2]

4.2 The Total Quality culture should be actively promoted by the executive, lived at all levels of management, and should be intrinsic to everyone within the organisation. [Ch15]

4.3 An active Total Quality culture must be a live organism. It will be ever-changing to control new situations, and thus universal on-going education will be essential to its healthy development. [Ch15]

Management of People

Concepts

Principles

5 Positional significance

5.1 All should understand their position and purpose within the organisation as a whole, including the financial situation and relationships. [Ch6]

5.2 Everyone should understand the responsibilities and accountabilities involved with individual processes. [Ch5]

5.3 All internal relationships should be as a supplier and a customer. Everyone has a duty to demand good Quality and should never fail to give good Quality. [Ch13]

5.4 All should have the skills, knowledge, equipment and back-up resources to enable them to perform with pride and success. [Ch7]

6 Commitment

6.1 Trust, honesty and a high level of integrity should be assumed to be common throughout all levels of the organisation. [Ch7]

6.2 It should be assumed that all are motivated by firstly, the satisfaction of achievement, and secondly the receipt of material reward for that achievement. [Ch7]

7 Team work

7.1 Active team work, in which groups share responsibility, should be implemented wherever possible. [Ch6]

7.2 Process operation should always be perceived as the working of a team. [Ch8]

7.3 Interactive cooperation, rather than competition, should be the basis of both internal and external organisation. Competition should be reserved, in full measure, for the business rivals. [Ch15]

7.4 Leadership and followership are needed by everyone, and all should understand these concepts. [Ch4]

7.5 Every group and team should contain sufficient communication and interpersonal relationship skills to ensure its efficient function. [Ch10]

8 Education

8.1 Total Quality Education is essential for everyone. [Ch16]

8.2 The on-going education of everyone is in the interest of the organisation. [Ch4]

8.3 Multi-skilling of all personnel is the efficient way to use human resources. [Ch4]

8.4 Do not proscribe the development of personnel. Provide everyone with a career route within the organisation. [Ch7]

9 Open management

9.1 An open and honest management style should be the norm. [Ch3]

9.2 Business information, including financial data, should be accessible to all within the organisation. [Ch5]

9.3 The work environment contains many implied messages of worth and value. Everyone needs a pleasant and efficient working environment. [Ch7]

Management of Process

Concepts	Principles
10 Process planning	10.1 There should be a live, overall process plan, to locate each individual process within the overall process. [Ch8]
	10.2 Processes that have no financially sound part to play within the overall process, should be discontinued. [Ch8]
	10.3 All processes should be perceived to be of equal importance, that is vital to the overall process. All processes should be considered to be production processes. [Ch8]
	10.4 There should be integration between all departments and process areas, from design and manufacture, to sales and marketing. [Ch8]
11 Process control	11.1 There should be coherent overall process control mechanisms, regulating each process within an organisation-wide strategy. [Ch9]
	11.2 All processes should produce consistently acceptable results. [Ch9]

	11.3	All processes should be capable of producing virtually 100% acceptable results. (Cpk > 1.3), and the organisation should work towards this goal. [Ch9]
	11.4	Process control is achievable earlier, rather than later, within the overall process. [Ch8]
12 Process improvement	12.1	All processes should be constantly subject to improvement, forever. It is the responsibility of everyone to improve each and every process. [Ch10]
	12.2	No problem is insoluble, and no problem, once solved, should return. All problems should be one-offs and, therefore, new. [Ch10]
	12.3	All designs, both of product and process, should be subject to constant on-going improvement. [Ch10]
	12.4	Organisation-wide use of problem-solving techniques will progressively eliminate all problems that inhibit the proper functioning of processes. [Ch10]

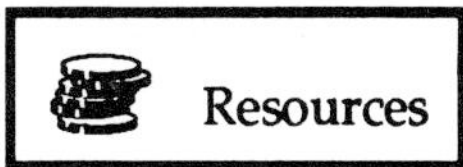

Management of Resources

Concepts

Principles

13 Wealth generation

13.1 All should appreciate the role that their processes have in the organisation-wide task of wealth creation. [Ch11]

13.2 Everyone should appreciate the overall trading (working) position of the organisation. [Ch11]

13.3 Everyone should have access to performance indicators, to compare past and present performance. [Ch12]

13.4 Teams, and other internal groups, should be aware of their operational costs, and other financial implications. [Ch11]

14 Cost of Quality

14.1 The Cost of Quality for each area, department and the entire organisation, should be assessed, broadcast and continually reduced. [Ch12]

14.2 Expenditure on prevention measures will nearly always reduce other Quality costs, that is the costs of appraisal, internal failure and external failure. [Ch12]

14.3 Supplier organisations, distributors and other corporate customers, are all part of the chain to satisfy the end-user. All share the same long-term interests, and their future security is closely linked to that of the organisation. [Ch13][Ch14]

15 Resource conservation	15.1	Everyone should appreciate the value of all of the organisation's resources, including people, money, material, energy, time and space. [Ch11]
	15.2	It is the duty of everyone to conserve the organisation's resources at all times. [Ch11]
	15.3	The consumption of 'internal energy' should be minimised. [Ch5]
16 Resource planning	16.1	Efficient planning can maximise the value of time, space, energy, materials, and all other aspects of the organisation's resources. [Ch9]
	16.2	Efficient processes will minimise the need for handling and storage of materials. [Ch8]
	16.3	The responsibility of the buying function of the organisation is only complete when the goods and services purchased have been fully utilised and their fruits passed to a satisfied end-user. [Ch13]
	16.4	The process of marketing and selling the products of the organisation should be fully integrated with the planning and production activities. Sales staff should be experts in the products, goods and services that they sell. [Ch13]
	16.5	There will be a service element that will be either technical, educational or knowledge-based within every transaction, whether internal or external to the organisation. [Ch13]

Principles and actions

Management of Quality

1. Quality definitions

Principle 1.1 **The organisation must identify the concepts, such as Quality, that are vital to its existence.**

and

Principle 1.2 **The definitions and meaning of these concepts must be available to everyone.**

Prerequisite for action:

- Identification and education of executive or senior management team. (1.1.1)

Suggested action:

- The executive, or senior management team, should draw up a list of the vital concepts, and arrive at acceptable definitions. (1.1.2)

- A suitable list might be: Quality
  senior management
  management
  competition
  leadership
  responsibility
  accountability
  honesty
  customer
  supplier

(definitions will be found elsewhere and in the glossary)

- The concepts, definitions and meanings of these terms should be included in the cascading Total Quality Education programme. [See Chapter 18] (1.1.3)

- Incorporate these definitions into every activity. (1.2.1)

On-going activity:

● The executive, or senior management team, should always use these concepts correctly, and insist that others follow suit. Loose terminology breeds dissonance of attitude and action. The list should be subject to periodic review. (1.1.4)

● It will be vital to ensure that personnel joining the organisation after the suggested Total Quality Education cascade programme has been completed are given similar educational inputs, to ensure that the terminology is kept pure. (1.2.2)

---

2. Total Quality Policy

Principle 2.1 **The organisation should have a Total Quality Policy, stating the centrality of Total Quality within its activity.**

and

Principle 2.2 **The Total Quality Policy should identify the Quality relationships of all those who work for, or with, the organisation.**

Prerequisite for action:

● An understanding of Total Quality Management theory by the executive and board. (2.1.1)

Suggested action:

● Establish a Total Quality team, possibly the senior management team, to present a Total Quality Policy. The team should include knowledge of all the organisation's activities. (2.1.2)

● Present, modify and create a Total Quality Policy, ensuring that it has meaning to everyone concerned with the organisation, either internally, or externally. (2.2.1)

● The adoption of a Total Quality Policy should be a board level decision, since there are considerable implications in becoming a Total Quality organisation. (2.2.2)

● Explore the full significance of the Quality Policy to each individual during the cascading Total Quality Education programme. (2.2.3)

On-going activity:

- The operation of the Total Quality Policy should be periodically reviewed, but only changed if really necessary. (2.1.3)

- Provide tangible evidence that all will benefit from the success of the organisation. (2.2.4)

Principle 2.3 **The Total Quality Policy should be published to all who have dealings in or with the organisation.**

Prerequisite for action:

- Establishment of the Total Quality Policy, and the accomplishment of enough groundwork to be able to demonstrate the organisation's intention of living up to it. (2.3.1)

Suggested action:

- Publish the policy. Display it prominently internally, and ensure that suppliers and customers have a copy, together with some explanation of the organisation's stance and intentions with regard to Total Quality. (2.3.2)

On-going activity:

- Internally, the Total Quality Policy should become the bill of rights, identifying the just cause in any internal dispute or question of priorities. (2.3.3)

- Externally, it should become built into the contractual arrangements with suppliers, and be part of the added value presented to potential customers. (2.3.4)

- The Total Quality Policy must be lived up to, if it is to have any long-term value. (2.3.5)

---

3. *Total Quality Strategy*

Principle 3.1 **Develop and maintain a strategy, indicating how the Total Quality Policy is to be achieved.**

Prerequisite for action:

- Senior management understanding of the concept of the strategy and the value of a Total Quality Policy. (3.1.1)

Suggested action:

- Identify a Total Quality Strategy group. It will probably be drawn from all areas, levels and concerns of the organisation. A group of between six and 11 is often appropriate. The executive should outline a specific brief for its work, and modify and/or ratify their conclusions. (3.1.2)

- The strategy group should identify the essential values of the organisation, and weld them into a framework of activity that will lead the organisation towards Total Quality. (3.1.3)

- It will be important to identify responsibilities, costs and time-scales, either within the strategy, or in documents related to it. (3.1.4)

On-going activity:

- The group should meet regularly, as a watch-dog, to comment on progress, recommend actions, or suggest modifications to the strategy. It should report directly to the executive. (3.1.5)

---

4. *Total Quality culture*

Principle 4.1 **Quality should be a prime consideration within every decision and every action.**

Principle 4.2 **The Total Quality culture should be actively promoted by the executive, lived at all levels of management, and should be intrinsic to everyone within the organisation.**

and

Principle 4.3 **An active Total Quality culture must be a live organism. It will be ever-changing to control new situations, and thus universal on-going education will be essential to its healthy development.**

Prerequisites for action:

- A belief that Quality, as the central management concern, is necessary for commercial success. (4.1.1)

- An understanding of the concept of a Total Quality culture by the executive. (4.2.1)

Suggested action:

- Total Quality Education for all senior managers and managers. (4.1.2)

- Place Total Quality on the agenda of all formal meetings, so that all groups become involved with the progress review of the move towards Total Quality. (4.1.3)

- There are implications at board level, and it will be vital that directors become educated in the concepts of Total Quality. (4.2.2)

- Actively live Total Quality, tolerantly reminding others as they fall back into manifestations of the past ethos. Insist on the highest standards from everyone, whether of higher or lower status. All can defend their interests in Total Quality. (4.2.3)

- Cascade Total Quality Education throughout the organisation. Total Quality needs everyone. (4.3.1)

On-going activity:

- Quality should continue to be a prime consideration within every decision and every action. (4.1.4)

- All managers and senior managers should demonstrate, by daily example, their commitment to Total Quality. (4.2.4)

- Institute on-going Total Quality Education. (4.3.2)

People

Management of People

5. Positional significance

Principle 5.1 **All should understand their position and purpose within the organisation as a whole, including the financial situation and relationships.**

Prerequisites for action:

- An understanding by the senior management that people need to feel personally located within an organisation. (5.1.1)

- Senior management prepared to divulge financial information. (5.1.2)

Suggested action:

- Firm up positional charts and internal communication systems to establish a coherent organisation-wide structure. (5.1.3)

- Make everyone aware of their position within the organisation as a whole, via the cascading Total Quality Education programme. (5.1.4)

- Ensure that everyone has sufficient understanding of financial matters to be able to comprehend the financial information being presented to them. Again, this will form part of the cascading Total Quality Education programme. (5.1.5)

- Establish formal communication links to provide the information necessary for a wide understanding of the business. (5.1.6)

- Create purposeful communication to ensure the positive involvement of everyone within the Total Quality development. (5.1.7)

On-going activity:

- Managers should be encouraged to periodically assess the confidence with which people work. This will indicate their positional understanding. (5.1.8)

- Regularly update everyone's understanding of the commercial activity of the organisation. (5.1.9)

Principle 5.2	**Everyone should understand the responsibilities and accountabilities involved with individual processes.**
and	
Principle 5.3	**All internal relationships should be as a supplier and a customer. Everyone has a duty to demand good Quality and should never fail to give good Quality.**

Prerequisites for action:

● Clearly define processes in all areas. (5.2.1)

● A general understanding of the concepts of responsibility, accountability, process and internal customer relationships. (5.2.2)

● An appreciation of the concept of internal customer relationships. (5.3.1)

Suggested action:

● Strengthen the links between people and their processes, so that the team responsible for a process gains knowledge and becomes expert at that process. (5.2.3)

● Establish exact responsibilities and accountabilities for each process. No-one should be responsible for a process over which they have no control. Where possible, the responsibility should be shared by the team involved with the process. (5.2.4)

● Develop horizontal lines of communication and responsibility between processes, so that direct customer relationships can be established, with immediate feedback. These will include communication links with outside suppliers and customers. (5.3.2)

● Review the efficiency of each process, and consider potential improvements. Such a review can be conducted informally at little additional cost, and will often highlight fundamental improvements. (5.2.5)

On-going activity:

● Provide everyone with expanding opportunities to extend their knowledge of processes adjacent to their process. (5.2.6)

- Actively encourage direct supplier/customer relationships between all processes and all areas of the organisation. (5.3.3)

- Arrange continuing education to give the necessary skills for easy customer relationships between processes. (5.3.4)

Principle 5.4 All should have the skills, knowledge, equipment and back-up resources, to enable them to perform with pride and success.

Prerequisite for action:

- Associate particular people with actual processes. (5.4.1)

Suggested action:

- Identify and provide skills training as necessary to develop expertise in each task within a particular process area. Everyone should be a process expert. This training may be conducted on-the-job. (5.4.2)

- Provide all the education necessary to increase the knowledge of everyone within particular process areas. This education requirement may be partially covered in the cascading Total Quality Education programme. Everyone should be a process expert. (5.4.3)

- Identify, and assess all the additional equipment and engineering necessary to allow success to be achievable within each process area. Everyone has the right to good Quality equipment. (5.4.4)

- Identify the back-up needs for each process to ensure continued and uninterrupted production of good Quality outputs. (5.4.5)

- Establish personal performance indicators to enable every person to be able to recognise his success, and so be able to take a pride in his achievements. (5.4.6)

On-going activity:

- Institute regular updating of skills, via refresher courses, for all process experts (5.4.7)

- Formalise communication links to ensure that knowledge can be transmitted to and from each process area. (5.4.8)

- Ensure that those concerned with a particular process have access to information concerning developments in the equipment they use, and periodically review the provision of this equipment. (5.4.9)

- Develop a team work structure, so that the team becomes aware from whom assistance may be requested, and give it the status of a customer to obtain that assistance. (5.4.10)

- Establish department performance indicators to enable every person to recognise their department's success, and so be able to take a pride in their joint achievements. (5.4.11)

---

6. *Commitment*

Principle 6.1 **Trust, honesty and a high level of integrity should be assumed to be common throughout all levels of the organisation.**

Prerequisites for action:

- Common understanding of the concepts of truth, honesty and integrity. (6.1.1)

- A belief, at senior management level, in the integrity of all the people working for the organisation. (6.1.2)

- An understanding that the consideration of 'process failure' is always of benefit, whilst consideration of 'human failure' becomes associated with blame, and is thus damaging to the organisation. (6.1.3)

Suggested action:

- Establish an 'open access to information' policy throughout the organisation, whereby anyone may know anything, unless there is a sound reason for withholding the information. (6.1.4)

- Include a study of the concepts of honesty and blame in the cascading Total Quality Education programme. (6.1.5)

- All managers and senior managers to trust everyone until they show themselves unworthy of trust, rather than trust only those who demonstrate their trustworthiness. (6.1.6)

On-going activity:

- Gradually erode the vestiges of any previous blame culture. (6.1.7)

- Ensure all future managers have sufficient Total Quality Education before they start to manage within the organisation, to prevent them rediscovering the blame culture. (6.1.8)

Principle 6.2 It should be assumed that all are motivated first by the satisfaction of achievement, and secondly by the receipt of material reward for that achievement.

Prerequisites for action:

- A belief at executive and senior management level that everyone seeks job satisfaction, and that this is the prime motivator. (6.2.1)

- An appreciation of the need for financial reward for efforts made on the organisation's behalf. (6.2.2)

Suggested action:

- Ensure that nothing stands in the way of each person's opportunity to acquire job satisfaction. (6.2.3)

- Teach all managers the necessary motivational techniques. (6.2.4)

- Establish the means whereby managers are able to listen to the concerns of those they manage. (6.2.5)

- Also, establish the means whereby managers are able to represent the concerns of those they manage, to the decision-makers. (6.2.6)

- Include in all team work training, the skills necessary for team self-motivation. (6.2.7)

● Introduce methods by which the workforce can be rewarded for its increased commitment to the organisation. This might be from stronger contractual arrangements or share ownership. (6.2.8)

On-going activity:

● Develop team work. (6.2.9)

● Formalise the representational links between teams, groups, management and senior management. (6.2.10)

---

7. Team work

Principle 7.1 **Active team work, in which groups share responsibility, should be implemented wherever possible.**

and

Principle 7.2 **Process operation should always be perceived as the working of a team.**

Prerequisite for action:

● The principles of team work should be understood by senior managers. (7.1.1)

Suggested action:

● Educate all managers in team work methods, responsibilities and relationships. (7.1.2)

● Educate groups of people involved with like processes, in team work methods, responsibilities and relationships. (7.1.3)

● Establish team work situations. (7.1.4)

● Even where team work is not instituted, encourage the identification of a group of people responsible for each process. (7.2.1)

On-going activity:

● Develop the team work concept across the organisation. (7.1.5)

● Establish process improvement groups. (7.2.2)

Principle 7.3 **Interactive cooperation, rather than competition, should be the basis of both internal and external organisation. Competition should be reserved, in full measure, for the business rivals.**

Prerequisite for action:

- The nature of, and place for, competition should be appreciated by all senior managers. (7.3.1)

Suggested action:

- Eliminate all formal mechanisms that create artificial competition within the organisation. (7.3.2)

- Create facilities to encourage and facilitate negotiation between suppliers and customers, whether internal or external. (7.3.3)

- Ensure that the customer/supplier relationships with all supplying organisations achieve the highest level of efficiency. (7.3.4)

- Ensure that all external suppliers are paid within the negotiated credit period. (7.3.5)

- Ensure that the customer/supplier relationships with all the organisation's customers achieve the highest level of efficiency. (7.3.6)

On-going activity:

- Breakdown barriers between departments within the organisation. (7.3.7)

- Encourage everyone to perceive themselves as production staff. (7.3.8)

- Arrange visits and on-going personal contact between external suppliers' personnel and the organisation. (7.3.9)

- Likewise, arrange visits and on-going personal contact between external customers' personnel and the organisation. (7.3.10)

Principle 7.4 **Leadership and followership are needed by everyone, and all should understand these concepts.**

Prerequisite for action:

- The executive should understand the concepts of leadership and followership. (7.4.1)

Suggested action:

- The concepts of leadership and followership should be included in the cascading Total Quality Education programme. (7.4.2)

- Clear zones of responsibility should be established. (7.4.3)

- Team exercises should be included in the cascading Total Quality Education programme. (7.4.4)

- Team leaders' courses should be run for selected personnel, as team work is established. (7.4.5)

On-going activity:

- All managers and senior managers should display daily, by example, the value of both leadership and followership. (7.4.6)

Principle 7.5 Every group and team should contain sufficient communication and interpersonal relationship skills to ensure its efficient function.

Prerequisite for action:

- The executive should understand the importance of interpersonal relationship skills. (7.5.1)

Suggested action:

- People from every group should attend courses in communication skills. (7.5.2)

- People from every group should attend courses in interpersonal relationship skills. (7.5.3)

- All managers and senior managers should become proficient in modern communication skills. (7.5.4)

● All managers and senior managers should develop their interpersonal relationship skills. (7.5.5)

---

8. Education

Principle 8.1 Total Quality Education is essential for everyone.

Prerequisite for action:

● A belief in education as the essential force for change. (8.1.1)

Suggested action:

● Cascade a Total Quality Education programme throughout the organisation. (8.1.2)

On-going activity:

● Assess the educational needs of all new entrants to the organisation, at whatever level. (8.1.3)

● Provide further Total Quality Education, as required. (8.1.4)

Principle 8.2 The on-going education of everyone, is in the interest of the organisation.

Prerequisite for action:

● Implicit belief in the value, and potential, of people. (8.2.1)

Suggested action:

● Enhance (or establish) a training function within the organisation to extend and disseminate the skills and experience available within the organisation. (8.2.2)

● Implement the 'One more theories', by making education and training available for everyone. (8.2.3)

● Make the resources available to allow personnel to visit, and learn from, sources outside the organisation. (8.2.4)

On-going activity:

- Once the skills and experience have been acquired, always promote from within the organisation, rather than recruit from outside. (8.2.5)

Principle 8.3 Multi-skilling of all personnel is the efficient way to use human resources.

Prerequisite for action:

- An appreciation of the value of multi-skilling. (8.3.1)

Suggested action:

- Institute skills training as an on-going and continuous part of the organisation's operations. (8.3.2)

- Develop the team work concept, so that tasks, responsibilities and skills are shared. (8.3.3)

On-going activity:

- Include personal interaction and leadership skills in future personnel education to ensure a secure resource for future management positions. (8.3.4)

Principle 8.4 Do not proscribe the development of personnel. Provide everyone with a career route within the organisation.

Prerequisite for action:

- A belief in the human resources of the organisation. (8.4.1)

Suggested action:

- Design the titles and positional factors for each employee to provide for a single status organisation that will not inhibit people's self perception. (8.4.2)

- Conduct regular appraisal sessions, with everybody, to be aware of ambitions and the organisation's developmental need of human resources. (8.4.3)

- Negotiate with individuals the correct extension education and training package, that meets their requirements and expectations, and those of the organisation. (8.4.4)

- Give everyone an opportunity for a career, rather than a job. (8.4.5)

- Consider the local community, the area from which the workforce is recruited, as a mine of human potential. Ensure that the local community has knowledge of the organisation's achievements, understands the potential success of the organisation, and has a pride in its association. (8.4.6)

On-going activity:

- Develop the ability to provide for the educational needs and expectations of the workforce. (8.4.7)

- Foster strong community links. (8.4.8)

---

9. *Open management*

Principle 9.1 **An open and honest management style should be the norm.**

Prerequisites for action:

- An understanding by the executive of open and honest management styles. (9.1.1)

Suggested action:

- Senior management education in open government theory and techniques. (9.1.2)

- Senior management to practice open government theory and techniques. (9.1.3)

- Open government theory and techniques to be included in the cascading Total Quality Education programme for all managers. (9.1.4)

- Establish communication and feedback networks. (9.1.5)

On-going activity:

● Encourage a general knowledge of, and pride in, the organisation's achievements. (9.1.6)

Principle 9.2 Business information, including financial data, should be accessible to all within the organisation.

Prerequisite for action:

● Agreement of the board. (9.2.1)

Suggested action:

● Establish formalised means of conveying up-to-date business information to the entire workforce. This may be via briefings, newsletters, or visual presentations. (9.2.2)

● Create informal means of conveying up-to-date business information to the entire workforce, by making information freely available. (9.2.3)

On-going activity:

● Develop the ability of groups, teams and departments to broadcast their own successes. (9.2.4)

● Encourage a general knowledge of, and pride in, the organisation's achievements. (9.2.5).

● Institute realistic, and easily appreciated, performance indicators for the whole organisation. (9.2.6)

Principle 9.3 The work environment contains many implied messages of worth and value. Everyone needs a pleasant and efficient working environment.

Prerequisites for action:

● Appreciation by senior management that people spend more time at their workstation, than in their lounge at home. (9.3.1)

● Understanding by the executive that the provision of a good working environment is a cost effective means of reducing Quality costs. (9.3.2)

● Someone with taste within the organisation. (9.3.3)

Suggested action:

● Employ someone,from outside each department to give an objective view of the working environment of that department. (9.3.4)

● Establish department working parties to recommend environmental improvements. (9.3.5)

● Make good housekeeping a matter of performance Quality. (9.3.6)

● Encourage a responsibility for the general environment within everyone. This can be included in the cascading Total Quality Education programme. (9.3.7)

On-going activity:

● Include representatives who will be working in an area with all future process planning for that area. (9.3.8)

● Environmental management should be perceived as synonymous with Quality management. (9.3.9)

Management of Process

10. Process planning

Principle 10.1 There should be a live, overall process plan to locate each individual process within the overall process.

Prerequisite for action:

● Appreciation by senior management of the need for one overall coherent process. (10.1.1)

Suggested action:

- Draw up an overall process plan, detailing flow of work, including:

  design
  process inputs
  customer relationships
  communication links
  resource requirements
  staff
  materials
  materials handling
  maintenance, etc.

(Whilst there are sophisticated computer software programs to assist with this activity, it will probably be done better by pencils and paper in the first place.) (10.1.2)

- Encourage discussions between process personnel to identify methods of reducing materials in storage, and handling problems. (10.1.3)

- Examine ways of exerting a pull on work through the processes, rather than the push of production. (10.1.4)

On-going activity:

- When chains of processes have been brought into control, producing a continuous flow of predictable results, institute Just-In-Time methodology. (10.1.5)

- When most of the processes throughout the organisation are in control, institute MRP2 philosophy, via computer software. (10.1.6)

Principle 10.2 **Processes that have no financially sound part to play within the overall process should be discontinued.**

and

Principle 10.3 **All processes should be perceived to be of equal importance, that is vital to the overall process. All processes should be considered to be production processes.**

Prerequisites for action:

- Senior management understanding of: what processes actually exist; and the cost and value of each process. (10.2.1)

- Senior management should appreciate the totality of the organisation's productive effort, encompassing every activity. (10.3.1)

- The term 'production' should be used to mean the 'production of wealth', and as such, is applicable to every part of the organisation. (10.3.2)

Suggested action:

- Each department should be asked to assess the value of each process, and ensure that nothing is occurring unnecessarily, or at an overall cost to the organisation. (10.2.2)

- Each department should justify, in real terms, any process identified by the senior management as a possible drain on the organisation's resources. (10.2.3)

- The cascading Total Quality Education programme should teach the single nature of the organisation's productive effort, thus encouraging a single status of activity throughout the organisation. (10.3.3)

- The rhetoric and language used by all managers, at all times, should reinforce the single purpose of the company: to produce wealth. (10.3.4)

On-going activity:

- Establish that it is the duty of everyone to question the net value of every activity. (10.2.4)

- Develop a single status organisation. (10.3.5)

Principle 10.4 There should be integration between all departments and process areas, from design and manufacture, to sales and marketing.

Prerequisites for action:

- The term 'production' should be used to mean the production of wealth. (10.4.1)

- Senior management should appreciate the need to remove barriers between departments. (10.4.2)

Suggested action:

- Integrate design and manufacturing activities to produce a joint responsibility for finished products. (10.4.3)

- Integrate manufacturing and assembly activities to produce a joint responsibility for finished products. (10.4.4)

- Integrate manufacturing and sales activities to produce a joint responsibility for customer satisfaction. (10.4.5)

- Encourage horizontal communication links between all aspects of the organisation's operations. (10.4.6)

On-going activity:

- Develop multi-skilling, so that people appreciate the skills involved in all other parts of the business. (10.4.7)

---

11. Process control

Principle 11.1 **There should be coherent overall process control mechanisms, regulating each process within an organisation-wide strategy.**

Prerequisite for action:

- Organisation-wide vision. (11.1.1)

Suggested action:

- The concepts of process control should be included in the cascading Total Quality Education programme. (11.1.2)

- Remove barriers, so that all functions of the organisation are considered as production processes. (11.1.3)

- Remove barriers, so that all functions of the organisation can interact directly, thus achieving the highest degree of immediate control at process level. (11.1.4)

On-going activity:

- Continually develop the concept of one overall process. (11.1.5)

Principle 11.2 All processes should consistently produce acceptable results.

Prerequisite for action:

- Process thinking. (11.2.1)

Suggested action:

- Include the need for stable processes and consistent results,in the cascading Total Quality Education programme. (11.2.2)

- Begin a rolling introduction of Statistical Process Control (SPC), with education, process stabilisation and implementation. (11.2.3)

- Establish Accepted Quality Levels (AQLs) within all process parameters, including all non-manufacturing processes. (11.2.4)

On-going activity:

- Tight control of all processes. (11.2.5)

- Development of other Quality methods dependent on predictable process control. (11.2.6)

- Introduction of Taguchi theory. (11.2.7)

Principle 11.3 All processes should be capable of producing virtually 100% acceptable results. (Cpk > 1.3), and the organisation should work towards this goal.

Prerequisite for action:

- An understanding of SPC terminology. (11.3.1)

Suggested action:

- Institute SPC as the accepted control mechanism. (11.3.2)

- Conduct regular capability studies in all processes. (11.3.3)

- Regularly review the capability of each and every process. All incapable processes should be redesigned and made capable. (11.3.4)

On-going activity:

- Increase the capability of all processes. (11.3.5)

Principle 11.4 Process control is achievable earlier, rather than later, within the overall process.

Prerequisite for action:

- An understanding of the principle of earlier process control. (11.4.1)

Suggested action:

- The concepts of process control should be included in the cascading Total Quality Education programme. (11.4.2)

- Strengthen links with suppliers, both internally and externally, to assist with tighter process control. (11.4.3)

- Strengthen links with the design and planning functions, both internally and externally, to assist with tighter process control. (11.4.4)

- Introduce Failure Mode and Effects Analysis (FMEA). (11.4.5)

On-going activity:

- Design out process and product failure. (11.4.6)

12. Process improvement

Principle 12.1 **All processes should be constantly subject to improvement, forever. It is the responsibility of everyone to improve each and every process.**

and

Principle 12.2 **No problem is insoluble, and no problem, once solved, should return. All problems should be one-offs and, therefore, new.**

Prerequisites for action:

- Senior management's appreciation of the definitions involved with problem-solving. (12.1.1)
- Senior management's ability to delegate cost effective improvement action to individual areas. (12.1.2)
- The ability of decision-makers to think laterally. (12.2.1)
- The acceptance of principle 12.2 by senior management. (12.2.2)

Suggested action:

- The concepts of constant process improvement should be included in the cascading Total Quality Education programme. (12.1.3)
- Integrate all functions, including design, engineering, maintenance, administration, accounting and manufacturing, to ensure a totality of understanding about problems. (12.1.4)
- Establish Quality improvement groups in areas where Quality improvements are essential. (12.1.5)
- Establish Quality Circles. (12.1.6)
- Cost all failure and all improvements. Broadcast the results. (12.1.7)
- Encourage every individual to be cost conscious, and to act on the organisation's behalf when potential improvements are perceived. (12.1.8)

On-going activity:

● Spread problem-solving and process improvement activities into all areas of the organisation. (12.1.9)

Principle 12.3 All designs, both of product and process, should be subject to constant on-going improvement.

Prerequisite for action:

● An understanding that designers design processes to manufacture products, rather than just design the products themselves. (12.3.1)

Suggested action:

● Initiate joint projects between design and manufacturing functions to review the critical parameters on items with a history of Quality problems. (12.3.2)

● Provide education in the theory, techniques and practice of FMEA. (12.3.3)

● Establish FMEA as a regular technique within the design area of the organisation. (12.3.4)

● Establish FMEA as a regular technique within several process areas of the organisation. (12.3.5)

On-going activity:

● Develop Failure Mode and Effects Analysis as an everyday technique within all areas of the organisation. (12.3.6)

● Introduce Taguchi's 'Design of experiments'. (12.3.7)

Principle 12.4 Organisation-wide use of problem-solving techniques will progressively eliminate all problems that limit the proper functioning of processes.

Prerequisite for action:

- Senior management's appreciation of the resources needed to institute problem-solving activities. (12.4.1)

Suggested action:

- Provide education in modern problem-solving techniques for all managers, as part of the cascading Total Quality Education programme. (12.4.2)

- Integrate these techniques into the everyday life of the organisation. Cost and broadcast the results. (12.4.3)

On-going activity:

- Constantly up-grade and spread problem-solving skills within the organisation. (12.4.4)

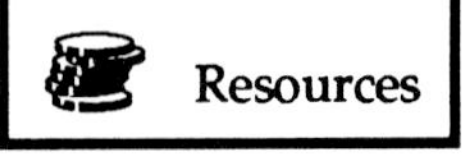

Management of Resources

13. Wealth generation

Principle 13.1 **All should appreciate the role that their processes have in the organisation-wide task of wealth creation.**

Principle 13.2 **Everyone should appreciate the overall trading (working) position of the organisation.**

and

Principle 13.3 **Everyone should have access to performance indicators to compare past and present performance.**

Prerequisite for action:

- Availability of live, easily digested financial data for the organisation as a whole. (13.2.1)

- Availability of live, easily digested financial data for individual departments and areas. (13.1.1)

- Senior management understanding of performance indicators. (13.3.1)

Suggested action:

- Establish an organisation-wide chart of related processes, including inputs from suppliers and product outputs to potential customers. (13.2.2)

- Establish communication systems to inform everyone of live business details, customers, suppliers, contracts, etc. (13.2.2)

- Establish personal performance indicators. (13.3.2)

- Establish area performance indicators. (13.3.3)

- Establish organisation-wide performance indicators. (13.3.4)

On-going activity:

- Integrate the use of performance indicators into the staff appraisal, and departmental appraisal activities. (13.3.5)

Principle 13.4 Teams and other internal groups should be aware of their operational costs, and of other financial implications.

Prerequisites for action:

- Provision of basic financial skills in all areas of the organisation. (13.4.1)

- Provision of basic financial data in all areas of the organisation. (13.4.2)

Suggested action:

- Establish activity costing in key areas of the organisation. (13.4.3)

On-going activity:

- Establish activity costing in all areas of the organisation. (13.4.4)

14. Cost of Quality

Principle 14.1 The Cost of Quality (COQ) for each area, department and the entire organisation should be assessed, broadcast and continually reduced.

Prerequisites for action:

- Appreciation of COQ theory by senior management. (14.1.1)

- Accounting resources and ability to cost activities. (14.1.2)

Suggested action:

- Educate everyone in COQ theory, as part of the cascading Total Quality Education programme. (14.1.3)

- Establish COQ projects. (14.1.4)

- Be totally open, honest and scrupulous with all dealings within the internal customer/supplier relationships. (14.1.5)

On-going activity:

- Reduce the COQ in each and every activity of the organisation. (14.1.6)

Principle 14.2 Expenditure on prevention measures will nearly always reduce other Quality costs, that is the costs of appraisal, internal failure and external failure.

Prerequisite for action:

- Understanding by all, of the concepts of prevention, appraisal, internal failure and external failure. (14.2.1)

Suggested action:

- Cost individual process failures, eg. cost of scrap, rework, down time, administration, etc. (14.2.2)

- Establish performance indicators that are indicative of the prevention costs, appraisal costs, internal failure costs, and external failure costs. (14.2.3)

● Establish performance indicators that are indicative of the indirect Quality costs. (14.2.4)

● Institute preventative maintenance throughout the organisation. (14.2.5)

● Establish process improvement groups in Quality critical areas. (14.2.6)

On-going activity:

● Regularly review the 'cost of conformance' versus the 'cost of non-conformance'. (14.2.7)

Principle 14.3 Supplier organisations, distributors and other corporate customers are all part of the chain to satisfy the end-user. All share the same long-term interests, and their future security is closely linked to that of the organisation.

Prerequisite for action:

● An understanding within the organisation's external partners, of its Total Quality Policy, definitions, methods and commitment to Total Quality. (14.3.1)

Suggested action:

● Establish close Quality links with all supplying organisations. (14.3.2)

● Minimise the additional non-product costs of doing business with all suppliers. Simplify, harmonise and increase the efficiency of the relevant procedures. Make all payments in the negotiated manner, and within the negotiated credit period. (14.3.3)

● Minimise the additional non-product costs of doing business with customers. Simple and efficient procedures are the least expensive. Demand that you receive all payment in the negotiated manner, and within the negotiated credit period. (14.3.4)

● Be totally open, honest and scrupulous in all dealings with corporate customers, and indeed everyone else. (14.3.5)

- Request from all suppliers, all relevant Quality information in their possession, such as capability studies of a product or related processes. (14.3.6)

- Develop joint training schemes in Quality methods, for the suppliers personnel and those from the organisation. (14.3.7)

- Select criteria by which to assess the Quality performance of the supplier organisations. Assess their performance and discuss the results with them. (14.3.8)

- Offer assistance to improve their Quality performance. (14.3.9)

- Set up a system of preferred supplier status. (14.3.10)

- From mutual discussion, establish standards of process control and methodology to be considered essential for all supplier organisations. Make this mandatory in future contractual arrangements. (Where industry standards already exist, use or modify, and constantly review these.) (14.3.11)

- Keep all corporate customers closely informed about Total Quality activities, including relationships with the supplying companies. (14.3.12)

- Where the organisation is in need of assistance from a larger corporate customer, to achieve the desired Quality level, ask for such assistance. (14.3.13)

- Pass to the customer all relevant Quality information, such as capability studies of a product or related processes. (14.3.14)

On-going activity:

- Develop ever closer relationships with suppliers. (14.3.15)

- Review the Supplier Quality ratings and the preferred supplier status listings on a regular basis. (14.3.16)

- Award all future business on a Quality confidence basis. (14.3.17)

- Develop ever closer relationships with customers. (14.3.18)

15. Resource conservation

Principle 15.1 Everyone should appreciate the value of all the organisation's resources, including people, money, material, energy, time and space.

and

Principle 15.2 It is the duty of everyone to conserve the organisation's resources, at all times.

Prerequisite for action:

- An appreciation of the financial cost of all material, energy, time and space. (15.1.1)

Suggested action:

- The appreciation of the value of all of the organisation's resources, including people, money, material, energy, time and space, should play a central part in the cascading Total Quality Education programme. (15.1.2)

- Initiate performance indicators on the conversion of purchased material into saleable product. (15.1.3)

- Establish SPC on all energy consumption. (15.1.4)

- Initiate energy saving measures, in which everyone is responsible for the minimisation of all business costs, including energy costs. (15.2.1)

- Review the use of space within the organisation. For instance, develop a nominal cost per square metre of:
  1. Office space.
  2. Heated manufacturing space
  3. Non-heated internal space.
  4. Open space. (15.2.5)

- Institute time management. (15.2.6)

- All senior managers should preach by example, respect for, and conservation of, the value of subordinates time and effort. (15.2.7)

On-going activity:

- Continued reduction of all Quality costs related to the organisation's resources, including people, money, material, energy, time and space. (15.2.8)

Principle 15.3 The consumption of 'internal energy' should be minimised.

Prerequisite for action:

- An understanding of the concept of internal energy. (15.3.1)

Suggested action:

- Educate everyone in the need to reduce internal energy consumption as part of the cascading Total Quality Education programme. (15.3.2)

- Eliminate by example, the practice of criticising people and identifying human failure, and replace them with criticism of task, and process failure. (15.3.3)

- Take all measures possible, to make working within the organisation fun. Work should be challenging, enjoyable and rewarding. (15.3.4)

On-going activity:

- Establish performance indicators to monitor the cooperative climate of the organisation. (15.3.5)

16. Resource planning

Principle 16.1 Efficient planning can maximise the value of time, space, energy, materials, and all other aspects of the organisation's resources.

Prerequisite for action:

- Organisation-wide planning ability. (16.1.1)

Suggested action:

- Include resource planning theory in the cascading Total Quality Education programme. (16.1.2)

● Hold all managers accountable for the efficient use of time, space, energy, materials, and all other aspects of the organisation's resources. (16.1.3)

● Develop organisation-wide resource planning routines. (16.1.4)

● Establish resource planning performance indicators, such as overtime as a percentage of manpower bill, area yield levels, and intermediate stock levels. (16.1.5)

On-going activity:

● Establish Manufacturing Resource Planning (MRP2). (16.1.6)

Principle 16.2 Efficient processes will minimise the need for handling and storage of materials.

Prerequisite for action:

● An understanding of the concepts of push and pull methods of production. (16.2.1)

Suggested action:

● Identify areas and manufacturing lines in which the processes are in statistical control. (16.2.2)

● Institute Kanban-type systems. (16.2.3)

● Reduce all intermediate stock levels. (16.2.4)

● Discuss Just-In-Time arrangements with suppliers and customers involved with materials for, or the products of, these lines. (16.2.5)

On-going activity:

● Institute Just-In-Time. (16.2.6)

Principle 16.3 The responsibility of the buying function of the organisation is only complete when the goods and services purchased have been fully utilised and their fruits passed to a satisfied end-user. (16.3.1)

Prerequisite for action:

● An appreciation that the Quality of all products, goods and services offered by the organisation is dependent on the Quality of all incoming materials, goods and services. (16.3.2)

Suggested action:

● Include purchasing procedures in the cascading Total Quality Education programme. (16.3.3)

● Issue all purchasing personnel with details of Quality requirements and procedures. (16.3.4)

● Make Quality the central issue in all purchasing contracts. (16.3.5)

● Ensure that the purchasing department retains responsibility for materials and services until fully utilised. (16.3.6)

● Cost the purchasing procedure, and reduce this cost. (16.3.7)

On-going activity:

● Review procedures of purchasing department to respond, as suppliers, to the other areas of the organisation. (16.3.8)

Principle 16.4 The process of marketing and selling the products of the organisation should be fully integrated with the planning and production activities. Sales staff should be experts in the products, goods and services that they sell.

Prerequisite for action:

● An appreciation of the sales department's task to maximise the return on the organisation's potential, that is to convert its talents, abilities, skills, expertise and plant, into wealth. (16.4.1)

Suggested action:

● Include sales and marketing procedures in the cascading Total Quality Education programme. (16.4.2)

- Issue all sales personnel with details of Quality procedures and achievements. (16.4.3)

- Make Quality the central issue in all sales contracts. (16.4.4)

- Develop the understanding that it is the fruits of Quality processes that are being purchased, not mere products. (16.4.5)

- Integrate the sales department with the manufacturing environment to ensure that sales reflect the ability of the organisation to produce. (16.4.6)

- Establish the customer's expectation when a quotation is requested, and do not respond outside this expectation. Decline work that cannot be achieved to a high Quality standard. (16.4.7)

- Cost the sales procedure, and reduce this cost. (16.4.8)

On-going activity:

- Review procedures of sales department to respond as a customer to the other areas of the organisation. (16.4.9)

Principle 16.5 There will be a service component that will be either technical, educational or knowledge-based within every transaction, whether internal or external to the organisation.

Prerequisite for action:

- An appreciation of knowledge, and the value of live data. (16.5.1)

Suggested action:

- Educate everyone in the place of knowledge within supplier/customer relationships as part of the cascading Total Quality Education programme. (16.5.2)

- Develop the principle of direct internal negotiation between internal suppliers and customers. (16.5.3)

- Establish procedures for the interchange of expectations and data in all internal customer relationships. (16.5.4)

- Integrate the sales department with the manufacturing environment to ensure that the sales department has a technical appreciation of the products being sold. (16.5.5)

On-going activity:

- Increasingly meet the customer's requirements and expectations in every respect. (16.5.6)

- Become the best. (16.5.7)

Summary

The TQM blueprint

Management of Quality
1. Quality definitions
2. Total Quality Policy
3. Total Quality Strategy
4. Total Quality culture

Management of People

5. Positional significance
6. Commitment
7. Team work
8. Education
9. Open management

Management of Process

10. Process design
11. Process control
12. Process improvement

Management of Resources

13. Wealth generation
14. Cost of Quality
15. Resource conservation
16. Resource planning

Last thoughts ....

The only constant in industry is change.

Chapter 18

Total Quality Education

Human history becomes more and more a race between education and catastrophe

– H G Wells

Education makes people easy to lead, but difficult to drive; easy to govern, but impossible to enslave.

– Lord Brougham, House of Commons 1928

Route-map

This final chapter explains the concept of a cascading educational programme, and suggests a method for a typical company, whilst stressing that each organisation should design the programme to suit itself.

A sample list of contents is given, and the chapter finishes by stressing the need for expertise, resources and vision.

Company orientated programme

Whatever educational programme is introduced to the company, it will stand the greatest chance of success, and have the greatest potential for change, if it is designed specifically for the company.

It should make good use of the company's resources, and purchase in those that are not available. The design and resourcing of the programme will determine its success. The programme should take full account of the present company culture, and the desired changes. It should be optimistic, and contain a built-in assumption of success. It should contain education in all the activities, techniques and methods that are deemed necessary for the introduction of Total Quality. It should touch and interest everyone.

Cascade

The concept of a cascading educational programme delivers education to everyone within the organisation, in a cost effective manner. It has the additional bonus that the operation of the programme plays a significant role in the cultural development of the company.

The substance of the programme, that is the theoretical content, the methodology and the attitudinal input, originates from the centre, and cascades outwards, to every individual person within the company.

The phases of this sample programme are:

Phase 1 Executive briefing

It is most important that the executive and senior decision makers of the company are aware of the full importance, benefits and implications of Total Quality Management. This briefing should cover all these aspects and sketch out the cascading method of disseminating education. The strategy team should be formed soon after this briefing, to establish the Total Quality Policy and the Total Quality Strategy.

Phase 2 Senior management education

The main aspects of Total Quality are covered in depth, based on the four fundamental aspects of TQM. It is important that the senior management is fully aware, committed and involved from the outset. A member of the senior management team should be established as a TQM coordinator.

Separate, and additional, educational inputs for senior managers and managers, are justified by the intrinsic nature of TQM. The move to Total Quality will change the culture of the company, and will have a considerable influence on the role of the management. Senior management's priorities and decisions will be crucial. A more professional approach will be required by all managers, together with an enhancement of their motivational and leadership skills. This will enable them to develop the Total Quality culture necessary for TQM to thrive.

Phase 3 Management briefings

An overview of the TQM theory and practice should be presented to all managers, so that they are fully aware of the programme and its contents. It is important, at this stage, to identify the Quality Policy and Strategy, and to define all the central terminology.

Phase 4 Facilitator selection

The organisational structure of the company or organisation should be considered, and divided into groups of between 12 and 20 people. Each group should have a facilitator, who must be a person with the ability to inspire, lead and facilitate a Total Quality education group. Skills, knowledge and methods will be provided, but the facilitator must have some natural ability.

The management should be similarly grouped, into management education groups, each with a facilitator, who might be a senior manager. Individual managers will find themselves in both types of group.

Phase 5 Facilitator Total Quality Education

The facilitators, from both types of group, are given Part 1 of the facilitator education programme. This imparts the necessary interpersonal skills and communication methods, together with a complete overview of the programme.

Later, they will be taken through the Total Quality Education programme in a series of sessions, interlocked with the Total Quality Education group sessions that they themselves will facilitate. These sessions will enable them to pass on the education to their own groups.

Phase 6 Management education groups

TQM is a culture demanding positive managerial participation. The unifying of the company will be best achieved at this level. Groups of between eight and 16 managers should each have a facilitator, preferably from the group.

Phase 7 Total Quality Education groups

Regular meetings of the Total Quality Education programme groups are arranged. The pattern of these will reflect the organisation and facilities of the company. The facilitator conducts the education. It is vital that facilitators are provided with all the necessary materials and resources. They pass on the education from the previous facilitator session. (The author provides such material commercially.)

Phase 8 Cascading education programme

The TQM coordinator arranges the education of the facilitators, who cascade the education to their groups. The management cascade occurs simultaneously. It is vital that all the necessary resources and facilities are provided, and that all groups cover the same topics and with the same understanding, definitions and priorities.

Phase 9 Representative interaction

At the end of the courses, representatives of each group meet to discuss the results and intended follow-up methods and practices. The groups offer each other assistance and interact with information and methods.

Phase 10 On-going seminars

From time to time, additional seminars on particular points, methods or techniques are introduced, for representatives from each group to attend, and then report back to their group.

There will also be the need to update all new entrants to the company, at whatever level, to ensure that the culture does not become diluted with past bad habits and practices from elsewhere.

The content

There is not space here to give anything more than a list of the topics to be covered. Clearly, the timing and balance will be of great importance, and will need to reflect the present culture of the company.

Experience highlights the dichotomy, whereby those companies with the greatest changes to be made often assume that these changes can be achieved with the least input of resources. Clearly, this is irrational, and demonstrates a lack of understanding of Total Quality, its benefits and implications.

Total Quality Education programme

Management of Quality

Quality definitions and statements
Directional Quality
Customer satisfaction
Cultural change
Concept to customer chain
Internal customer relationships
Internal energy
Financial implications
Knowledge-based environment
The Quality Policy
The Total Quality Strategy

Management of Process

Two levels of process
Single status activities
Macro process considerations
Micro process consideration (6Ms)
Ever earlier control
Inspection v control
SPC, FMEA, MRP, MRP2, JIT
On-going process improvement
Increased individual process skills
Purchasing implications
Sales and marketing implications

Management of People

Motivation
Communication methods
Interpersonal skills
Leadership/followership
Honesty/blame
Open management
Organisation
Team-work
Team exercises
One-more theories

Management of Resources

Resource conservation
MITEMS
Data analysis
Financial analysis
Cost of Quality
Activity costing
Evaluation of resources
Energy conservation
Environmental considerations

Total Quality Management

Responsibilities within TQM
Benefits of TQM
Implications of TQM

Certification

There is considerable value in the certification of any educational activity. It recognises the additional effort and energy expended by the participants, and it becomes a visual record of their achievement.

It emphasises to everyone that the company takes seriously the academic pursuit of excellence.

Making it work

It is easy to be committed, but difficult to get results. The list above is but a collection of suggestions. It is intended to focus concentration on the important issues. The organisation of a cascading educational programme is skilled work, and most companies will need assistance, if they are to reap the potential benefits.

In this age of specialism, companies should avoid devoting resources to designing the vertical circular moving mechanism, pivoted in the centre, and with a smooth surface equidistant from the pivot point – the wheel has already been invented!

Course material exists, and can be easily purchased.

Educational expertise exists, and can be purchased.

The design, resourcing and implementation of the Total Quality Education programme, cascading throughout the organisation, is easy. The difficult part is lifting the eyes to the horizon. As Edward Gibbon said:

> *'Every man who rises above the common level has received two educations: the first from his teachers; the second, more personal and important, from himself.'*

Every company needs to take a long cool look at its medium and long-term business. Total Quality has to be the route.

Summary

Total Quality Education programme

Cascade through the organisation, using Total Quality facilitators: a suggested method and content are outlined above.

Education needs expertise and resources: both exist.

Last thought ....

Let's make work **fun**!

Quality through People

A Blueprint for
Proactive Total Quality Management

Glossary

Glossary

These explanations should be considered as tools, rather than dictionary definitions. Use words and concepts dynamically. [nos in brackets indicate the chapter in which the term is most used.]

Accountability — A management function, whereby managers, or management teams, explain the functioning of processes, for which they have the responsibility to facilitate. [7]

Activity costing — A means of tracking the costs of any process or activity, by treating it as a mini-business. [11]

Appraisal costs — The costs involved with all activities undertaken to check during and after the process, that the process has conformed and given satisfactory results. Such costs are a 'Quality cost' rather than a 'production cost' [12]

Attitude — The stance taken as a result of the perception of reality. It embodies the judgement of the individual, based on limited knowledge. [7]

Attribute — A characteristic that can be counted or checked whether it meets, or does not meet, a given requirement, (on/off, pass/fail, go/no go). [9]

Blame — An expensive commodity designed to divert the understanding of processes. [15]

Brain-storming — A method of quickly emptying minds of all possible thoughts on a particular subject. It is best performed by individuals in temporary isolation from others. [10]

Capability — The measurement of the ability of a process to produce acceptable results. Capability relates process performance to specified tolerances, and the most common Capability Index is Cpk. [9]

Cause	An input to a process, leading to an effect. The cause is a condition or action that is present, or takes place, prior to the process. [10]
Cause & Effect diagram	Method of solving problems. Sometimes called an Ishikawa diagram after Dr Kaoru Ishikawa, or fishbone diagram after its appearance. [10]
Competition	Others that seek the same source of wealth. [8]
Concept	An original idea. [1]
Conformance	Performing to produce acceptable results. [12]
Control	The degree to which process inputs are known, stable and predictable. [10]
Cost of Quality	The sum of all resources expended to ensure that acceptable results are produced, plus all the production lost as a result of non-acceptable results being produced. These will not all be known, since lost reputation and opportunities can never be calculated. [12]
Culture	The generalised sense of reality within which people make decisions. [15]
Customer	A customer is the recipient of the fruits of a person's work. [1]
Customer care	Defined by the principles: Cooperation, Confidence, Continuity and Quality. [13]
Design failure	A failure that can be attributed to an inherent design fault. As such, its occurrence should be considered as inevitable until a design change is accomplished. [10]
Detection	The ensuring that a defect in a process will be found prior to the results leaving the location. [10]

Diffuse structure	The structure of a company with departments and areas operating with different sets of values, agendas, priorities and objectives. [5]
Direct & indirect costs	Direct Quality costs are those that are incurred within the location of the company, and hence can be found. Indirect Quality costs are those that are consequential to the failure, such as lost reputation, and hence will seldom be accurately known. [12]
DNPL	Demand Now Pay Later, the out-dated and expensive accountancy practice, whereby money is demanded within the negotiated credit period, but retained as long as possible from suppliers, thus breaking their negotiated agreement. [14]
Effect	An effect is the result of a process. It is the condition prevailing after the process is complete. [10]
End-user	The customer who makes use of the product. It is usually the end-user who converts the product into wealth. [13]
External customer	A customer who is outside, and is thus served by, the company. [13]
Failure	A failure is the inability to produce the desired Quality level. All failures are either design or process failures. A potential failure should be considered to be a failure. [10]
False competition	The setting up of quasi competitive situations between people, or groups of people, who will benefit from cooperation in the acquisition of wealth, and will share the wealth so acquired. [8]
FMEA	Failure Mode and Effects Analysis is a technique that prioritises improvements to design and/or process. [9]

Fundamentals of TQM	The four management aspects that combine to give Total Quality Management are the management of Quality, people, process and resources. [3]
Honesty	An open approach that gives the company a person's full potential. [5]
Human failure	An unhelpful and expensive means of allocating blame, associated with a misunderstanding of the concepts of process, and management.[10]
'I only' syndrome	The self perception that a task or process has a low status, or is peripheral to the main company activity. [3]
Industrial citizenship	A culture wherein employees actively live their responsibilities and duties with regard to the provision of Quality to internal customers. [1]
Integrated structure	The structure of a company with departments and areas, with one set of values, priorities and objectives; the company's. [5]
Internal customer	A customer who is inside the company. The person whose work is dependent upon others Quality outputs. [13]
Internal energy	Energy expended by a company, internally, in the act of doing business with itself. [5]
JIT	'Just-In-Time' is the manufacturing principle, by which nothing is done until it is needed, thus reducing the inventory of work in hand. [9]
Kanban	A Japanese system of applying push and pull to work in a factory, thus ensuring an effective Just-In-Time system.
Manager	The facilitator of a process, or several processes. The manager's task is to ensure that all the manpower, machine, material, methodological, measurement and environmental requirements are fully met. [3]

Four 'A's of management	A mnemonic to describe good management. They are Access, Action, Attitude and Activity. [3]
MITEMS	A mnemonic to orientate people in wealth conservation. It identifies Money, Information, Time, Energy, Materials and Space. [11]
Motivation	To stimulate attitudes and actions to produce high Quality work. [7]
MRP	Materials Resource Planning is a system that organises the efficient use of materials. [9]
MRP2	Manufacturing Resource Planning is a system for organising all the variables necessary for efficient manufacturing, including materials, staff, plant and equipment. Pioneered by Oliver Wight. [9]
6 Ms	A mnemonic to describe all the aspects of any process, or all the possible inputs or effects of the process. They are Manpower, Machine, Method, Materials, Measurement and Milieu (the environmental conditions). [3]
Negotiation	Purposeful discussion to determine the expectations and requirements of a customer, either internal or external. [1] A negotiation will include the expectations and requirements of the supplier, who will become the customer immediately after the product has been supplied. [14]
One more theories	Suggest that everyone should have an additional skill, or area of experience, than is needed for the present job. Also, for every skill and position of responsibility, there should be one additional person within the company than is needed at present.
Pareto analysis	A graphical analysis of information, in which groups of similar data are arranged in order of magnitude. It is used to identify priorities. [10]

Peer group Those people, usually of the same status, who exert an influence over an individual. [7]

Preferred suppliers A list of suppliers who can display the ability to perform to a high Quality standard, and with whom the company seeks a long-term relationship. [14]

Performance indicator A measure of present performance compared with the past. This may be applied to a company, department, team or individual. [12]

Prevention The virtual elimination of the causes of a problem. [10]

Problem A process or design failure. The problem inhabits the active inputs to the process, rather than its results. [10]

Problem fix Sufficient action to obtain a temporary solution, but not preventing further recurrence. [10]

Process The dynamic change of something. [1]

The *Macro* level of process is the overall process, from concept, or raw material, to end-user. [8]

The *Micro* level of process is an individual process, and is governed by the inputs (6Ms), Manpower, Machine, Materials, Method, Measurement and Milieu. [8]

Process failure Some aspect of the process that produces, or potentially produces, unacceptable results.

Process thinking A concentration on the dynamic activities of a company, in preference to the static results. [8]

Production costs The sum of all the necessary expenditure to produce the goods and services of the company. These will not include those costs incurred to ensure that high standards of Quality are maintained. [11]

Productivity The conversion of the fruits of the company assets into wealth. Assets can be listed under the 6Ms, evaluated and compared with the output of products and services, to arrive at a unit cost. [4]

Quality The meeting of the negotiated requirements and expectations of the customer. [1]

Quality Circle A meeting of those involved with a process to identify, analyse and solve job-related problems. [10]

Quality Policy The statement to everyone concerned, both inside and outside the company, of its intentions, with respect to Quality. [1]

Quality Strategy A written set of actions that together will enable the Quality Policy to be accomplished. [1]

Responsibility Having the control of a process, which an individual or a team is employed to operate. [7]

Senior manager A manager contributing to decisions concerning company strategy and which policy. [3]

Solution A solution is a combination of:

- An understanding of the causes.
- Remedial action, and
- Preventative action. [10]

SPC Statistical Process Control is the control of process inputs by understanding what is actually happening during the process. It is achieved by sampling process data and using a simple statistical analysis. [9]

Statistical control A stable condition of a process, from which the results can be predicted. [9]

Suppliers A partner who provides goods and/or services.

Superlative — Judgement with a single ill-defined definition, such as the best, the quickest or the cheapest. [1]

Team — A group of people sharing responsibility for a process or set of processes. [6]

Team work — The organisation of people to work in teams. [6]

Unemployment — *Frictional* unemployment is caused by the normal movement between jobs of individual people for personal reasons. It is met by people finding alternative employment. [4]

Structural unemployment is caused by the change in type of employment available, due to products and skills becoming out-dated, and unwanted. It is met by re-education, to provide skills that are needed. [4]

Unified company — A company with an integrated structure, wherein departments and areas live by a single set of values, priorities and objectives. [5]

Unitary thinking — A concentration on numbers. These tend to be results, and thus uncontrollable. The opposite of 'process thinking'. [8]

Appendices

Appendix A

DESIGN FMEA - OCCURRENCE

Occurrence Rating	Possibilities of Occurrence	Statistical Probability of Failure	
1	remote	zero	
2	low	1 / 20,000	one in twenty thousand
3	low	1 / 10,000	one in ten thousand
4	moderate	1 / 2,000	one in two thousand
5	moderate	1 / 1,000	one in a thousand
6	moderate	1 / 200	one in two hundred
7	high	1 / 100	one in a hundred
8	high	1 / 20	one in twenty
9	very high	1 / 10	one in ten
10	very high	1 / 2	one in two

Appendix A

PROCESS FMEA - OCCURRENCE

Occurrence Rating	Probability of Occurrence	Statistical Probability of Failure	
1	remote	1 / 10,000	one in ten thousand
2	low	1 / 5,000	one in five thousand
3	low	1 /2,000	one in two thousand
4	low	1 / 1,000	one in a thousand
5	low	1 / 500	one in five hundred
6	moderate	1 / 200	one in two hundred
7	high	1 / 100	one in a hundred
8	high	1 / 50	one in fifty
9	very high	1 / 20	one in twenty
10	very high	> 1 / 10	greater than one in ten

Appendix A

PROCESS FMEA - SEVERITY

Severity Rating	Severity	Comments
1	very low	no noticeable effect
2	low	slight customer annoyance
3	low	no noticeable loss of performance
4	moderate	some customer dissatisfaction
5	moderate	some customer dissatisfaction
6	moderate	noticeable loss of performance
7	high	customer dissatisfaction
8	high	some performance failure
9	very high	serious safety and/or legal implications
10	very high	death and/or serious damage could result

Appendix A

DESIGN FMEA - SEVERITY

Severity Rating	Severity	Comments
1	very low	no noticeable effect
2	low	slight customer annoyance
3	low	no noticeable loss of performance
4	moderate	some customer dissatisfaction
5	moderate	some customer dissatisfaction
6	moderate	noticeable loss of performance
7	high	customer dissatisfaction
8	high	some performance failure
9	very high	serious safety and/or legal implications
10	very high	death and/or serious damage could result

Appendix A

PROCESS FMEA - DETECTION

Detection Rating	Likelihood of defect reaching a customer	Statistical Probability	
1	remote	1 / 10,000	one in ten thousand
2	low	1 / 5,000	one in five thousand
3	low	1 / 2,000	one in two thousand
4	low	1 / 1,000	one in a thousand
5	low	1 / 500	one in five hundred
6	moderate	1 / 200	one in two hundred
7	moderate	1 / 100	one in a hundred
8	moderate	1 / 50	one in fifty
9	high	1 / 20	one in twenty
10	very high	> 1 / 10	greater than one in ten

Appendix A

DESIGN FMEA - DETECTION

Detection Rating	Likelihood of defect reaching a customer	Comments
1	remote	something obvious
2	low	something noticeable
3	low	only a fair chance of the fault being detected
4	moderate	only a fair chance of the fault being detected
5	moderate	poor chance of the fault being detected
6	moderate	poor chance of the fault being detected
7	high	a very poor chance of the fault being detected
8	high	a very poor chance of the fault being detected
9	very high	an extremely poor chance of the fault being detected
10	very high	defect will not appear during manufacture

Appendix B

Formulae for Control Charts

SPC Chart	Formula	Plotted value
Variables Mean/Range	$UCL_{\overline{X}} = \overline{\overline{X}} + A_2\overline{R}$	$\overline{X}$
	$LCL_{\overline{X}} = \overline{\overline{X}} + A_2\overline{R}$	$\overline{X}$
	$UCL_R = D_4\overline{R}$	R
	$LCL_R = D_3\overline{R}$ (if –ve, use 0)	R
	$\sigma = \overline{R}/d_2$(approx)	

Constant	Sample size (n)								
	2	3	4	5	6	7	8	9	10
A_2	1.88	1.02	0.73	0.58	0.48	0.42	0.37	0.34	0.31
D_3	0.00	0.00	0.00	0.00	0.00	0.08	0.14	0.18	0.22
D_4	3.27	2.57	2.28	2.11	2.00	1.92	1.86	1.82	1.78
d_2	1.128	1.693	2.059	2.326	2.534	2.704	2.847	2.970	3.078

$\overline{\overline{X}}$ is calculated as the average of a number of $\overline{X}$ values

$\overline{R}$ is calculated as the average of a number of R values

These should be taken over a representative period (min 100)

Appendix B

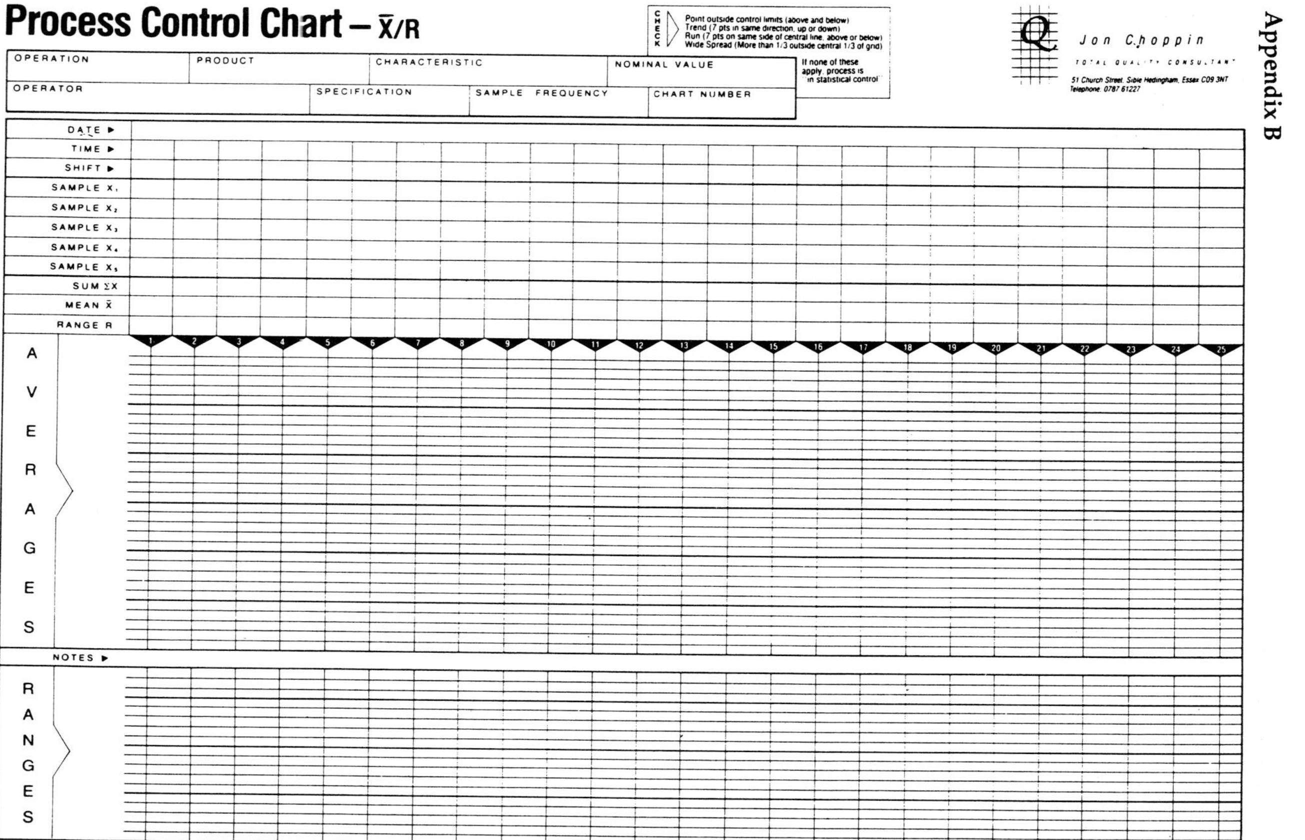
Process Control Chart — $\bar{X}$/R

OPERATION	PRODUCT	CHARACTERISTIC	NOMINAL VALUE
OPERATOR	SPECIFICATION	SAMPLE FREQUENCY	CHART NUMBER

CHECK
Point outside control limits (above and below)
Trend (7 pts in same direction, up or down)
Run (7 pts on same side of central line, above or below)
Wide Spread (More than 1/3 outside central 1/3 of grid)
If none of these apply, process is in statistical control

Jon Choppin
TOTAL QUALITY CONSULTANT
51 Church Street, Sible Hedingham, Essex CO9 3NT
Telephone 0787 61227

DATE ▶
TIME ▶
SHIFT ▶
SAMPLE X_1
SAMPLE X_2
SAMPLE X_3
SAMPLE X_4
SAMPLE X_5
SUM ΣX
MEAN $\bar{X}$
RANGE R

1 2 3 4 5 6 7 8 9 10 11 12 13 14 15 16 17 18 19 20 21 22 23 24 25

AVERAGES

NOTES ▶

RANGES

Appendix C

Quality Cost Priority Rating

COST OF CONFORMANCE

RATINGS

	Signif.	Improv.	Cost	QCPR
PREVENTION				
Prevention costs associated with people				
Prevention costs associated with process				
Prevention costs associated with product development				
APPRAISAL				
Appraisal costs associated with product development				
Appraisal costs associated with process failure				

Appendix C

Quality Cost Priority Rating

INDIRECT QUALITY COSTS

	RATINGS			
	Signif.	Improv.	Cost	QCPR
LOST OPPORTUNITY COSTS LOSS OF CUSTOMER GOOD WILL EROSION OF MARKET SHARE PUBLIC LIABILITY				

QUALITY COST RATINGS

SIGNIFICANCE

(How significant to the company is this particular Quality Cost?)

Very high cost to company	5
High Quality cost	4
Moderate Quality cost	3
Only slight cost to company	2
No significant Quality cost	1

IMPROVEMENT POSSIBLE

(How much improvement would you expect to be possible?)

Virtually all the Quality Cost	5
Considerable improvement	4
Somo improvement	3
Only slight improvement	2
Almost none	1

PROBABLE COST OF IMPROVEMENT

(How much will it cost to improve this Quality Cost?)

Virtually no cost needed	10
Only small initial expenditure	9
Some initial expenditure	8
Some initial expenditure	7
Moderate expenditure	6
Moderate expenditure	5
More than moderate expenditure	4
Considerable cost to company	3
Probably high cost involved	2
Very high cost involved	1

Quality Cost Priority Rating = Significance Rating X Improvement Rating X Cost Rating

- Highest priority should be given to processes with highest QCPR,
- Also to any individual rating with maximum score.

Appendix C

Quality Cost Priority Rating

COST OF CONFORMANCE (APPRAISAL)

	RATINGS			
	Signif.	Improv.	Cost	QCPR
Appraisal costs associated with product failure				
COST OF NON-CONFORMANCE				
INTERNAL FAILURE				
EXTERNAL FAILURE				

Quality through People

A Blueprint for
Proactive Total Quality Management

Index

Index